Now, Faith
is the
Substance
of things
hoped for,
the
Evidence
of things
not seen.
Hebrews 11:1

Faith
~ Knows ~
God

William Thompson, Jr.

Copyright 2018

By; *William Thompson, Jr.*

PUBLISHED BY

Write Everlasting Tips,

Publishing company

Printed in the United States of America

ISBN -0-9755994-7-X

ISBN 978-0-9755994-7-1

To contact the author, write

Write Everlasting Tips Publishing Co.

7525 Arbor Hill Dr.

Fort Worth, Texas 76120

Unless otherwise indicated, all Scripture

quotations are from the King James Version

of the Bible.

Table of Contents

Dedication

I Love "God"; The Father; God the Son Je~sus Christ; God the Holy Ghost; and for the Love that He has for me....

I submit the successful finish of this work of knowledge of the Kingdom of God; to the Body of Christ.

I have been so blessed as to have been trusted to pen such an eternal mystery of God's established truth! I dedicate this work to Faith and to the Faithful Body of Christ in the earth; everywhere!

To my own Faithful Family; Mrs. Sharon; Misty; Aaron; & William III.................

You know that I love you all***

F
A
I
T
H

"Faith;"

~ Preface ~

"Consistent; Errors of Faith; Now Result in No Faith"

Is it really a must for the sake of your expedition of reading that as a writer I pen only that to which is most familiar to simple reasoning and easy understanding, most likely consistent to what you might have already read? Is it only the desire of some, that I write attempting to give a pre-authorize dialogue on "Understanding Faith?" Is it really necessary to say that of which had already been said?

Why is it an indictment against me to transcribe the infrequent unfamiliar unspoken definition of faith that has been revelatory confirmed through the written word of God to me, by the Holy Ghost?

Who has the right to determine that my composition ought to be parallel to the information and to the style of inscription of other writers? Those are the books that rest upon the shelves of acceptability and of a more basic recommendation; even though the authors may not even be Holy Ghost filled people of faith in God; themselves?

God never raises up duplicates or clones, as He is too perfect to ever make a mistake, or to fall short of creating. I am chosen of God to write this book; "Faith; Knows God." The need to understand that faith is not necessarily what it has been taught to be for even centuries and decades now, is in urgent need of total clarity, as the Lord Jesus Christ is so close now to returning to receive the church out of the world!

Judgement is so much closer than whenever we at first believed and turned our lives over to the salvation of the Lord Jesus Christ.

That which has been specified for me to write is by unction of the Holy Ghost! The sweetly articulated mystery aroused my spirit and intellect, intensifying the sensitivity of the skin of my entire body. For the benefit of everyone living on the land, just as the sun freely gives off its rays of sunshine without prejudice, I am so inspired to share the revelation.

Obstructions may block the rays of sunshine, but they never stop the sun from shining. Some who fall short of teaching faith have indeed hinder them from being able to receive the revelation of the scripture concerning faith; but it doesn't change the fact that the revelation has been given to me!

Many people read the word of God but they never receive it as being the only infallible written word of God that it is indeed! Without faith in God; there is absolutely no way that you are ever going to receive a revelation from God concerning His word. The bible is indeed God's spoken, written, and revealed eternal word to all mankind.

Other ministers, writers, instructors and biblical teachers are called to the body of Christ that will find and see what had been either missed or overlooked in the bible for the benefit of the saints in the churches. God have absolutely no reason to fear when releasing the very next minister or teacher to the Kingdom of God.

People that are not members of your church denominations or affiliation of religious organizations are called of God and endowed of the Holy Ghost to walk in the truth in the word of God; with power and authority!

Everyone that comes from God is not only right, righted, and upright; but they have been endowed with the ability to show forth the glory and the essence of the maker and the creator which is God! Many that are indeed in need of having faith in God have been handicapped and crippled, having been taught to reject the next anointed ministries and the faithfully dedicated messengers of God.

They are not at all blind; they naturally have great visualization or at least expensive eye-ware that enable them to see a spec of dirt on the beach; naturally they can see! They are often guilty of looking into the presentation of a brand new revelation but having their understanding safeguarded with very traditional old viewpoints of opinionated references.

The ideas were handed to them from very closed minded instructors and from teachers that taught them to shield their minds, refusing to allow others to teach them, or to disallow others the access to challenge the teaching that they had already received. Whenever one has truely given themselves to thorough study in the word of God; they are often wise enough to block out those whose determination is nothing more than to cause confusion.

People who suffer from mental illnesses often have very good eyesight even though they have damaged psychological awareness where the true sight of seeing is located in the spiritman, on the inside of their being. I don't know that it is really possible to look at a good product and recognize it also as being the good thing that it is when seeing through the damaged mental perception of an ill spirit.

Our Lord and savior, Jesus Christ; laid his hand on a blind man eyes. He asked the man how do you see other men? The man answered; "I see men as trees walking." Jesus; touches the blind man's eyes again and everything was restored to normal, and the man that was indeed blind; now being healed he saw things as he should see them.

What people are seeing is not always in sync with what the spirit on the inside of them is saying and speaking about the images they are seeing. The blind man's eyesight was fixed, but how he saw things was distorted as result that he never had visual sight to identify images causing his understanding of what he was seeing to be misled, and misinterpreted. He was neither misinformed or misguided, he never knew what to look at, or what to look for until the master touched him; he had never been aware of the natural appearance of people.

For a truth, many people only want what they already have, as they are not looking for something that is more challenging to their intellects. Most are satisfied with their present understanding, whether the information that they have held mentally for years is found to be skewed and twisted, or simply unfounded all together. They are relentless never to give up on what they had been taught initially; of which is not always a bad thing when the teaching is found to be biblically sound; as the bible's information is indeed infallible.

The bible {la'biblia ~meaning Library} was never intended to be understood and received as an information recycle warehouse of age old insignificant pages of historical outdated documents. The awesome benefit of the bible concordance is that it reveals that the bible has so much more to say on a particular topic or subject to be exponentially researched.

It is not of the wisdom of God to believe, or to be led to believe that the bible no longer speaks to us as people on the earth. If the bible is ever at a stage when it is finish speaking to mankind, it will be the time when there is no more people on the face of the earth.

We have only begun to hear all that the bible has to say to us as the people of God; we have been so slow to surrender and to dedicate ourselves to praying and fasting. The purpose is for connecting with the spirit of God, putting our flesh aside, releasing our will to the will of the Father in Heaven.

The greater damage done to the average individual of a particular setting of an organized religious affiliation is that they purposefully deliver their own corporate spin on the scripture to aid the ideal message for faith and God; disregarding the complete understanding of the scripture that connects the entire spectrum of the Kingdom of God; bringing all people together in one faith and relationship with God.

It is heartbreaking that so many organizations have been formed for the intended purpose of dividing us, and maintaining the divide believing that they are leaving the reality of the separated who aspire to the one faith; to God.

A balance of the information on the shelves of the warehouse is not even com-parable to the books on the shelves in the library. The products of the warehouse may indeed be deemed as good material not worthy of being discarded and totally destroyed, but valuable enough to be preserved in archive for the sake of future references.

The books on the shelves in the library are available for reading and research; being judged as presently viable relevant material substance that is yet applicable to sustain a given format of historical balance for the establishment of our modern advancement.

"Intellectually Transformed; By Reading Comprehension?"

Others, determine what should be considered as good reading material for your literary consumption; whether the information is beneficial for you or not. The material may only be good enough to keep you intellectually, where you have always been relative to your level of reading comprehension.

So, we take it upon ourselves to read what has indeed been written and penned from various authors known and unknown, both past and present. The writers who failed to say what had been said already, have suffered their works to be put aside, if they were even lucky enough for the publishing powers that be to decide that the works needed not to be totally destroyed and permanently annihilated, their works were at least saved in an archive.

In all truth, every individual is only allowed to be as smart as the level of the reading materials of which they are willing to read and are able to comprehend. At the selective strength of the data that they have allowed into the intellectual processing annals of reasoning in their own understanding, the strength of the reading materials are absorbed. Strong minds are often only as strong as the strength to literarily digest any ingested resources accepted as benefiting for their intellectual integrity and growth.

Literary submissions to the library of congress, for the sake of national and even international archive recognitions and authorship status of ownership; bear the hidden scrutiny of examiners who peruse the data to make determination of authentic authorship to the copyright claimant.

Many will actually take what has been written and already published of another author, and package it and claim it as their own to reap the benefits of the sell which lawfully and actually belong to another original author.

When you are only in a since recycling what you have already been given that doesn't further stretch your understanding beyond what many of the instructors may not have been able to venture out into, you are becoming more acceptable to enter into the information thoroughfares to the non-expansive mental place of nowhere.

Very soon you will discover that you will have gone nowhere intellectually; although you might have had the feeling of traveling far and beyond the norm through the pages of the book that you had just finished reading.

Information explorations are already affixed to determine where the reader is going to be allowed eventually to arrive intellectually; as the information highways are often a multiplex of destinations where any traveler is capable of landing at diverse comprehensive platforms.

It all depends on which angle is applied to your reading expedition, whether or not you are positive or negative, whether or not you prefer to be entertained or seriously informed, secular or spiritual is going to determine which entrance or off ramp you are going to take from the highway of information.

While we read and explore the multi-facets of faith determinations by innumerable authors, we may arrive at what can only be founded as parking lots at the religion mal-manufactured; faith super stores?

Many of our churches have become parking lots having the bulk of the parking spaces labeled as Handicapped/Disabled parking. These are parking lots which have allowed for those who are faith-sick; maimed; and the crippled explorers of faith to have a closer entrance to the doorway of the entrance for faith shopping.

Only; such super stores of faith are at the lowest levels of faith shopping located on the same grounded levels of all that produce doubt and disbelieves in the superiority of Faith in God; above and beyond every other methodology to satisfactory eliminate and simultaneously manifest the quality of all human need. The average persons of the churches had already visited those places of the natural, but, most carnal experiences of faithlessness seeking to fulfill the desire of their needs.

A very sad, but also very true reality is that many of the churches had also become faith cemeteries. The seating in these churches is comparable to the burial plots for the dead; the people who occupy the seating spaces are sure to be right where they are for the years to come; they're dead to faith and they can never be moved. The faith understanding of these people has been so darkened and smothered being shifted away from the light of the word of God; nothing can reside there but death.

That of which had indeed been the driving force which caused them to seek and to search in such grounded places of the flesh and of the natural experience of the earth, has been all along the deep inner call of faith without them even knowing of it.

Many people choose faith as a last chance option, having had all of the former decision to fail at producing the needed necessities of their lives left in dissatisfaction and utter disappointment. The problems that many of the churches leaders of today have when attempting to teach the parishioners who attend their meetings, actually presents itself in the fact that they confess to have also been students of faith failure themselves!

As a result, in their teaching on acquiring faith in God; they feel it most necessary to apply the sympathetic reasoning of being understanding and sensitive to those who fail at successfully having their need met in the Lord, through faith. Erroneously; they set themselves to agree that faith may not always work!

So as people come into the churches already busted and disgusted relative to having faith in God; rather than being driven to get onto the runway to take flight on faith airlines, to soar to the heights of God in Heaven in all of the highest realms of the spirit, people are otherwise encouraged to find a parking space and rest there; or a cemetery plot; a final resting place and die there.

The erroneous messages are that as people of faith, perhaps they should prepare themselves because God just may not do it for them just because they have believed in faith, even though He can?

Nothing, at all more distressing to the idea of going shoping, than when you have reached your destination you can't even get out of the car to enter into the place that you have arrived because while seeking a parking space to park your car you enter into a crowded, fully occupied, parking lot. All of the parking spaces have been taken, and we find ourselves circling the parking lot hoping that someone else's shopping has ended?

You continue driving around the parking lot in the hopes that there is soon an empty space for you to park; this is the very realistic experience of the parking lot. Many said believers are having similar experiences with faith in the parking lot of the churches.

Many people are settling into the parking lot styled churches in this topic of discussion; but they are never exiting their cars (figuratively speaking), to enter into the faith super stores that are housed with everything possible to those that believe; according to the teaching?

Figuratively; they are driving through the services seeking a place to park, seeking to belong to what they believe to be gatherers of faithful members of the churches. Positioning themselves closer to the people in attendance over a period of time it is soon discovered that they are parked with the intent to be there for a while. Only they emerge from what might have been thought to be a shopping experience bearing absolutely nothing at all.

In a more common vernacular, we might enquire of a friend or more likely a family member when they returned from shopping; "hey what did you get; or bring back; or what did you buy?" Naturally whenever people go shopping they are going to come back with something; but in the spiritual realm too many people are allowed to seek, but finding nothing of direct interest to the need for having faith in God!

People are just going along for the excitement of all of the hype to see if there is anything real to all of the talk from the people in the churches concerning faith in God. They want to know; "does faith really work like they say that it does?"

See, they are on the failing decline as result of having no biblical reference to apply to their need to know. They are in the classes on the scheduled appointed times, but somehow they miss the teaching, or it just may be that the teaching is all together wrong?

I have discovered the truth about faith that I had never been taught before in the churches all of my life. Faith; knows God! We have all been taught the truth that God knows faith, but somehow or another we have been left to believe that we make up or create the faith that God will eventually know and be pleased with.

God had already created the faith that He knows and that would be the only faith acceptable and pleasing to Him.

With Much Love and Caring................ WTJR ~ 2018

"Faith" Was Implanted In The Garden of God!

In The Beginning Was The Word..........

xiv

Introduction

"FAITH" ~ "For/ All/ Is/ To/ Him"

"For All Is To Him"

The infinite wise God allowed for an ever, over-riding system of faith; eternally intented to be in place for mankind to be the unstoppable plan of action in the earth, as any man would adhere to believing God.

By revelation I have come to realize that the greatest attack ever launched against the move of God in the earth has been against what should be the definitive understanding of the true faith of God. The greater purpose against the movement of faith had been designed for hindering and slowing the process of allowing mankind to be faithfully informed and further exposed to the nature of God.

Figuratively speaking; faith has been through the wringer; like having been put through the spaghetti maker, whereas it has been strung into many elongated strands, as if to be eventually brought together in boiling hot water (the trying of faith) to make the serving of one dish for supper?

Eventually connecting the people of the churches all over the world, bringing them into oneness; as one church? Many will eventually teach the similar lessons on faith, however disregarding initially the error in the understanding that faith is of one faith, not many different faiths!

Equality is often found and fashioned as to be that of the natural existence of mankind in the earth, whereas the likeness is in the possibilities of our abilities to be and or to become whatever we may desire on the earth? We rarely hear any of these people declare that all men are created equally in the likeness and in the image of God!

The scripture clearly helps our understanding as to what level of equality that all men are created which establishes our equality even though men of all walks of life strive unconditionally to prove and to reign as the greater ones of their own surroundings, and even to be held as the more accomplished persons in the world.

People want greatness, but too often they lack the understanding relative to the drive that leads to greatness. They desire to be more than just another normal individual living on the face of the planet earth. People don't just want to be great, they desire to be the greatest of all, ever heard of in the history of all times.

To the likes of "Mohammad Ali" who declared that he was the greatest boxer of all times; only to have the industry of boxing's Hall of Fame to echo the declaration that he was indeed the greatest Boxer of all times!

"God is Great; and greatly to be praised!"

Whenever we look out over the plains of the land and over the vasstness of the sea, we are witnesses to the creative splendor of God's hand. Any individual can look into the mirror and see the handiwork of God's own hand; thus lending reason enough to desire God's greatness as an indelible part of the make-up of their own character and strength as a created being of the earth.

Greatness was never intended only to be that part of an individual's demeanor for other people to see who they are in the community, comparable to the accomplishments of any other people. We may indeed be great to certain other people; however in the eyes of a totally diverse people, we may be no more than trash in comparison to the people that they themselves hold as great in their own eyes!

I am; we are; great simply because God says that we are indeed great! He has awarded us the permission of His own will concerning us, to pursue greatness in the earth among men. Whatever the level of greatness that we are allowed to achieve, our accomplishment is for the purpose of spotlighting the greatness of God. Others are to be made aware that we are only great because our God is indeed great!

We were made to glorify God for all that He is; for who He is; for all that He has done, and for all that He is eternally able to do! Be it known and understood of all people; with everything that is within you; with every fiber of your being; to everyone one on the face of the planet right now that are living, and to everyone that has already been here but are now gone into the grave; from the very beginning, we were made for the glory of God.

As I look into the word glory; I see the word glow i.e. (glo)w... in its most informal form; look at glow – ree', whereas we have the word glorify (Glow-ree-fah-eey). We are made to intentionally amplify the attention on God; to spotlight the fact that God is eternally in the state of glorified greatness; radiantly shining over all of heaven and of the earth. Faith truthfully works for us when we determine that it's not about us, but that it's always about God! ~

Let your light so shine before men, that they may see your good works, and glorify your Father which is in heaven. {Matthew 5: 16}

Faith; expects for us as the created people of the earth; of every nationality and tongue, to do what we have been created by God to do according to the written word; which is to hope in God, to expect God to do all that we need for Him to do for us and through us; by faith.

We get caught up in all of the sin and the shame of living in this world, as a result we need the savior to free us from the bondage and from the penalty of sin, so as to be able to carry out our God given task as worshippers.

We need the savior; to redeem us back to God to activate our given measure of faith, {all planned by the Father}. In the Garden of Eden; Adam sold us out to sin and the curse of death was passed on humanity; as a result were in a sinful state just being born into the sinful nature of the flesh here in the earth. We are unable to get ourselves out of the sin nature without the redemptive work of Jesus Christ; on the cross at Calvary.

Faith; itself remains in the presence of God; the Father in heaven. As human beings, by our own choices we slip further and further away from the planned purpose and from the perfect will of God.

Striving after the personal selfish goals of the flesh, people become so worldly and earthly; never even realizing just how far they have drifted away from God, until they are forced to face the fact of needing a working faith to reach up to God! It can often be at a very detrimental period in our lives to discover that we have drifted away from true faithfulness in God.

As result of the penalty of sin being passed on to humanity; those who are passed on from living that are now dead without having receive the perfect sacrifice of Jesus Christ shed blood to redeem us, the ultimate penalty for them is hell.

Note: faith itself will not be going to hell with everyone who enters in to Hell; however the corruption and the sinful perversion attached to people for the purpose of redirecting us away from faith in God according to His written word, will definitely be in hell with those who are indeed going to hell as a result of denying the given faith of God.

I can prove to you that faith won't be going to hell and that it will not be burning in the lake of fire and brimstone! The word of God teaches us; that God; have dealt to every man the measure of faith. *[Romans 12:3]*

There is not an element of the spirit of God; that God has given to us that He is eventually going to destroy it in hell, because it was never good enough, or rather because you were responsible for corrupting it! God has given to every one of us life; you cannot corrupt life or living, but you can corrupt the manner of which you live. You chose the corrupt manner of living that reveals the fact that you have rejected Christ Jesus through the word of God.

Faith will be returned back to the father who sent it in the first place. Faith; has done well, it has done what the Father intended for it to do in the realm of humanity; faith never displeases God! It's on you, that you have never viewed faith as the wonderful measure of connecting us to the Father in heaven, to give us the expected end of our life. *[Jeremiah 29: 11]* Faith causes us to believe what God knows concerning us. *[I Corinthians 13: 7]*

As I began the ministry of praying for others, whenever I visited the hospitals and the nursing homes, and often in the churches the Holy Ghost made me aware of the fact that we in the ministry are often asking the people to do what they had never done before; which was to have faith in God! Many people are truly empty of the true knowledge faith, which disables them from receiving what they have needed from the Lord.

The statement that I am about to make may be painful to some readers; many of those people were in the states they were in because they purposefully denied having faith in God; on purpose!

Although we have all been given the measure of faith; not all people have been faithfully adhering to the given measure of faith. Many of the teachings on faith have left the people of the churches confused and distorted relative to the true definition of the meaning in the scripture; *{according as God has dealt to every man the measure of faith.}* not to be understood to mean that God has given to everyone their own individual scoop, or a personal bag of faith to use as they are pleased to do so!

Faith; or, Faithfulness; is not meant in its definition to be the chosen manner of religious practice that one may choose; as many of the religions of the world allow the people to believe that it is the true meaning of faith. Many religions allow the practitioners to adhere to faith as meaning; this is how we do it in this religion?

Religion in itself, does not have the power to define for us who God is; but rather it allows for us to adhere to and to learn about who are supposed to be to God! God is to us; relative to the sacrifice of the cross of Christ; and the shed blood of atonement at Calvary's rugged hill; our only hope of salvation and deliverance.

God have given to every man the equal access to the faith that pleases God! God established the plan of faith, whereas whenever we would come to Him in faith through the only begotten son of God; that it would be forever possible to commune with the Father in heaven, though we are still in the earth!

Most people, take faith for granted and they often doubt the power of faith as a result of giving a listening ear to worldly influences and negative detractors and distractions. When they are in a crisis, they reach for a faith they have never embraced or exercised. They are now empty and totally void of faith in God. Upon praying for such people, we make it our practice of asking them to have faith and to believe as we pray in faith believing for their healing and deliverance.

There are people who are repulsed at the very thought of having faith in the unseen, all powerful God! They think it to be more than foolish to allow them to be reliant upon anything or anyone who is intangible and unable to be handled or manipulated by them?

Relationships are often destroyed and upended through the inability to physically touch one another in the relationship, as the ability to touch each other bespeak of the truest desire for one another's affectionate company on a consistent basis favorably, and a more permitted basis for intimacy through the institution of marriage.

Thinking that they ought to have a more favorable access to the Father than everyone else, others make the mistake of thinking themselves to be more holy than the average person? They're a disappointment to faith being ignorant of the fact that they are not between faith and God; rather faith is between each and every one of us and God!

Faith is there between us knowing the motives and the intentions of our heart; when our prayer request to the Father is undeliverable as result of the faith hindrances within us, faith cannot speak for us nor deliver to us that which we think that we expect from the Father.

Clearly the scripture speaks of Jesus the Christ; as being our mediator, our go between to the Father on our behalf; but without faith Jesus doesn't even know that we desire for the Father to help us, to free us and to deliver us from our own selves, or from the power of sins aweful grip!

The churches are prone to have pre-introductory services of praise and worship; praise thanks God for what He has done for us and it even allow us to thank God in advance to whatever we might have asked Him to do for us. Worship; simply, only thanks God; for just being who' He is! If He never does another thing for us, He's yet worthy to be praised and glorified because; He is "GOD!"

It is our responsibility to make sure that all people on the face of the planet know that God is responsible for our being and for providing the things necessary for our daily welfare.

God; in His own infinite ability to produce and to create could only do so in total excellence! God expects for us as mankind in the earth to put the attention back on God; and that we not look to any man as being the one responsible for the things of which we are so marvelously taken to show our appreciation for.

The excellent splendor of God's creation is so captivating and arousing of our imagination and appreciation. It is no wonder that we as people can often be left speechless and breathless; it is commonly an human attribute to become so excited and overwhelmingly expressive relative to what our eyes are seeing; being forced to acknowledge the amazement in what we are witnessing!

Most people believe that it could not be possible at all for the things of this life to be in existence if it were not for the Lord! They do not all believe that; "All Is To Him"; which means that we are to give meaningful understanding to those who ask of us that are in need of knowing the truth, for the reasons that all things were made.

The egotistical arrogance of mere men of the earth, reveals that they believe that God put all things here on the earth for mankind to enjoy! So they are taking it for their own possessions, and what they choose to do with it is their own business for their own purpose and gain. In the mind, of the carnal minded individual; they feel that God left things here uncared for and available to be taken by anyone who wanted to have them?

It is not at all a naturally common thing among mankind to acknowledge God and or to even see Him in all things that are made here on the earth. God; is ignored and ruled out as the only creator of all heaven and earth; as if someone else might have been truly responsibly creative enough to have thought of the things that we see in our daily lives.

Many people are determined to think within themselves that they don't know where things come from and and they are satisfied to leave it at that without any possible research of the scripture through faith and prayer. Even the things that they see clearly, with their own two eyes, that are remarkable and above the manipulation of any human hands; they are still better off leaving things to question?

Looking on the beautifully colored feathers of birds and foul of the air, and the different styles of their feathers, I know that only God had the idea to design such for the purpose of identifying each bird type. Comparable to the array of plants and flowers in the garden, having the vastness of the types, shapes, and of colors.

Even the many different fish in the ocean and the seas; the different colors of the scales and beautiful hues of color that makes them to stand out from all other fish, no doubt has to be the work of God. There is a direct message in the colors of their scales and skin coverings which allows for them to reside in certain parts of the ocean to attract sun light and to adapt in certain temperatures of the water.

Even in respect to the things that are here on the earth to be found, discovered and had for a possession, many people are not assured as to who to give thanks to; as they themselves are not thankful people. They just want the credit is given to them as being the owner of certain said earthly personal effects. It is their ultimate position to be benefited in every way that is possible to mankind, and to be noted and cited for being the one who have those things.

It is most absurd to me that the very people that refuse to acknowledge God as the maker and the creator of all Mankind, and of all heaven and earth; they can be heard as acknowledging that man is to have dominion in the earth; they believe that men are the rulers of the earth! Now who taught them that? Where did they get that idea?

In our world of celebrity stars of secular music and of Hollywood Film stars; we hear them give reference to God for their talents and for their gifts of music when being awarded for their works in the industry?

They often credit the one who is greater than all of us here on the face of the planet earth, for their abilities to entertain and to amass such inflated financial increase, but don't get it twisted; everything that they have, had all been acquired for their own personal gain and had nothing at all to do with giving any glory to God in Heaven.

Some physicians will even credit God for their ability to perform very delicate surgeries on patients who could have died during the surgery, especially had there been even one of the slightest slips of the scalpel?

They will credit God for the availability of knowledgeable information to those who are willing to dig and to give elevated research and studies in higher learning institutions to acquire the information and the skill to perform such medical trade.

So many members of the scientific community may even give slighted references but with great reluctance, to God; only as a definitive measure undeniable to their ability to explain mind blowing phenomenon in the earth. Some things that even appear to be greater than that of anything that nature itself could ever produce.

Faith in God; stands as the curtain to reveal the stage and all of the players responsible for the greatness in the earth; that it is God who is responsible for their platforms and for their stages. Faith in God through Jesus Christ; is all that it takes to have the petition between all of mankind and God, rolled back.

There is a beauty to behold that the natural ability of the eyes of mankind will never be able to behold. God; desires for all of mankind to behold the beauty of the Lord and to enquire in His temple; of all of the beauty and the splendor of His creations in the earth and in all of Heaven.

Faith is truly the friend of mankind……………………..

FAITHFUL

XXV

"About The Author"

Born March 12, 1961 in El'paso, Texas, to the union of the late Rev. William Thompson Sr. & Rev. Daisy Y. Mclawler-Thompson; the family later relocated to Fort Worth, Texas in 1967 where he grew up in the church singing in the choir, learning to study his own bible, and participating in all of the youth activities faithfully.

He attended the Fort Worth Independant School District; graduated from P. L. Dunbar Sr. High, class of 79'. He was an honor student although he did not graduate with honors; his very best subjects where he excelled were English and Math, and everything Music. He was a Member of the Marching Band; Concert Band; Stage Band; School Chorus; his senior year he was the star of the Senior Play; "Roll Me Out To Sea" where he sang and played the piano. He was an initiator of the very first Dunbar Gospel Choir and musician; an after school project.

He attended Tarrant County Junior Colledge 1980, Vogue Bueaty Colledge 1981, and Dallas Theological Seminary 1986. Has spent the bulk of his time in coporate worship studies; multiple siminars on ministry, church ediquate, bible studies, music seminars for worship, revivals, conferences- pastoral, prayer, laymen, and of couse many conferences that cater to the total man.

He has been a partaker in several activities and auxilaries. Most of all he has been a servant to the body of Christ. An avid worker and a giver to the church unselfishly. He thoroughly operates impeccible as an anointed Prophet of God; whereas he has ministered to many people in the Kingdom of God across the country, and over the phone in India, Africa, and London. He is known and respected as a "True Prophet" of God.

He has been ministering the gospel since Feb. 7,1982, and has engaged in studies and training of the bible. He has been in the church all of his natural life and has the experience of a faithful churchman which lends the passion for which he ministers the gospel of God. He has been ordained since June 1998.

By the age of 3 years he had already began to express a passion to play the piano and to preach the Gospel. He is a talented instumentalist, and has composed many songs. He has ministered in music for ministries in the DFW Metro-plex, and OKC, OK. He has traveled with evangelist, and has been the guest musician for many revivals, musicals, weddings, conferences, recordings and etc.

His uncle; the Late Apostle Russell Thompson, laid his hand on him at the age of 11, from that point on he knew that there was more for him in the Lord. He moved to the next level of worship in an effort to get to that which he desired most of the Lord. Pastor Thompson has crossed the lines of denominational affiliations as a friend and brother, enabling him to be identified as a child of God and not Just a Baptist, a Methodist, a Pentecostal, or for that matter, just another member of the Church Of God In Christ!

He founded and pastored the Tried Whole Truth Foundation Ministry; in Fort Worth, Texas; As instructed by the Lord he later changed the name to The Spoken Word Center where he had 8 [1998-2005] years of successful ministry under both the names. Souls were indeed saved, people were filled with the Holy Ghost; we observed miracles of healing and deliverance; demons cast out; lives changed and many ministries were realized and answered to the call of God.

He founded and established the Spoken Word Center, School of Prophetic Excellence 2003. As of late as we are re-launching the ministry, we have again changed the name of the ministry to The Kingdom Impact Certen of the Spoken Word Church, Int. We have been instrumental in working with and for several different ministries since as of late 2005 until 2014. We have been commissioned to go on forward full force with the ministry of the Kingdom Impact Center of the Spoken Word Church.

He has since preached many revivals where deliverance and the manifested presence of the Lord are witnessed. He has become an avid teacher to those who are new to the body of Christ, instructing them to know and to practice the presence of God in pure worship and praise to our God; in Christ Jesus. He is a real true lover of people; especially to those who are of the household of faith across the board; if you can love him, and even if you can't, he's committed to loving you.

By the grace of God and divine providence, he found his way back to the grass roots of his own spiritual inheritance. Pastor Thompson hails from an extensive linage of dedicated ministers. He's a decendant of the Late; Reverend Vol William McLawler of Louisville, Kentucky; and of the first generation Church of God In Christ East Texas; have been active in Texas Northeast 1st Jurisdiction under the now late Prelate J. N. Haynes where he worked in the District; State; and the National music departments.

His endeavor is to serve the people of the Lord everywhere that will receive of the awesome gift of the Holy Ghost to which he has been endowed. Pastor Thompson has been married to Sharon Renee for 34 years and is the father of Three children.

Chapter 1

"Faith" ~ Knows God!"

*For in Jesus Christ neither circumcision availeth anything,
nor uncircumcision; but faith which worketh by love.*
{Galatians 5: 6}

[Love Is God]

"Discovering What Faith Actually Knows?"

BE IT KNOWN: Faith; knows God; for sure! All of the questions and the apprehensions that you are housing, both in your heart and in your mind causing you to reason and to ponder the reality of taking hold of faith and of the truthful existence of God; are inquisitive obstructions that are standing in the way blocking the flow of the spirit and the actual operation of having faith in God!

Faith knows that you teeter on the edge of doubt and disbelief while yet claiming to be a true believer, but only keeping your own selves from becom~

ing steadfastly assured of the necessity to know that GOD IS; and that He is a rewarder of them that diligently seek Him. *[Hebrews 11: 6]*...

Faith; is intrinsically informed of whether or not you actually walk with God; being aware always of where you are in your life and where you ought to be in the Lord!

Faith; moves with God; who is always in forward progression, moving towards the maturation of His own will for you while here in the earth.

However, as you are indecisively housing the apprehensions of faith and the power in God in your heart and in your own mind, faith obeys the assignment of watching you, and it is there available for you!

Faith; most conquerable and captivating through the awesome mystery in the ability to disregard any manifested results until the right spoken request is made out of your mouth through the written word of God from the heart of your own being to God; it must be known to faith that you know that He is God; and that He will answer you.

The intended working order of faith has always been founded upon the platform of God's Love.   It is therefore impossible to operate in faith, or for faith to be operable; outside of the Love of God.

So many have decided in their own minds that having faith in God is a hoax, or a great big joke of a scam to get people's money, so they act out according to their inward beliefs as they fake and fail at having faith in God.

The name on the big marquee sign out in the front of the building; or the name of the pastor; the denomination; and or even the designation of the denomination to which you may have chosen to adjoin your experience of worship is not at all the defining factor which determines to others that you have faith in God. Perhaps you might have a strong belief in the local church?

On many occasions I have had the privilege, even as a young man from the age of 18-24; to inform different people that it is not your church which determines whether or not I can serve the Lord. If your church represents a

different faith from that of which I am taught and informed in the bible, it's the wrong faith; as the bible states that there is but one faith; one Lord; one baptism… *[Ephesians 4: 5]*

Certain of the churches are viewed as being more of a circus that allow clowns and the wild animalistic behavior to be displayed during the services sometimes, like as to that under the huge circus tent; as some people are out of control!

The greatest mistakes ever made as it relates to the world, and of having faith in God through Jesus Christ our Lord; and Savior; is that people are now more than ever determined to mix-mesh the philosophical methodology of the world and the faith of God into one reality, as relates to living!

The community affairs to which you partake of as a member of your church may indeed be a good idea; but feeding the hungry and clothing the naked with no intention to share the love of God in Christ Jesus and the need for them to repent only places you in the same company as the atheist and the agnostics and all of the other religious people who reject Jesus Christ as the only begotten son of God.

"Habitat For Humanity" is a community effort which does have the ability to leave those who participate in building homes for those in need, in a very good spirit of brotherly love and caring for humanity; but it is neither the defining factor of having faith in God!

Although many who confess to having faith never ever participate in such affairs; as they are cited as having selfish agendas for the people of the churches and for the welfare of themselves. Many of the leaders are seekers of iconic status of celebrity, their greatest desire is to impress the people of the churches and the surrounding communities.

Much of the teaching in the churches is lacking the true definitive messages of faith to bring the hearts and the minds of the people to live faithful to God; increasing in their lifestyles according to the written word, once they have exited the sanctuary. This is the only reason that many of the people of

the churches are in the same place spiritually many years later as they were whenever they first came in.

You lack the knowledge of God; you lack the strength of the word of God; you lack definition of salvation and faith in God; you lack the ability to daily live with God!

The faithful society that we are supposed to create as the church; is not being produced when the agendas and the teachings or the lack thereof is not conducive for producing faith knowledge!

We are in a critical time in our spiritual history as the church, people are actually seeing less and less of the movement of God in the land among the people who gather for the sake of worshipping God?

It's about entertainment and social acceptance; it is not even about faith and repentance anymore, whereas people are more particularly interested in seeking the face of God; to be the light and the salt to the community of which they are a part of.

People of faith in God are interested in showing the people of the churches, the power and the presence of God in Christ Jesus; through the Holy Ghost (spirit)!

How can we possibly know what faith knows about God if those who have been called to teach and to instruct in the way of the Lord have a warped focus and another reason and determination for being at the helm of the ministry in the first place?

Too many people are really title struck like never before in the history of the call to ministry. Many wear the titles who never intend to do the work which establishes an authentic endowment of the call upon the life and ministry of anyone who bear the burden of the call of God on their life. Thus they lask the help of the Holy Spirit to teach and to lead the people to receive the knowledge of faith.

As of this late millennium reign; people are still yet in search of finding

the truth of faith in God through Jesus Christ. Like never before, religious groups are at war with each other, still trying to establish the right to be called the right church denominational organization for the people to follow and to attend.

I have been told by some certain people that I didn't have the right to operate as a faith-filled messenger of God simply because I didn't belong to a certain denomination, or even to a particular religious organization.

Faith knows what God wants all of us to know about having faith in Him; far too often faith itself has to sit aside and watch people fight and bicker over what someone else has told them that faith is, disregarding what the word of God has to say about the matter.

Some people have been arguing these issues for many years, never being sensitive, as faith itself taps them on their shoulders at certain instances, seeking to show them that it was indeed faith at work at that instance they had just witnessed.

One of the most disgusting things that I have ever witnessed was to be in a particular church where the move of God had just taken place but the pastor of that particular church stood up before the people to declare that God doesn't work like that anymore; discounting that what the people had just witnessed was not at all any possible move of God.

Amazingly many of the same doubtful people believe in magic and witchcraft? They totally believe in the tricks at the magic show; and Crystal ball gazing, and star gazing; but they are totally turned off at even the mention of the movement of faith at the church!

I understand such adamant determination to disbelieve the move of God being prevelent in a non-spirit led church; as much as I do that God is not going to be received from the outwardly perspective looking through lenses stained with sin and iniquity; un-forgiveness and hatred!

All of these elements shut the door on the working of faith whereas no

one will be able to see God at work in their lives. Lots of sin~sick people claim to have God in their lives attempting to associate paranormal activities and demonic manifestations as to the very same as the working power of the Holy Ghost; simply because they have not known God through faith and repen~tance.

Even many in the churches are heard themselves as quoting that faith without works is dead! And yes of course I know that the scripture says it in the book of James; but you cannot successfully show me faith in God without first having God in your own life!

We must all receive God by grace, but through faith whereby we are saved; but only after the fact of having God through Jesus Christ, will we ever be able to show true actual faith in God to others.

Faith has to show itself to others through the partnership of faith and the love of God! If you do not have it you can never show it! Faith is never at all lost about where it is and or about where it can and will be found; so when looking for the faithful ask God in faith and you will find them for certain. Faith is found in God!

The book of I John; in the scriptures of the Holy bible, informs us of the fact that Love is God; as God is Love! {I John 4: 16} So it is most necessary to ac~knowledge the very truthful fact that faith works by God; by the Love of God; which is by and through the only begotten son of God; Jesus Christ! Faith knows Love; the love of God; and faith knows the Love that is God!

The scripture informs us that faith continuously works by the very power of love; so in essence to your working or non~working faith, check out your love or the lack of love in your own heart towards others and towards God; and even your love of the written word of God.

Only them who have been transformed by the renewing of their mind through the spirit of God can stand faithfully in His presence. Faith stands in the presence of God accurately abiding with knowledge of each individ~ual; prepared to manifest the request to them that faithfully seek God. Faith

knows exactly what God knows about everyone individually; whenever the statement is made that God will do it for you in spite of you; you can believe that when you're living your life putting forth the efforts associated with faith to please the Lord.

No man, woman, boy, or girl could ever educate faith, possibly suggesting that there is neither a need yet for faith in our lives, or that we have gone too far away from the God of the bible for any faith to have an effect on our lives?

Faith knows the history of all mankind; Faith knows the bloodline and genealogy of all created beings that have ever been on the face of the planet earth; so who a person's family might have been, does not necessarily create a hindrance to be used by God; any individual who wants to live for God to please Him; can and will through faith.

Faith knows the tolerance and the stability of God's endurance, knowing how long the spirit of God will strive with mankind, in that He always was; and is; and that He always will be.

Faith knows that man is God's greatest creation in the earth having put forth the plan of salvation for man; being ultimately for the intended purpose of the Kingdom of God.

Not at any time did God pity man knowing that He placed the power and the authority to live in this world to dominate and to conquer living as faith filled people of God in the earth. In other words, God allowed mankind to bring a bit of heaven to the earth, but in a faithful manner.

Faith knows both the immeasurable span eternity and the limited activation of time; I personally believe that faith has been informed of the very end of time; faith sees the instance when the very last moment of time seeps through the bottom of the hourglass; as eternity rolls onward forever.

Faith neither loses track of time, nor has it forgotten the things of the past except in the face of the things which God Himself have forgotten!

Faith sees mankind as we desperately run to and fro throughout the earth

trying to keep up with the track of time; knowing that we may indeed see the clocks on the wall or the time on the watches that we wear on our arms, and other time pieces, but we have not held respect to God's timing of things in the earth according to the word of God in our own personal grasp!

Faith knows the wrath of God, and that even His unimaginable wrath is yet fueled by His eternal Love and compassion for all of mankind; whereas; the enemies of God are but on the time tables of much borrowed time!

Faith sees God's Love, willful to allow man unrestricted chance after chance to accept the perfect sacrifice of His own dear son and savior Jesus Christ. At each given day to continue living on the earth faith watches as people squander each chance that they are given to repent and to turn away from sin.

Man on the other hand only see God's patience to deal with the sinfulness of mankind as tolerance and an allowance to sin willfully as each man might be pleased within his own self will to do so! Even though they have been deceived to their own utter detriment and eternal destruction without repentance!

Faith knows that the call of God is but for a time and a selected season for each and every man to carryout the assignment of his own calling for the benefit of the Kingdom of God.

Faith knows that God has never given to man the authority to dictate the movement and space of time; as time is but a gift to man; the allotted span to go after and to conquer the things which were afore the beginning of time in the heart of God for mankind to do in the earth.

Faith knows that the hell spoken of in the scripture is of the incendiary wrath of God being a fire unquenchable to all mankind, and of every other spirit known and unknown to mankind!

This is the reason that the very presence of God must be acceptably invoked through faith and prayer; so as to allow God to show up in the essence

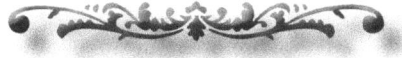

of His greater Love; the Love of God is greater than the wrath of God.

There has never been a storm or a cosmic shower from space; a volcanic eruption; tsunami; earth quake nor anything known to mankind as being so unimaginably terrible, that could ever be compared to the presented wrath of God!

Faith sees mankind as a whole as we are prone to take God for granted; disregarding the love that He has for us as nothing more than His responsibility to us?

Many people believe that God in some way or another owe us something for allowing us to be born into this world. However; silent faith sees and know of the other millionth percentages of sperms that were never chosen to be you; they will of course never make it to the face of the planet earth to worship God; to give glory to His name.

Faith knows of the opportunity that has been given to you and I to know God in the beauty of His own character; which is Love.

Faith knows that we are not serving and or living for a God that can be erased on a whim at the desires of any non-believing ungodly people of the secular sinful society.

People have wished for many years now for a more common approach to having faith; even if it means that someone else exists as a faith stand-in for you, in your place; if it were possible?

People now more than ever like to think of themselves as being very smart innovative new aged thinkers, who are capable of taking the ideas of faith in God, to a more common level of lesser biblical principles and churchy regularities, into more world friendly acceptance of much more inclusive secular atmospheric surroundings.

There is nothing at all common to the word of God and to living righteous according to the written word of God; King James Version; that scientific ideology of so-called advanced thinkers of the world among mere mankind;

relative to having faith in God that has now been left to the laboratory find-ings and understanding that allows faith into every household, else everyone would be faithful; but without God.

As of late; that is of course within the past century or two; people, mean-ing Theologians, Scientist and even Sociologist have taken it upon themselves as authoritative analyst to definitively give common meaning to faith, and or having faith, and God.

Erroneously they have determined that faith is believing without evidence or proof; only they have also failed to know and to understand that faith is the evidence and eventually the proof of both God and of what any individual might have asked God for!

They thought it not to be the very best for common man to find that God is; through the written word of God and the spirit of God. Secular mankind found out a long time ago that the true acquisition of Faith in God meant a spiritual take over even in secular society. People would see their sinful be-havior transformed into that of a much godlier lifestyle of righteousness.

I will admit that these now fools who think that they have majorly thrown a wrench in the acquisition of faith in God, are announcing to all that will hear, that there is no God?

Such fools; were all of the way back in the historical writings of the bible. {Psalms 14:1} They, themselves; were forced to realize the mistakable error of their ungodly findings.

What is so amazing to me is how that the very people who reject God as the all supreme being; the maker and the creator of all heaven and earth; feel that they have the authority to direct others especially the leaders of the reli-gious communities, in what they have determined according to their research and subsequent findings; what they suggest that faith ought to be?

These people are often observed having extremely puffed up confidence when giving their own definitions of faith over the media platforms of any

of the networks.

There is no way on the earth that their research should have led their inquisitions to look outside of, and away from the written word of God.

Faith; is founded upon God; within and through God; rather mankind can appreciate that fact or not, faith is not even a religious thing, it is a God thing! Faith; has God's attention perpetually, it moves God to immediately respond to the call of mankind in the earth; it causes God to totally eradicate and to annihilate sicknesses and diseases for those who faithfully believe and ask for healing.

Everywhere you look in the direction of God, you will see faith all over God; faith in what He says; faith in whatever He does; wherever you find Him; and of course within all of the created realm of the Kingdom of God's Dear Son; the atmosphere is painted with faith.

In the earth, faith is found in the children of God who are truly blood washed and forgiven; changed from sinfulness to righteousness; through Jesus Christ our Lord.

The truth is that there are some certain practices of what is referred to as faith found in most of the churches; but be it true or false practices, faith is also suggested as being the basis for the reasonable premises in all religious establishment. Not many religious customs and practices are significant to true faith in God!

Most of the churches are now teaching that God in some way or another has changed in the manner of which He responded to faith in the bible?

It is also now more openly suggested that it would be worthless to expect for God to do whatever He did in the bible; as people simply don't believe that way anymore? But why not, since faith is definitely the same as it was since God created it; God is still the same!

As we hear people over the television media in movies, talk shows, and other forums of social media; we hear the discussion of the danger of reli-

gion, and how it has corrupted the free thought of the human mind, relative to the free will of living as one may choose to do so?

I beg to differ with that particular analogist rhetoric and the hidden agenda of those who prefer to dissuade others from adhering to the faith of God; as the penalty of living as we choose to do so is sin, and sin separates us from the love of God and all that He has provided for us to live in the earth.

The true understanding of faith now for many decades have been terribly marred and disected to the point that it is no longer understood as the methodology to take hold of, to bring the desired results of that which we expect from the Lord into fruition.

Here in America; many of the big business corporations are now outsourcing the manufacture of their product goods; so as a result, many jobs are depleted leaving the household providers indigent to care for their families.

The American people who have been effected by the decision of the big corporation to move work and jobs to another country for whatever the reason; they are not guessing, they know for sure that their dependable employment has been taken away without their consent!

Corporate heads of the big business corporations are not concerned with the welfare of the American workers; they are only concerned with the cost of production and the revenue of the product to which they are responsible to produce.

They see the loss of jobs and the financial welfare of the lower people as spoils of the corporate wars. The citizens who have lost their income, many of them are forced to turn to another source for the welfare of their families; and that's a real situation!

Some are blessed to find other forms of income; some were wise enough to have saved back some of the income; others went into business working for themselves now; while others simply sank to the bottom alike the Titanic on the ocean floor; they have no other hope for making a living.

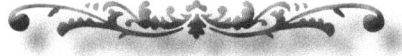

On a daily basis many people are forced to deal with this kind of thinking on their jobs only to face the very same thinking mindset of people on the boards of the churches?

It is no wonder that so many people are now hopelessly living without faith in God? Even the messages across the pulpits are ingrained with the resonance of corporate secular colloquialism whereas the people of the churches are left to be responsible for their own spiritual wellbeing and growth as a born again believer of Jesus Christ.

Very stiff measures of doubt and unbelief are served as the meal for the meat at the churches table of discussion during a sermonic delivery.

Those who are now more determined to believe that the church is to like-wise operate as a business, they are more rapidly turning away from faith in God as the true source of supply for the needs of the people of the churches, and they have turned to other sources outside of faith in God; even turning to the devil as a source.

We now have more conferences and workshops in and around the church communities, with ideas of teaching the people of the churches how to make money; so that the people and the churches will have the money to depend on as a competitive source of supply with the rest of the people in the world, and the churches.

It is detrimental that the churches have lost sight of the faith that we are required to have in God as we endeavor to live the life of Christ Jesus in the presence of this unbelieving world.

We often need to be blinded to the ways and the methodology of the people of the world who live totally to the left of the word of God and faith.

Should we just begin to poll the penitentiary and other systems of correction and so-called justice reform; the truth that is levied upon you here will soon be realized!

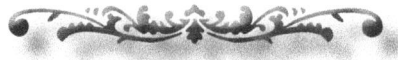

"Faith Knows The Enemies of God!"

As the children of God; we have been attacked as of late with what has been referred to as the "Ministry of Inclusion!" Which, in my own observation; has proven to be most dangerous to the manner of which people in the body of Christ think and choose to now believe, as many were very weak in the faith to begin with.

The bible instructs us to come out from the world and to be separated from the mindset of the world's process of thinking; however some have come along having been deceived and possessed by the devil to believe God is responsible for everyone and that He must be a friend to everyone; since He's the creator of everything and of everyone; no matter what?

The problem with many people is that faith did not appear to work for them in other places and situations outside of God? As in the company of true non-believers and in the presence of those who practice as a way of living, the doctrines of devils; Satan; faith will have no place!

While in the company of people making all sorts of ungodly pledges and taking of oaths and other blood rituals, and demonic rites; based on erroneous teachings about faith; people are led to believe that there are no boundaries or forbidden places that will hinder our faith from reaching out to God!

With the exception of getting us out of there for the sake of our own spiritual wellbeing, and to bring us to the place of repentance, faith will not work for us there.

Such deceptive teachings are the reasons that so many people are choosing to think and to believe that faith in God doesn't work! People don't want faith in God to work for the purpose and for the will of God; people want faith to work like the Hocus-Pocus of casting spells and working magic.

No matter of what their plans are, they just want faith to work to deliver the desires of their heart, even if it is not at all the plans of God for their lives. People want faith to work illegally against the word of God? The attitudes are to the like of asking God to just put a blind fold on the devil so that he won't

see that God just disregarded His own word for their sake.

On the contrary to what you might just be thinking about whether or not your faith worked, my friend, faith did work, but it rather worked in God's favor according to his will concerning you!

Faith in God doesn't work in your behalf to fatten you and to make you extremely well for the sake of God's enemies! Don't be so gullible as to think that the faith of God is not always as all-knowing as is God who gave the faith to us.

Too many are teaching subjects relative to having blind faith; blindness is an enemy to faith, and to the faithful. Blind nothing in this world is ever at any time capable of leading you to anything and for certain not to God.

Stupidity and ignorance are enemies to faith in God; because people lack definitive understanding of the word of God; inadvertently stupidity is assigned to accompany faith itself and even to the acquisition of faith in God; in the minds of those who are willfully illiterate to the word of God.

Faith is not stupid; there is never an unseemly act nor behavior of faith whereas it will cause you, the child of God to behave ungodly or out of the sorts of a faithful believer.

You may choose to put the blame on faith for such unbecoming behavior; but you will never be able to show any supporting foundation of your behavior in the written word of God.

Most people of the churches never discipline themselves to read and to study God's word, and most never really pray at all accept when they are faced with a crisis.

Without faith, it is totally absurd to even think of fasting and praying as a necessary discipline to be used of God in this faithless and perverse generation of people.

All of itself, faith is knowledgeable of the things that we need in an effort to discern the enemies of our faith and of God.

It is a major mistake to think and even to believe that whatever your condition is; mentally, physically, and even spiritually; that it is the exact same condition of the faith that is within you.

While you may be in a bad condition unable to benefit yourself or anyone else around you in any manner; faith itself is always in the very optimum condition, able to deliver to you that which God has intended for your life, the very same as it was when it was first delivered to every man!

"Faith Is!"

God works through faith, therefore faith can never be an unworkable element which stands in the way of God, blocking Him from being able to meet our need!

Through faith the sight of the blind is recovered; the lame walk again; the deaf hear again; even the dead are raised!

Faith could never be in the condition of any of the needs afore mentioned; else it would be totally impractical and impossible for God to work through faith to deliver and to heal those who were in need.

Faith have nothing to do with being mentally incompetent or psychologically emaciated or deficient; as God has no problem with the faithful being able to think or to use the skillful thinking of their own minds; it is not about so much of a concern as to what an individual might be able to think, it more so relative to where it is that your thoughts are gleaned from, as all thoughts are not conducive to the working order fo faith in God.

Faith is not at all indigent of counting numbers, of accounting of situational occurences as they happen and are manifested in our lives; faith is accurate and extremely powerful to document the instances of when we are trusting and believing that God will see us and hear us and meet our need right as we have aligned our hopeful expectation to get and to receive the help of the Lord God in our most urgent times of need.

Faith is God at the helm of our own personal systems of belief; knowing that we are totally incapable of bringing our own desires to pass, and of solving our own problems, and or of being able to heal our own bodies.

God is there in the assurance of faith to successfully settle us and to establish us having all of our need provided, as a result of having asked of Him to do so for us in faith.

Faith is not ever sick, or riddled with disease, nor infected with any type of germs or bacterial intrusions; as these types of things are only to touch the flesh, but never the spirit of any individual. Faith can never be demonically influenced; oppressed; depressed, or possessed!

All of the spiritual oppositions to the spiritual balance of every human being are also enemies to faith in God; whereas they are always found fleeing or setting up resistance to Faith in God.

The moment that faith has been established in the life of any individual, no enemy has the power to stand against the life of the believer in Christ Jesus!

Faith is strong enough; powerful enough; close enough to God; in touch with the universe and all of the people who live here; faith is smart enough; faith is joyous enough and pleased to be here with us and for our own benefit; wherever love is indeed pleased to be in the realm of humanity, so is faith also pleased to be there.

Faith is an awesome world of reality and splendor of God, left with us since the beginning of the creation of the heavens and the earth.

Faith is actually more awesome than everything that was made indeed; it is only that we are able to see other things, visualizing them with our given eyesight to the point in fact that we are most apt to verbalize the excitement for having the experience of seeing something else that our God has created for us in the earth; so we think of so many other things as being greater than faith itself.

Faith is greater! As reality of living in the realm of the earth, we have many things which come upon us to try us at levels that we are most unfamiliar and unaware of, for which we need a much greater substance or an even greater reality to help and to deal with that erected reality that is troubling us.

Faith can never be weaker or less than what is needed for our present benefit, else it would never be us on the losing end of things, it would be faith that would have lost the battle or faith would have been on the failing end to have conquered the situations for us!

As faith was initially created to be conquering and most powerful and smart; the continuous never ending reign of faith is as it has always been from the beginning. The continuity of faith is as awesomely splenderous to that of the continual reign of the marriage covenant, only with the absence of the divorce decree.

It is so awesome and powerful to know and to realize that there is absolutely no such thing as a divorce from faith; although any individual can in fact deny the faith of God.

For an instance; if you were required to give back everything that you had acquired as a result from faith; could you? Would you? What would you even have left that you will have gotten on your own?

If you were required to separate from faith, where would you go where faith in God is not there; and of course where would you send faith to be away from your presence?

The scary thing to theses questions is that many people actually think that they have a suitable answer; you would be shocked and totally blown away at the surprise of the fact that faith is not only there, but also that it was there before any of you ever arrived!

You have only chosen to do other things in that place instead of allowing faith to have precedence and to do it's perfect work in that place concerning you.

Faith is instant; it would seem that faith would ride on the backs of opportunities and of circumstancial situations where the people of the earth need to apply faith to get whatever is needed from the Lord.

However, I need for you to understand that without faith, opportunities and circumstances would never even have a reason nor occurrence to be in the realm of humanity.

It should be better understood that it is not faith that is looking for and instance to be applied to humanity, as it is already connected and attached to humanity; and affixed to every opportunity to ask the Lord for everything.

Faith never stand in the presence of humanity asking for a chance to be chosen; we find often that it is humanity that leaps and jumps at the presented chance opportunities to choose faith as the manner of getting God's attentiveness to our present situations, and need for repentence to save us.

Contrary to what many have been led to believe, faith is not standing idle and doormant in the isles and the annals of human pathways, crying, rejected by mankind. Saying to itself; "that only if they would choose faith their lives would be so much better?"

No; faith just continues to stand in the presence of God; as the perfect doorman or the liason to the coridors in the realm of the spirit to usher us to the presence and to the provisions of God's grace.

Faith stands as the traffic officer that directs us to the right turns and to the exact parking lot for resting in the appointed place of God's intentions for us to rest while He purposefully provides for us!

Faith stands as the elevator attendant who directs the elevator to the exact floor of the building where we have been directed to go for the benefit of being ourselves, elevated.

Faith is durable; it doesnt get tired and worn out as result of the people of God always leaning on faith and looking to faith; faith has the durability of a trillion Rhinoceros all moving at an instance, and then some; there is nothing

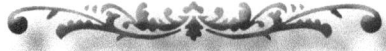

that faith can't move out of the way of every child of God!

Even after we will have taken faith into the battle with us, we will never have to look back at faith only to realize that faith needs a medic or a surgeon as a result of haven taken a bullet, or from the shrapnel of an explosive inference of some kind?

Faith can stand the test of any attack; whenever faith has been attacked, it is not faith which suffers from the attack, it is however that one who levies the attack that suffers for the fact that faith will not be lending the support to assist that individual for whatever their need might be.

They are surely going to need faith before faith will ever need them; as the assignment and the role for each party never changes, nor is it ever rendered neutral or powerless in that it no longer have the ability to produce!

God empowered faith to produce for them that call on the name of the Lord trusting and believing that God is able to do whatever they need for Him to do.

The never ending powerpack of faith is never to be compared to or confused with that of a battery pack which have the ability to last for extended periods of time needing to be recharged as result of being drained after the time of usage will have expired.

Finally; Faith; has no time of expiring or of being used in totality to the point that there is no more faith to be used.

Faith will even outlast you and I; as we rest in our graves, faith is still at work in the lives of others; faith is still moving in the thoughts and in the idealogical inquisitioning of the people around the world who might have been a bit slow adhering to the acquisition of faith in God;

Whether we will like it or not, only God will have the last say on the fact of who will and may not be awarded the benefit of faith in God!

Remember that it's God's Faith; Not Your's!

Chapter 2

"Faith; Before The Beginning"

Through faith we understand that the worlds were framed by the word of God, so that things which are seen were not made of things which do appear. {Hebrews 11:3}

"By Faith It All Happened"

More and more we are beginning to understand the awesome power of faith as we see faith respond to the command of God. The opening chapter of the book of Genesis; what is most remembered and realized is that; "God said!"

I hear lots of people who refuse to acknowledge faith in God; as they even adamantly refuse to confess that Jesus Christ is come in the flesh; I hear them disputing that the bible has any facts written in it!

They are dead set against anyone believing that what we read in

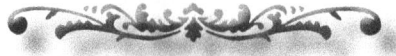

the word of God that it is indeed factual; not only were they not here on the face of the planet during the reported times of the scripture; they were not even present during which times that the bible was translated into the English language.

They omit to acknowledge that they don't even have concrete evidence to dispute the validity of the biblical accounts which have been penned and documented as historical record for every believer and unbeliever alike to take account of for the sake of being able to choose whether or not they are going to accept the written truth or to discount it as the truth and totally deny it!

I am amazed at the late comers who came to be as a result of God; who are in existence because God said so for us all to be! Many of them could not even tell you what happened to them last year unless they documented the accounts themselves accurately; so as not to misconstrue the details of their occurrences?

Yet they have the mitigated gaul to discount the documented re-count of the move and actions of God and the people of God who followed His narratives to live upon the earth.

As always it's not just that these people are refusing to allow the truth of the word of God to take root in their hearts, they are con-sistently working on the heart and the minds of others; as many as they are able to influence; to get them to turn a deaf ear to the mes-sages of the scripture, and to throw away the bible all together.

Faith; as it is, as seen both inside and on the outside of the church-es is intellectually contained as only a thing of selective choice of an individual's rights to choose!

Be it known right now that faith was not at all given for us to have belief in faith; but rather faith was and is given for every hu-man being on the face of the planet to have strong trust in God! Whether they choose to believe and to receive God or not, faith was

yet given to spiritually benefit all mankind.

Many believe that faith doesn't even exist unless they create a since of mental reasoning in their own mind, so as to instigate a rightful reality to make sensible truth out of faith.

How wrong they are to believe such thinking; as many who are even in the pulpits don't seem to have much more of a grasp on the actuality of faith and the truth about faith's origin and its true func~ tion in the earth's realm among people.

I know that since we are going to teach faith, that we ought se~ riously to know what faith is, in depth, and also that we ought to understand that faith comes from God!

My argument is that if it were so that we as mankind were pres~ ent to see faith generated and defined to function among mankind; then perhaps we might have more of a validated reasoning to say what faith is and how faith is to be used among us?

It doesn't really matter to me that people have a fixed idea of faith, whom are not even believers that are open to seek God's word about faith's origin and to receive the truth about how faith works!

It matters to me that so many people of the churches who pur~ port to pray, to study their bibles and to believe the word of God; that they allow so much of the secular mind-set to influence their idea of faith in God.

Most people; adhere to as to what they have been told that faith is, although they have no experience of a faith that works the ex~ traordinary manifestations from God, and even dumbfounds the minds of mere people of their everyday surroundings.

They have only heard about miracles; although through faith they have never been the witness to the miraculous occurrences in the earth. Far too many people have only a weak understanding

of faith that allows for them to go to church once a week or maybe once a year?

Thank God that I have come to realize that faith is so much more than just that!

Faith; has been selectively given to every man in the existence of time without prejudice; but understand that faith has never been left in the earth's realm as a selection, at man's own discretion having the right to choose faith.

Man; has been given the right to choose whether to act on faith or to ignore faith all together! The scripture admonishes us according to {Ephesians 4:5}, that there is but one faith; not many faiths as we hear across the pulpits and over the television screens reporting that there is indeed many faiths!

I believe the report of the scripture, THERE IS ONE LORD, ONE FAITH, AND ONE BAPTISM!

People are determined to apply the biblical principles of faith to their natural lives, although their behavioral actions of faith are intentionally and purposefully void of the spirit of God. That one faith that has been given to every man, by God; is not at all what they are believing to exercise.

Their preference of an account of faith is what they believe to be exerciseable on the outside of the church; and separate from those people who confess to being saved by the grace of God.

How often do we sit in a chair that we do not confidently trust that the chair will hold us as we rest the total weight of our bodies in the seat?

How many of our steps as we walk, do we journey believing that it may actually be our last step, in that we will not make our destination; even when we are only walking across the floor to the other

side of the room that we are in already? We actually believe in all of the abilities that we had been given at creation as a human being.

We believe in the activities of the limbs our bodies at all times until if and when they actually give out and refuse to operate as normally expected and most definitely desired for them to work for us.

We believe in the ability to raise our hands attached to our arms to brush our teeth; to comb our hair; and even to simply take up a pencil or a pen to write with our hands.

We accept that it is our natural ability to do these things; often disregarding the fact that there are so many others who had been born lacking the natural ability to use those limbs as everyone else who had also been blessed to do so!

And let's not disregard the ones who were indeed born with all of their natural abilities who lost them some way or another along the way while living on the earth?

As of late, we have been experiencing the openings of sink holes and landslides unexpectedly in places where we could never have been prepared for them to happen or appear!

In my opinion; those occurrences have been blatant disappointing failure to the trustful acceptance that people have mobilized their belief senses to come to the place of actual retirement or rest upon.

We drive down certain streets or highways believing that these are the pathways that are going to deliver us to our neighborhood destinations and the communities here in the earth.

When shown how to read and to use the directions on a map, we believe that the highways are the direct pathways to the next state in the country? We just follow the directions on the map in total

belief.

Houses are built on certain plots of ground that we would never believe would one day out of the blue just happen to fall or to sink out from beneath us taking the house or at least part of the house with it?

We don't go to bed at night expecting to wake up in the morning; opening the door preparing to go out, only to realize that all of the earth that was in front of the doorway when we laid down to sleep, is fallen away to oblivion through the night?

Though it is never really intended that we are using faith to believe while we sleep; we yet believe that the world as we know of it will be here when we are awakened to see the next day; or only hours after a brief nap.

Faith seems to disappoint the expectations for some people when they are required to apply living through faith intentionally! See, just because an individual may never choose to live by and through faith, doesn't erase the actuality and the truth about faith and definitely about faith in God!

In fact, if it were really left up to certain people; whenever they had actually done what was supposed to have wrecked and destroyed an individual's faith, there would not have been any more faith left for anyone else!

In spite of the way that others have acted in response to faith, other people are yet grasping and taking hold of faith by the scores? There is a reason for that!

"Faith is Not at All Left Up To You! However, Faith; Has Been Left Here For You!"

There are lots of liars who falsely lay claims to faith with the

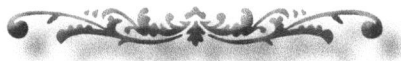

uttermost intent to deceive others concerning faith, of which in my own opinion had been the motivation for persuading people to segregate themselves from others to perform certain religious acts of what has been called worship; but true faith itself will never lie!

Many people have been so deceived that they believe that all they need is to be a part of a certain denomination, and their ticket to heaven would be awarded to them? They now believe that they are set to enter into Heaven with the Father for eternity!

Regardless to what the bible says about us believing and receiving of the word of God and of the spirit; people more easily adhere to the deceptive voices of other people to believe that there has to be another way to reach God; totally disregarding the commandment to receive Jesus Christ our Lord and savior; through faith!

My friend, suppose the spirit of God were removed from the earth's realm; exactly how would you ever go about making an attempt to reach God, or even to reach out to Him; through a spirit-less sense of faith?

It is the spirit filled faith; itself, that helps our understanding as we defy the natural behavior of most mere men of the earth, as we pray to an unseen God; believing that He hears us as we pray; believing that He sees us every moment of our lives?

We rise from our knees after praying looking for things to happen or even for invisible things to show up with physical attributes.

God; in His own ultimate wisdom and Godhead; placed faith for all of mankind from before the time of the beginning of creation, in an effort to keep us all connected to the Father in Heaven.

It was never God's intention that heaven would be separated from the earth; faith my friend is the only method of which we are able to go about making the reconnection.

Even as God has released His most powerful angelic being into the earth's atmosphere; though they are invisible; without faith those angels will never aid us in our needs.

God will do great things for us that will always enable us to know that He is the only one responsible for the mighty deeds done for us in the earth.

Faith allows us to be separated from Satan indefinitely; whereas His plan for humanity is destruction and total separation from God; eternally.

We are God's greatest creation in the earth's realm; only through faith are we enabled to bring the spiritual into our natural experience.

Time rides on the very back of faith, as it is faith that was here first in the beginning with God. Time never stops; should all of the clocks in the earth cease to operate and quit working altogether, it would have no effect on time!

The clocks only tell us what time it is, as time dictates to the clocks whenever we inquire of the clocks; but it is God who made time allowing faith to speak to the very movement of time itself?

Clocks are often wrong, set to the wrong time whether it is minutes or hours; there are times that the clocks indeed report to the people of the earth in error.

But, there is never an instance when time itself is wrong; time is always right just like God! No matter how biblically astute and literarily sound and educationally correct you may be, you cannot deny this truth! Though many may try?

How could we even believe the time of the day or of the night without faith? God knows that we as people certainly rely on the timeclock when it comes time to begin and to end a work schedule.

As untimely that we as people in general are with many of our daily affairs; we have certainly become timely as it relates to having any type of a service at the church where we should invoke the presence of God.

We will often tolerate starting the service late, but almost never are we as tolerable when it comes to dismissing the service so that we can go about our personal plans.

We schedule the times of our personal affairs, whether we are responsible for the scheduling or someone else, but not realizing that every single event of penning a scheduled affair for us to attend, that faith is likewise included at the helm of that schedule!

There have been times that we could hardly fall off to sleep anticipating the arrival time of any particular scheduled event of our lives.

We have allowed faith to be overlooked and disregarded in our daily affairs, though this is not the truth at all. Some see faith as an intrusion to their daily affairs and to their livelihood, for the simple reason that faith is associative to God being present wherever we are!

Faith is here whether we want or desire for it to be here; it doesn't matter that you have refused to inquire of God for the presence of faith, and even if ultimately you would prefer if it were never here at all.

Some people believe that they would like to see for themselves that faith had been annihilated and totally eradicated from the presence of this world. Even the discussions of faith in the churches is disturbing to some people to the point that they are disgusted, made to feel nauseated in their bellies at the mere mention of faith in God.

Doctors who are consistently looking for the exact causes for migraine headaches would be blown away if they knew that the cause

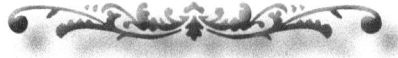

of many of the migraines are happening because people are trying to deny the truth of faith in God?

The truth of faith is so powerful that it could cause your heads to literally explode into fragmented pieces as you try to deny it; were it not for the mercy and for the grace of God.

However, I have seen too many people who would rather suffer with the migraines, taking the prescription medications knowing that the drugs are no real remedy to the headaches, rather than to trust and to believe God through faith to be healed.

You and I were never created to deny faith nor to live faithless in any manner of the expressions of our beings. Others, who don't try to deny faith, only seek to have faith in other sources and things and in other people.

Some people seem to feel as if it is their intelligence that allows for them to deny whatever faith is or is supposed to be. They accuse faithful people as being ignorantly stupid and deceived for their choice to believe God. While others only choose to believe in the existence of God; I believed, to know God!

As easy as it is to believe that breath and breathing was here from whatever a beginning might have been, because all living plant life and creatures breathe to this very day, it should be just as easy for you to believe that faith was also here from the beginning.

My friend, where did eating originate, and to what do you associate as being the authority of trust and faithful reliance to engage in such necessary behavior of the human body?

Are we to acknowledge that we are certain as to whether or not the practice of eating was passed on to plant-life from humanity; or were it passed to humanity from the plant-life? As we feed the plants, it is a fact that the plants in return feed humanity!

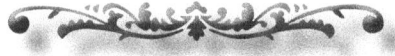

We know through scientific evaluation and personal studies that animals of all origins feed and nourish their abilities to live in the earth's realm; and likewise as we faithfully feed and nourish animals and fish of the sea, they in turn feed and nourish humanity as we partake of them and eat.

Faith allows for us as people to follow through with eating and ingesting certain foods, as we don't all culturally share the same diet and desires for food. Some things that I have seem others eat should certainly require faith in God? My Opinion..........

"Faith;" Came First!

There is a danger in humanity associated with the egotistical arrogance of the flesh which drives us to desire and even to demand aside from God that we'd be in charge of everything that happens and or occurs in our lives.

The most eminent danger is that we have great tendency to believe in our own chosen beliefs, though they are most often unreliable and prone to make us even more irresponsible than we've ever been before!

Some have even forgotten where they acquired the structured but baseless information that they refuse to distance themselves from upon learning the truth?

We are truly capable of believing in things until the death of us; like as to those who have chosen to think that they believe that it is unnecessary to take hold of any such thing as of faith in God.

Though foolishly they have said in their own hearts that there is no God; according to the scripture! Doesn't matter that people are often shown the error of untruth in the things that they have believed, they are not going to relent believing what they have indeed chosen to believe; even when it means that they are hell bound as a

61

result.

So my question for you is; Was it belief; or was it faith? I am not going to judge those ministers of the churches who consistently teach belief; and believing; as being one and the very same things as of having faith.

Belief, is but the doorway to the entrance of faith? In an effort for us to really have faith in God; it is also imperative that we seek definition for the sake of our own comprehension, in that we will come to know what it is to truly believe.

Belief; is but the starter ignition to get us revved up to move out and to move forward into faith! Belief; if you will allow me is but the initial step to decide on faith; but we have got to determine within ourselves to continue moving forward refusing to stop, in an effort to realize faith for what it really is.

Many have thought themselves to have believed, but after being inside of the matter, they soon discover that they no longer believed in the matter after all; they had a change of heart. If you can indeed just only believe, you can also allow for yourself to be found in disbelief!

Many; who had also confessed to have believed at one time or another, have also walked away from the church, and they often confess that they have also walked away from God. They truly walked away from what they thought themselves to have believed; although it is evident that they had never really believed God;

The intimate, personal experience with God alone is too powerful to allow us just turn from His Peace and His Love and walk away as if God never existed? Not when you have really gotten to know Him for whom He really is!

Such shallow erroneous teachings, so many of the people of the churches are encouraged to stand at the entrance of faith; never

really finding the true depths of faith in God. The bulk of people in the churches can truthfully say that they have believed; but most of them cannot show you real true faith.

For God so loved the world, that He gave His only begotten son, that whosoever believeth in Him, should not perish, but they shall have everlasting life.
{St. John 3: 16}

The key in this verse is the word; "Believeth" ~ of which in our English language, suggest to us that according to the suffix, "eth" it means that there is to be a continuance…..

Understanding that belief leads to faith; the continuation of believing leads us to realize and to aggressively adhere to faith, and of course to being faithful!

Once we are adjoined unto faith, with the mindset and the determination to go further and deeper into the knowledge of faith in God; we become as affixed unto God in Christ Jesus; even as the ground is permanently attached to the earth!

Most people are busy making choices to believe certain things for which they have never applied the choices to faith in God. Faith must establish a reason to adhere to any belief beyond question and scrutinizing beneath the surface for validation.

Faith settles us to the foundational rest of any inquisition to know about things, whereas, questioning keeps us uncertain and consistently seeking to know why the previous whys of the questions asked before, are there in the first place.

People just keep on asking questions for reasons that they may not even understand themselves; they just want to know why?

It has been my understanding, as I have come to recognize the true demeanor of people who prefer to stay in question about ev-

63

erything; purposefully they have intentionally denied the reality and the truth about faith in God.

Faith always eliminates the questions, faith alleviates the need for questions; especially when the layers are peeled back to reveal that God is standing thereby as the only reason that whatever it is that is there, is there!

Faith pulls back the curtains and removes the partitions between what we are able to see as it relates to truth and God.

So many others prefer to only deal with what is true among people and all that is indeed tangible and physical in the earth's realm. However, all things that are true are not all truth!

It is possible to find that many of the things that we have been shown to be true, can often turn out after all to be false, and an outright lie, or an optical illusion!

But, you will never be able yourselves, or find that anyone else has been able to overturn the truth! Truth stands eternally upright and correct in its integrity.

It is necessary to come to grips with the truth that God is; in an effort to know that faith is; also! Outside of God; there is no real need for faith as it is written in the word of God!

Because the word of God is eternally established in Heaven; the need for faith itself is likewise eternally established as a need for all mankind in an effort to fulfill every individual purpose and to complete the ability to establish a right relationship with God; through Christ Jesus.

We as people should really stop trying to change the order of things as God ordained for them to be.

First things always come first! We have not been given the rightful ability to alter things in life, although we often finagle and stress

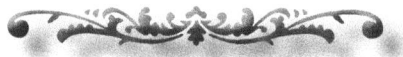

the natural order of things only to reveal the great mess of things that we will have indeed made trying to play God.

The original linage of which God ordered for all things to be, must be left at rest, so as not to disrupt the natural flow and the assigned rest at the proper time.

Faith; is the established order of God in that it stands and it rest at the head of the line in place before everything else; whereas faith must be applied before you look so as to ensure that either you know that what you are looking into that it is of God, or that you know to turn away from whatever it is that you have set your focus upon realizing that it is not of God, at all.

And for certain, we have learned to put faith before hearing anything spoken in the churches and in the atmosphere that may indeed have the ability to dampen our desires to grow and to increase in faith.

The problems of so many people in the churches; is that they have bibles under their arms and in their hands, but they are refusing to connect their bibles with the faith of God.

To me it is out right hideous to see people read the bible, which is all about God; but they refuse to see God in the bible as being anything more than a historic figure.

Even in many of the pulpits worldwide, many of the pastors and the ministers alike outright refuse to make the connection of the word and the spirit of God.

Brethren, my heart's desire and prayer to
God for Israel is, that they might be saved.
For I bear them record that they have zeal
of God, but no according to knowledge.
{Romans 10:1-2;}

There is absolutely, positively, no way period to know God without faith! No matter how intelligent you have been told that you are, without faith you are slipping and missing gravely!

Smart brilliant interpretation does not and will not allow revelatory entrance into the word and into the knowledge of God; as only faith will unlock that doorway entrance of the word to you through praying and fasting.

I'm totally blown away and disgusted whenever I see people in the churches who attempt to lay hands on the people of the churches, and or to preach and to teach the truth of the word of God; who are obviously denying the power of faith in God; which ultimately reveals to all in attendance that they have also denied the power of God!

Pray, that your own heart may be faith-filled, to the point in fact that God is pleased to release the powerful presence of the anointing in the atmosphere so that the work of faith can be loosed where the manifestation of the scripture can be realized and experienced in the lives of the people who are present in that same atmosphere.

Where God is; so is His powerful presence; but without faith there is no way at all to experience the essence of His powerful presence.

We assumed that the people come into the sanctuary of the churches to experience God; but because of so much zeal and not at all enough faith, people get an entertaining show.

Truthfully, faith has been kicked into the corner; and the falsehood of religion is being erected and ushered to the forefront as what is thought to be the rightful order of worship.

First faith; then praise and worship; without faith there is just a whole lot of singing and musical expression.

One of the most annoyingly disgusting things to happen in the

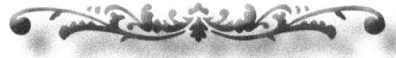

churches is to sit through so-called praise and worship under the guise of a faithless non-anointed worship leader who is determined to go on and on; so as to complete the audition for some sort of talent scout, or a record agent in the house. Totally Faithless!

Finally, the experience of the so-called Apostles and Prophets that are indeed faithless and absolutely void of hearing the master's voice, have gotten to be ridiculous!

People who are given the chance to stand with the microphone are so bold now; they no longer fear the Lord God in the sanctuary and anywhere else.

Not only do they lack the faith of God; but as you are jumping up and down at the words spoken out their lying mouths, they are assured that you lack the faith of God also, as you are too easily deceived.

For there shall arise false Christs, and false prophets,
and shall shew great signs and wonders; Insomuch
that, if it were possible, they shall deceive the very elect.
{St Matthew 24: 24}

Faith demands that we first and foremost follow after the scripture! But it's impossible when no faith is applied to the word of God; whereas there is no hearing of faith; or hearing in faith!

Many pastors think themselves to be spiritually on track, as they admonish the people of the churches that there are false prophets in the land; when in fact they themselves are fake pastors who had never been called of the Lord to preach, and for certain to pastor.

Faithless, check receiving salary pastors, who have been to the theological seminary, but have failed to meet God at the altar of their own hearts, can never lead you in the direction of faith to hear the truth in the word of God, and to the truth of the Holy Ghost.

Their greater determination is to get you to increase their salary, so they are entertaining your emotions to get you to feel better just as you are?

They are often seeking to assure the people of the sanctuaries of the absence of needing any longer to seek the Lord for greater faith to change and to live lives that are indeed pleasing to the Lord.

It is urgent that we the church get about the business of faith!

Chapter 3

"Understanding And Faith"

Wisdom is the principle thing, therefore get wisdom, and with all thy getting get understanding.
{Proverbs 4: 7}

UNDERSTANDING — *under–standing ~ {to intellectually assume a mental position of reasoning beneath the bottom of the foundation. To scrutinize the elements that makes up the facts at the bottom; find the meaning of a thing; to support the established platform.} Look up from down below to see the top of the bottom to be able to comprehend the reasons why, when, where, and even how....* Author's definition;

Understand —Transitive and intransitive verb;
1. Having the ability to explain; knowing the nature or the meaning or cause of somebody or something.
2. To realize or become aware of something.
4. Recognize somebody's character or somebody's situation, especially

in a sympathetic, tolerant, or empathetic way.

5. Interpret something in a particular way, or to infer or deduce a particular meaning from something.

6. Believe something to be agreed, settled, or firmly communicated.

7. Gather or assume something on the basis of having heard or been told it.

8. Assume information or a meaning that is implied but not expressed directly.

"Fat Heads Assume; But, They Often Over Reach, Often Missing the True Meaning of Faith"

Not many people really seem to care whenever a fraud has been exposed for being the fake that they really are, even though they have been going along with them in some capacity or another.

However, many people are rattled to the core of their being whenever it has been revealed that an individual has been declared a certified genius.

People will go all out of their way to try and prove that another individual is really not that smart, even though they often fail to disprove the previous findings of the individual of which they had been found to be jealous of.

A revolting fact for many of the collegiate educators and higher education instructors is that many people are extremely intellectual with the skill and the wisdom to properly execute putting their knowledge to work for them in the right timing, place, and in the exact order; they are smart.

I am of the opinion that higher learning institutions really do not teach the students as much as they are responsible for exposing them to the pathway of greater knowledge. It is the responsibility of the student to take advantage of the open access of the information.

I am rather appreciative of smart people who are not only studious, but their ability to maintain data and information is remarkable.

It's amazing to me how that almost little to none effort is put forward to intellectually stabilize the information, they just seem to be like a vacuum or an information magnet just pulling information into themselves.

These certain people are often found to be information heavy; full of all types of knowledge; I'd like to think of their brains as being swollen and just big; overflowing with knowledge!

Now what it is that we are finding relative to this particular subject matter is that many of our very smart people are over-shooters and over-thinkers when it comes to faith.

Some people have gotten to be so informed; they feel that understanding knowledge and faith can just be forged into the same reality.

Bear in mind, that there is a difference to the knowledge that you may have acquired and the actual knowledge that faith has; not including your own acquired knowledge of faith.

Faith; is not a dead head of cabbage or of lettuce, and neither is it just some sort of a fluff as to the likes of a cloud. Even fluffy clouds are filled with rain and lightening, ice and snow; but we don't even know how it all happens.

While we can see the clouds and are witnesses of the rain sleet snow and of the lightening, we even hear the thunder which roars out of the clouds, we cannot see faith naturally. That which comes out of faith is seen upon its manifestation to us in the natural realm.

Faith; is an alive, active gift from God; that responds to God; communicates with God concerning you and me, and it is perpetually

positioned between man and God.

Many of our pastors that are quite intellectual and smart think that they can just teach faith from the platforms of their own imaginative perspectives of what they have believed that they understand faith to be. But, often missing the scriptoral messages on faith that brings the clarity that we need each day of our lives.

Then of course many of the followers of their ministries are eventually rebuked and accused of not being obedient followers of the teachings of faith in that ministry?

I have found that many people from the churches are obedient followers of the teaching, but they are following hypothetical formulas of faith that never line up with the written word of God.

Being an adult now I am of the opinion that the teachings of faith need to be started when the little children are at the kindergarten stages of learning.

Thus we are more apt to jump start their ability to begin to mentally mark keepsake data and to configure many things about understanding; and to develop reasonable concepts of understanding faith in God.

Should we engage the children at earlier ages, as the people of faith in God we would be responsible for curtailing many of the negatives that will indeed visit their little lives. We can definitely teach them to look to God initially rather than to wait until the devil will have crept into their affairs of living.

The churches are guilty of waiting on the secular school systems and television to begin the thinking process of our children. Although we of the churchges are guilty of waiting on the schools to teach the children to read; we are even more guilty of waiting on the children to age having learned many very negative things of fear and of failing, before we even take an interest in teaching them

about faith in God.

The deception of the churches is that it seems that people are not ready to absorb the teachings of faith in God, until they have been ripped and torn to pieces by the cares of the world?

Someone told the people of the churches that people are not responsively appreciative to the teachings of faith until they have been beat down by Satan, and every possible negative thing that could ever happen in their lives.

Faith; allows for us to not only to believe in the covering grace of God, but it enables us to accept God's covering, preventing Satan and the things hurled at us from even being successful at touching us.

Had we been taught successfully at early ages to embrace faith in God; I'm sure that there are some painful experiences that we would have never known.

So as it relates to the strength and the skill of maintaining a sharp understanding; while most children are actually born to have very vivid imaginations; the children are left to themselves to think a lot of things that they never are really developing much of an ability to understand, much less to really understand the information and the knowledge that they have been given.

It is most common for the average young person to grow up being at best, just another product of their environment, even when their environment had been one of early childhood educational development and training.

Many youth are also products of the very surface, washed out, weak, and incapable teachings of faith in God. So many people in the churches are taught of a sense of faith that will eventually work for them if they only continue to believe that it will one day?

Some of the younger people are blessed to emerge much sharper and even more determinate of acquiring data and information on a much higher level than to that of which had been the norm of their own environment and community.

Many are actually gifted to learn who are not necessarily likewise as gifted to thoroughly understand all of which they have learned?

The paralleled actualities of truth, of the natural and of the spiritual realms in effect have caused the very same levels of learning and of understanding the things taught in the churches to be obtained, but not often always completely understood and totally comprehended.

Not at all suggesting that the people of the churches are any less intelligent than the people of the secular society!

Many of the leaders of the churches did not just come out of the woods desiring to take the helm of the churches, but they grew up in the churches void of the truest understanding relative to life and living?

Most of us have confessed that if we had the chance to do it all over again, we would definitely do some things differently. The message underneath it all is that they would have worked a bit more aggressively to understand life, living, and the word of God as it relates to us as the people of the Lord.

Most who teach faith are determined that the people in the churches being taught need to be prolific in understanding faith. The problem is that most people have not come to the point in fact of understanding faith themselves suitable for successfully teaching it to others.

I can remember being taught by my pastor, who wasn't an educated man, but he was quite a man of godly wisdom and of faith; he taught us that you cannot live above and beyond that of which you

are able to understand or above the level of the knowledge that you have.

Even many who themselves may be astute bible instructors have found themselves to be stumped and even confused when their own supposed manipulative grasp of faith seems to evade them; or faith might have appeared to have disobeyed their own personal faithful command over a situation in their life?

To speak with many people you will soon discover that not many of the instructors were actually filled with the kind of knowledge which taught their students to apply faith and to have faith work for them, because they lacked the true understanding of faith in God.

They failed to understand that the scripture says that the letter killeth; but the spirit maketh it alive.{II Corinthians 3: 6}

In other words; without the Holy Ghost, there will be no activation of the word to bring it alive in the bellies of those who have read it, thus also leaving the activation of faith inactively unable to be discharged.

People from all walks of life in all religions and denominational churches world-wide, are walking the planet thinking that they have the proper understanding of faith.

But, alike the others who also believes that their understanding of what faith is and of what it is that faith can do, they are all in debate believing that as soon as the other people come under their biblical instruction, their' message is the exact level of clarity to define faith.

The churches; worldwide need to be biblically aligned for the sake of unifying us all as the body of Christ. {Ephesians 4: 13}

I will admit that great effort have been applied in the churches so that people will be able to come to the understanding of faith.

However, in total honesty many people of the churches are known and recognized for being those who lack the gift of just naturally understanding things and people.

It is impossible to be a true witness when you have not understood that things that you are to witness to. Most people are too willing to omit stuff and to overlook the details in the things which take place in their presence.

In an effort to truly get a real true comprehensive grasp on understanding, one would most definitely need to spend time getting to the bottom of the meaning of what it means to be ignorant. You can not spend a balance of your time ignoring things and have an understanding at the same time.

Gaining an understanding will require that we come forward to apply the total attention of our minds, even at times to apply our motor skills in effort to grasp the reality of that of which we have comprehended.

I have been in the church long enough to recognize that the average people in the churches have no issue at all of the fact that it is a common practice for most people who come on over to the church to ignore the corporate study of the word of God in the churches during weekly and nightly sessions of teaching. And they also overlook the need for prayer, thus standing in the need of prayer on a daily basis; but, also for the very same things.

While the more studious members of the churches do find it most necessary to study the word of God, thus getting and maintaining a grasp on the written word of God concerning faith.

Many times they themselves have been found to be only at the surface, disappointed and unable to put forth the manifested evidence of faith as the bible says it.

It's been my determination to encourage them that there is noth-

ing at all wrong with faith, as their knowledge of faith may actually be biblically sound and accurate according to the scripture.

The problem lies within the manner of which they are intending on applying faith, and the motives behind their reasoning. It has also skipped their understanding that faith is a spiritual thing of which require the spirit and power of the Holy Ghost to actually set faith in the place of manifesting God!

The finite limit of our human ability to understand is most often the initial partitioning divide hindering our ability to work faith at optimum levels of non-contradicting actualities of manifestations from God!

As we allow ourselves to run rampant in circles through the bible seeking to know about faith to the point that we think that we truly understand faith, without even realizing it, we intellectually back ourselves into corners and into blind dark spaces where we could never see the truth, relative to true faith in God!

It is my true heart's desire to encourage as well as to literally lead us into the necessity to abandon the determination to understand faith itself; learning to understand and to comprehend what it means to have an understanding firstly.

Understanding, itself; have the power to allow for the windows of heaven and the doorway to the enlightenment of our minds, for the sake of making the right connection to faith, to be opened. Being able to comprehend the purpose and the meaning of faith to us as children of the Kingdom of God; to be opened unto us.

"How About Understanding What You Know"

A common recognition of people from all over the world is that they are filled with either lots of information or lots of knowledge; rarely do many of them know the difference.

Many people have what I will refer to as "swollen memories; flooded; enlarged; memories alike a river, a pond or a lake that has taken on more gallons and cubic feet of water than its capacity to store the water." Thus we see the water all over the place in places that it shouldn't be as result of taking on too much.

Knowledge is wonderful and suggestive of being powerful itself, but to know a thing of knowledge because you can say that you have comprehended it and that you do understand, is far better.

Things swell up real big and are at times enormously inflated when it is over-contained and or left unattended in heightened temperatures, as on an extremely hot summer day out in the shed; or maybe left out in the car on a sweltering hot day.

Some people that I have met along the way are just so overwhelmed with being able to learn something more that they never knew before; only they have never really done anything with the knowledge they have already stored up in their minds.

They have libraries in their homes that are stocked to capacity, with no more space for another book. Others have stock piles of books all over the house in corners and around the wall of the rooms of their home. People have knowledge and information and the text books to refer back on the information should the need arise.

Our societies have heightened the acquisition of learning, acquiring knowledge, and obtaining College degrees as being that of the greatest accomplishments in the earth for any individual.

We willingly likewise embrace the idea and it is a reality that knowing some things makes for a better employment possible for being able to sustain oneself to amass a decent financial income.

On average; those who have applied learning to acquire scholastic recognition, are often rewarded with the higher job positions and much larger pay grades.

Be it better resolved; that the ultimate purpose for getting understanding would actually be to establish our positioning around the matter of fact of living at hand.

We need to get to the bottom of the matter to relieve the stress of believing that the issues that confront us are elevated and stacked on top of us.

The only real reason that we are so stressed out, being paralyzed in our ability to move forward in our lives daily, is simply for reason of the fact that we have allowed our own thinking to suggest that we're on the bottom of the things that we should be on top of.

Many of the said believers are struggling with faith and of course of being faithful to faith in the word of God; faithful to their salvation and to the savior; and they are allowing for themselves to be defeated in their walk of faith in God.

They spend time focusing on the ability to flee and to run from the opposition and the spiritual warfare that comes against them, only never seeking understanding of their position against their opposition. Too many don't understand the positions that we are in as a result of our victorious savior, and our redeemer; Jesus Christ.

Not that we are to become so anal that we can't take the moment and seize upon the opportunity presented to us; but we should seek to be people who know who we are, what we're doing, where we're going, and for certain what we are to do whenever we get to where it is that we are going.

One of the greater tragedies in my own opinion is to see people in the body of Christ who are consistently void of understanding! Too many people in the churches are clueless and incapable of benefitting the Kingdom of God.

It is not that they are uninformed, but lacking the true intelligibility to understand when they need to be taught, they avoid the

greater sessions of the ministry which are the calmer more serene gatherings of the people of God; to be taught and made to clearly understand the word of God; and the purpose of the churches among the communities.

They need a much greater understanding for the purpose and the reason that they have indeed been saved and washed in the blood of Jesus. People need to understand that there so much more to being saved than just going to church now that they have come to Christ.

It is not possible to just leave God in Christ Jesus; at the church so that He will be there the next time that you decide to be there. Living alone will teach you why it is that you need to be with the Lord mentally, physically, emotionally, and spiritually everywhere you go!

Many of our believers totally freak out over the spiritual warfare that arises since being saved, almost everywhere they go. They have never experienced anything like this before!

While associating the new occurrences to the change that has happened in their lives, they ignorantly apply extreme negative reasoning to salvation and to churches, not realizing that those who will live godly shall suffer persecution. *{II Timothy3: 12}*

It's an understanding that has not been truthfully conveyed to the new comers; being saved now means that you have become the devil's target. Satan will do every evil thing possible to cause you to change your mind and to walk away from the Lord.

"It's The Questions Why; That Get the Very Best of Us"

Good stern biblical teaching and proper understanding will let an individual know that the real reason that such intense warfare has risen against them is because there is something right with them; not at all something wrong. I used to spend days and weeks trying

to understand why certain things were happening to me?

Then again I used to be very angry with God, while trying to figure out why it was that so many people seemed to be very glad and outright over-joyed at the fact that things weren't going very well for me?

Understanding soon reveals that there is a great deal more to see than what you are actually looking at, and are able to recognize!

One of the greater detriments of the people in the churches as it relates to the scriptures is that there are certain scriptures that are poignant and straight ahead to mean exactly what they say!

But people come together to reason and to create an objectionable dialogue when there is really nothing at all to discuss. There is to be no debate of the scripture, deciding as to whether or not we are going to believe this particular scripture or not.

I do believe that we should go all of the way into the necessity of having understanding, as it will be the vehicle to take us all of the way to our destiny and allow for us to glean everything that there is to be received, as a result.

Lots of people are right there, right now, standing in the midst of their assigned place; they have made their arrival to the place that they have been seeking for many years in prayer and fasting; but they lack the understanding to know it!

Understanding, stops the merry-go-round of looking at what everybody else is doing, to determine if that's what you are supposed to be doing also?

Understanding, relieves you from the need to measure up to everybody's opinion of you!

It will even allow for you to see when those who are measuring you, that they don't even measure up to themselves. They are

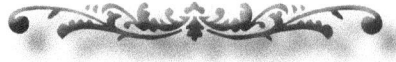

requiring something of you that they have not even been qualified to give of themselves! They actually know for sure that they can't measure up; they just think that they want to know if you really can?

So many people are literally disintegrating on the inside of themselves, as a result of warring against the whys that evade their abilities to understand!

Although we see and hear of suicides frequently in the natural, there is more spiritual suicide taking place than we are aware of! Whereas, people kill their own spiritual abilities to hold on to faith in God, even though this is done unintentionally.

What we see is that most people are strengthened in their weaknesses rather than being strengthened when they are weak. Ignorantly people are being encouraged and assisted in their moment of falling and failures, while others are being despised for being strong enough to take a stand and a determination to be unmovable, standing in faith!

The confession of the people in the churches, are not necessarily statements of faith that are encouraging to others in the church to push them forward to stay with the Lord even through trying times.

In other words, there are not enough replicas of faithfulness to lend to the average member of the body of Christ to cause them to be stronger in the Lord. Not many people are able to confess these days to receiving help from their fellow brothers and sisters in the churches.

People are succumbing to the attacks and to the feelings and emotions that is frequently calling for them to quit trusting in faith in the word and to leave God.

The bible is chocked full of the explanations needed for the benefit of sustaining us through the attacks from the enemy, but most

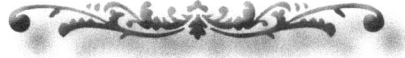

people are so out of touch with the truth of the word and the power of faith.

They allow the idea that the things of God through faith, that they are too far detached from the present reality of the things that are plaguing them.

We are often led to believe that once we know the reasons why the things are happening to us that we will have a better understanding to forge onward to our destinies.

But, I have learned that questioning only leads to more questions! Once we seem to get an answer for one reason, we then seek other answers to support the previous answers that we had received, and on and on........

It is possible to continue asking questions and seeking to know why, that we are actually led in to becoming questionable individuals.

Those who are left in the middle of the road asking questions are never going to be the persons who take action as result of having believed and trusted in the Lord. If you continue to ask questions, somebody is going to supply answers for you!

Only, they may often be deceptive dishonest people who happened to be at the church. You believed that you had actually been seeking them to assist you in finding the answers that you have needed.

The truth is that they have actually been seeking you! The world styles such people like you as a mark; you've been setup to be tricked and deceived.

Growing up in the church, we were taught that trials come to make us strong; but unless you have the ability to properly seek understanding and to wait on the Lord when we don't get an immediate answer, that that should make you strong will break you down

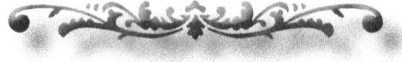

and eventually kill you faithfully!

"Let the Afflictions"

Many are the afflictions of the righteous: but the Lord delivereth him out of them all.   *{Psalms 34: 19}*

In many instances we wouldn't mind pain or being hurt, if it were not for the afflictions which cause the situation to be? We wouldn't mind going through the battles and the grievous experiences in our lives were it not for the afflicting causes which landed us right smack-dab in the middle of the heartache.

God knows that it hurts you deeply when certain afflictions come upon you and catch you unexpectedly unaware that they were even coming.

Yes of course God could have blocked it and stopped you from experiencing those things. But then neither would you be able to grow and to be stretch to further trust in the Lord.

Through each and every trying experience of our lives we are being prepared to go to the next levels of our ministries and of our realities of living with the Lord.

Many of the afflictions that try us are for the purpose of quality control and not necessarily for character destruction as some might want to believe.

God believes in us, it is His will and desire that each one of us succeed and completely fulfill our purpose with excellence.

We don't have the ability of the spirit to say when we have reach that next place in the Lord which qualifies us for the next place that God has ordained for us in the realm of the spirit.

God knows that we will never ask for Him to perfect us, as we are so prone to think of ourselves as being more than we may actually

be in Him. Since He knows where the flaws are in us, He also know just where to break us and to reshape us, suitable for the master's use.

The real problems of the people in the churches is that some are indeed qualified, but others are even more qualified, while none of us are ever over-qualified for the work of the ministry.

But so many over inflated egos hinders us from working together to make the Kingdom of God the place of reality for the next convert of Christ; preparing us all for the eminent return of Christ to receive us out of this world.

Too much lack of understanding among those of us who are thought to be the faithful people of the Kingdom; people are falling out over what is often refered to as misunderstandings.

Which is exactly what the problems are; for many reasons the understandings of what is truly needed and expected as result to the present need of the churches is missed! So it's more so to the likes of the experiences from missed understandings!

People are quitting the churches and walking away from faith in God all because of the things that are happening with the people of the churches.

The more spiritual that you become, you develop the awareness of the fact that there are things happening in the spirit realm that are angrily resistent to the will and to the word of God.

There is nothing at all wrong with you, and no you're not crazy; you are not as knowledgeable in the things of the spirit as you may think or even as knowledgeable as you may need to be!

Christ Jesus is not the only one interested in watching us and seeing us for who we really are in Him. Sinners and the ungodly; people of other religious persuasions are watching us at every turn

and at every move of our lives.

They are determined to be there to show us if it is possible when~ ever we fall or sin against our testimony and against the word of God; that we are not all that we think that we are; we're not better people than they are.

While they do everything to throw a wrench in the flow of our faith in God; they only wish that they were responsible for the afflic~ tions that tear us apart on the inside of ourselves.

Satan is using them as he is the one responsible for their behavior towards us, but even Satan is only being used to reveal the power of the Holy Ghost invested in us, against all the kingdom of darkness and the devil.

Afflictions do not point to the fact that there is something foul about you that is displeasing to God concerning you. Let's work the understanding of an affliction here to gain a much clearer compre~ hensive grasp.

AFFLICTION – *distress; a condition of great physical or mental dis~ tress; something that causes great physical or mental distress.*

INFLICTION – *cause suffering; to be the cause of something harmful or unpleasant such as loss, injury, or damage to somebody or some~ thing; force on somebody; to impose something burdensome or incon~ venient on somebody.*

Most people usually only choose to focus on the distress of hav~ ing been afflicted; they're in a place of spiritual and even of physi~ cal discomfort.

Commonly, most people would do almost anything to avoid the discomfort of being afflicted.

It makes great since to want to avoid afflictions at all cost, if it were possible; but, to avoid being afflicted and hurt as a result

doesn't at all produce the extreme power of understanding the faith of God in Christ Jesus, that we possess and live by.

I hear a lot of teaching and preaching that makes people feel good and comfortable in the churches that they attend. But to follow any of those people you soon discover that as a result of avoiding the application of faith that stirs the devil to attack, they are powerless and incapable of any ministry of deliverance or healing.

Satan is not your friend, and his attacks against you are not ever going to be friendly when launched at you. The right afflictions teaches an individual to be violent against the devil; never being afraid of hurting the devil's feeling or offending any demon spirit.

We're in a war and if we are going to win against the enemy; we have got to get violent in an aggressive way against the total agenda and the kingdon of Satan.

There is no such thing as a passive little pew member of the churches who are good and saved but prefer not to get involved with any devils or demons.

It's the people in the churches who feel this way that are struggling with the fact that the devil has gotten involved with them and their affairs.

People have been deceived about being saved and indeed spirit filled! You're the ones that Satan is coming after; troubles are looking to find you, whether you want it or not.

No need at all to allow yourselves to be embarrassed about what you are going through, as if you are the only ones going through the trouble that you are having.

If you would just search the scripture you will discover that you are in good faithful company with all of the people in the bible who suffered as you do or even greater than you; but they held on to

their testimony and to the faith of God.

Saved people all over the world are going through just like you even though it may not be the exact same trial description as to that of your's?

In effort for there to be real afflictions, there must at first be the inflictions, or the inflicting causes that ripped the hole in the flesh or the spirit of an individual.

The greater struggles are the spiritual things which take place in our lives as we are not able to manipulate those types of things in any manner.

Many of the physical things we are able to see them, as we try and ward them off from getting to us; but they are over-powering and often evasive of any tactics that we could ever put forth to try and to block the intrusions.

At other times the afflictions rush in and take us by storm even before we are able to realize that they had touched us internally.

This is the reason that we are so offended and or painfully stricken at the occurences; at most times we were going about our lives without any trouble or without what we might consider to be confusion or drama.

Afflictions may have also come upon us to cite the fact that we have allowed for ourselves to be filled with pride and great arrogance.

Some people are led to believe that because they have lived as closely obedient to the word of God; obedient to the teaching of their churches, that they ought to be beyond the afflictions which swept through their lives.

People omit the promises of the scripture, and they are swollen with anger and grave disappointment. They are mad at God; feel-

ing that He didn't protect them from the onslaught of the enemiy's attack against them.

Even the Lord's own disciples weren't exempt from the attack of the enemy and afflictions. They were on a boat haven obeyed the master's command to go to the other side of the coast, only to encounter a terrible storm.

I know, but you say; I didn't derserve this! Oh but how often did I even utter those words about the things which happened to me! But you see, even along with the Apostle's of Christ; and the Apostle Paul who declared that it was good for him to have been afflicted; I am in total agreement!

There are things that I know about God that I would only still be trying to believe had it not been for the fact of seeing the hand of God move on me and to work in my situation.

There is no other way of getting to know of the power of God to move in your life in many dire circumstances. God is way too powerful to just go around slinging His power through the earth for no reason?

Afflictions are the types of things that create the occasions and situations necessary for the power of God to be witnessed, experienced and appreciated. It is also the reason that we have the prsonal knowledge of God; to testify of the truth that He is real and all powerful.

Take notice of the scripture; it is reported that Jesus raised certain people from the dead. But you will also realize that Jesus did not just go through out the country raising everyone who died.

There is a method and a purpose for what God does; it is never done just because He is God; everything is done for a reason, with a divine purpose attached to it.

Please understand that God never allow afflictions in your life just because He wants to see you squirm; or to see just how well you are able to deal with and or to conquer being hit with very painful occurrences.

However my friend, God does need for us to be knowledgeable of the fact that He is able to do above and beyond all that we could ask or even think of. *{Ephesians 3: 20}*

The things that we are knowledgeable of asking the Lord for, even the things that we have learned to think of whenever we go down on our knees to pray are the result of the afflictions that we sought the Lord to deliver us out of them.

Consider the fact that; the deliverance from the afflictions had not been to the likes of magical disappearing acts, to whisk those things away.

But as we allow for God to step into the situations with us, The Lord blesses us to see Him working to the point that we are forever made knowledgeable of what the Lord has done, and of how it was that God did it.

Even though the things that God did for us, still we will never be able to do those things for ourselves ever! Even if those same things were to reoccur in our lives, it would still require the help of the Lord!

God intends for us always to depend on Him; it's by design that we know from now on that if there is anyone who can get it done for us; God Can! As a result of the afflictions that we have been through, now we know for sure that God is able, through it all.

An affliction may hit your life at times out of the blue, but the greater benefitting design is for the purpose of alerting you that the wrong thing has been allowed to attach itself to you!

Even when we are saved and we become sanctified, we have to be watchful of the people inside of the churches that we allow ourselves to be attached to.

As the spirits to which many of them may enhouse inside of themselves, they travel and leap onto another individual like ticks and flees leap from one dog to another; especially onto them that are weaker and not very well developed in prayer and praying.

The truth is that some things in your life you will never look for them to be attached to you, niether would you ever take necessary measures to rid yourselves of them because you never intended or expected for them to be attached to you.

When we are not as watchful as we ought to be, we become like anybody else of the churches and not as much like God; whereas the other people are just fine to have you to conform to their ways and likenesses as a member of the church.

Not everyone in the churches; but some people just love having little clones and conformants to them. Even denominational persuasions have tendancy to shape the behavioral aspect of the people who attend their churches, through the teachings and the frequent fellowship gatherings of the people.

At every occasion the people are required to meet for the benefit of getting to know the people and for the occasion to get to experience the behavior and the mannerisms of the people that they are in church with.

Something, someway, or even someone will always be trying to mold you into a desired form and particular status as a believer; not necessarily as a faithful, believer.

When you are unaware, God is aware of what is taking place concerning you, that may in fact be actually happening which might have slipped upon you.

But, He Loves you way too much to leave you developing in the wrong manner, which will actually deflect the spirit of the living God on our lives.

In the scripture God has already assured us that we would have many afflictions as being the people of righteousness; but He also promised us that He would deliver us out of them all.

Watch your arrogance; you're not that righteous all of your own will and ability to live and to choose righteously. If God doesn't work righteously in us developing the righteousness of Christ in our beings; we don't know righteousness; and for certain we will never know how to walk in the righteousness of Christ.

Many are the afflictions of the righteous: but the Lord delivereth him out of them all.   {Psalms 34: 19}

Look now; the scripture says; *"but the Lord delivereth {him}out of them all."* It is the reference to him; in the scripture that you have to get an understanding of. I am; You are; we are the righteousness of Christ; it is He the Lord who is the righteous one in us, that holds the attentiveness of God the Father in heaven.

We are absolutely nothing without Christ in our life; and sadly because of the lack of understanding many have embraced the mind set that they are even still nothing now having Him in their lives!

Whatever comes upon you as a saved and sanctified, blood washed child of Christ's, also comes upon the Christ in you! Whenever you get into trouble, that thing is actually seeking to trouble the Christ in you.

The sickness that you are suffering, is actually ignorantly trying to sicken Christ in you. Christ in us is still God; with all power and authority; whatever afflicts us being Christ's has to be removed be-cause Christ is not going to be removed from us!

I have said this before but I must say it again; God will never leave God in a mess! Since God is in us and we are in God; our afflictions and our trials don't stand a chance of enslaving us to the point that we are forever; eternally trapped under the weight of the afflictions.

See, there is no need of killing ourselves, ending our own lives at our own hands for feelings of dispair and hopelessness; at a set time in due time God is going to deliver us out of whatever it may be that we are plagued with.

That's the reason that we desperately need the afflictions to come in our lives. The power of our God is unimagineable and incomparable to that of anything other that my have been thought of as being a god; or and entity of a power source.

Just imagine what you would be lacking of the knowledge of God if you had never been in a situation which called for the need of God's direct power and Love to deliver you?

How successful do you really think that you would be as a witness if you had no real testimony of God's power, of His Grace; or of His Mercy?

Whenever you do share with other people of the glory of God; what do you have as evidence of God's truth and reality that will leave other people wanting to experience the same God that you have just spoken of?

I know that we are taught to rightfully speak of God's love; but you as well as to the people that you are speaking to need to know and to understand that God have not ceased to love them simply because of an affliction of some sort which came in their lives.

As witnesses of the church, too often we are taught to give the people fluff and softer stuff to make it appealing to them, hoping that it will make them to want to come into our churches.

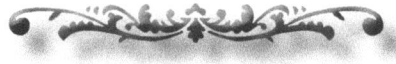

But, even whenever they come into our churches and are saved and spirit filled; they experience the trials and the afflictions and any sort as a member of the church; and they can't seem to mesh the simultaneous truth about themselves as a born again, blood washed child of the Savior; Jesus Christ.

Many people begin to say within themselves; well isn't He supposed to be the all powerful God?

The answer to those questions is; Yes He Is; the all powerful Omnipotent God; hold on and you will see that He is indeed for sure all that you thought of Him to be, and everything that you could have never even imagined that He is!

Oh Yes He's God; His great purpose and strategy is to develop relationship with you. God is kind in that He'd much rather share the truth and the Love of Him with you personally; being the only real reason that He wanted others to tell you about Him.

There is so much of Him; being God; that He wants to sit down on the inside of you, that will change the reflection of you to those who have even known you best and for the longest of time.

God desires that when others look upon us that what they see is God. As we open our mouths to speak, it should be that God leaps forth out of our mouths.

Whenever we lay hands on the sick and the demon possessed individuals, the God in us will be commanding that the ungodly thing move for the lives of the people that we are ministering to, immediately!

It is God's plans for us that we never fail at showing forth the God inside of us; and that we win and succeed at our God given assignments to love through the ministry of God according to our calling and the anointing.

Only God knows what it takes really to stretch your ability to rely on faith in God; and to remain faithful as a citizen of the Kingdom Of God's Dear Son.   Now Understand this in Faith..........

Chapter 4

"Infinite ~ Everlasting Integrity of Faith!"

And the Lord said, Si'mon, Si'mon, behold, Satan desired to have you, that he may sift you as wheat: But I have prayed for thee, that thy faith fail not: and when thou art convert-ed strengthen thy brother. {St. Luke 22:31-32}
Knowing this, that the trying of your faith worketh pa-tience. But let patience have her perfect work, that ye may be perfect and entire, wanting nothing. But let him ask in faith, nothing wavering. For he that wavereth is like a wave of the sea driven with the wind and tossed. For let not that man think that he shall receive anything of the Lord. A double minded man is unstable in all of his ways.
{James 1:3-4; 6-8}

"Faith is Always and Forever; in Place!"

The admonishment of the scripture relative to us as the in-dividuals of faith in God; directs us to be consistantly mind-ful to do the things which keep us dedicated, exercising faith.

I have not found instruction written in the scrip-ture which speaks directly to faith; saying without man it is impossible to please God? Neither admonishing faith to always be constant as it has been since God created it?

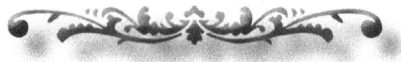

But, through the word of God we are reminded that without faith it is impossible to please God.

We are the given assignment of faith; forever! Without us; faith would never have a reason or a purpose to even exist in the realm of the earth. As disgusting as people are prone to be relative to having faith, it has never been apparent at any time that faith had been led to drop the assignment of us and leave.

Faith remains available, in spite of the most offensive behavior of mankind. God; and Faith; are more knowledgeable about humanity than anyone of us could ever even conceive.

Although we are egotistically hyped to think of ourselves as intelligent and smart, we can never even fathom God's knowledge of faith and neither faith's knowledge of God and humanity. I believe that there is a realm of knowledge that would cause our brains to be fragmented if we were to be made aware of so great knowledge?

You never have to search for faith; just surrender to it! Faith; when you first discover it, remarkably it is strong and powerful; but as you continue faithfully, you realize that it is even greater than when you first surrendered to the ability of faith!

For the sake of trying me relative to my faithful adherence to God, I made it through many trials and tribulations. I have had all sorts of trouble and hard battles, from the people in the churches and from people of secular influences alike.

However, through the scripture I've learned that I've been in very good faithful company. All of the patriarchs of our faith in God were tried and persecuted for having faith in God.

As a general rule of instructions we are taught to look to the word of God for the sake of the written accounts of the docu-

mented biblical experiences of the people during those biblical times; nothing at all wrong with the perspective interest of the people of God in the bible.

However, we often fail to see and to receive the unspoken and silent messages of the faith that they all each worked with to make it through all of their test and trials.

As many of them were tested to the point of utter failure and almost to the point in fact of denying the faith; the undeniable, unfailing, eternally affixed faith of God; never failed them nor ever sought to get out of the trying ordeal with them.

Should faith ever fail in the middle of testing and trying times; how would anyone who is in the test being tried, ever come out of the trial successfully?

Faith stands firmly affixed to the assignment of being available to us to assure that we are faithful as we are determined to please the Lord; receiving the reward as result of diligently seeking the Lord!

In every trial, faith knows who is being tried whether it is us; or an attempt to test faith itself. The only true way to test faith is to trust faith, applying faith in God; to our every need and request of the Lord.

As faith is then proven, it is also revealed of the sort and of the ability that it has been endowed to never fail humanity; faith is always there for us; not just posturing, but standing alert for the benefit of all who call on the Lord.

Many people have often felt that God had left them citing His silence in the midst of their trying situations and circumstances. We hear of these types of testimonies often; but I have never heard one individual ever say that they felt as if faith vacated

their circumstances, leaving them void and incapable of reaching out to God for the help they needed?

They know that they reached out in a sense of faith at least, to the best of their knowledge; they're just frustrated and a bit bewildered that God had not answered when they had expected for Him to answer for them?

Faith is awesome; though often taken lightly and disregarded as a necessary demand, yet it stands to complete the given assignment of the Father to help and to assist us at all times.

Being human beings; we are more apt to give recognition to the people who stand faithfully when being opposed and physically attacked, but neither do we or they themselves, stop to give God thanks for the awesome faith which allowed us stand unmovable and steadfast in Him.

It is the natural behavior for us to speak of the strength and determination of the people who withstand, to believe God; waiting on Him for deliverance from the onslaught of the enemy.

Even whenever life just happens to one of us, and we are found yet standing firmly affixed to faith in God, naturally we are cited as being strong in the faith of God, and unwavering. We are working with a faith in God that will always work for us!

I'm agreeable to the analogy of the people that we have recognized as being faithful to God. It is commendable to be unmovably affixed to the professions of our faith in God; but it is likewise remarkable and simply outstanding to know and to realize that we have a faith that itself can never be shaken or otherwise removed from its platform adherence to God!

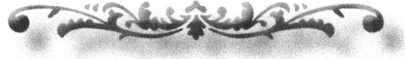

The enemy's opposition comes along to shake us from holding on to faith in God if we allow it to be possible; however, faith knows that there will be oppositions from the enemy at every turn.

Faith stands affirmed to see what you and I will do and how we will respond, recognizing that while we know and comprehend that we are the people of faith; we're already on the winning side. In God we win, and we never lose!

Faith itself is prepared for us to speak the word of God to the situational opposition, so that the angelic protection and covering can be activated and released into the atmospheric circumstances for our benefit.

I'm talking about an avowed faith; a faith that only knows yes to the Lord! Faith has a communication with God in heaven; although it has been intentionally released into the earth's realm to allow the people of the earth, to be reconnected with the Father in heaven.

"Fixed ~ Eternally Sound Faith"

Faith is in the bible from Genesis to Revelation; it is not until we as people of the faith in God, learn to recognize faith for what it truly is, that we are able to realize that it was indeed faith working on the behalf of the people of God even from the beginning of our time of existence.

Jesus our Lord and Savior; came along in the New Covenant of the scripture to reveal to us what it was that had actually been working in the hearts and in the minds and the spirits of people; He called it faith!

Remember, a Centurion soldier came to meet Jesus; to ask for

his servant to be healed, and that he would not die; he exemplified such reverential respect and trust in the fact that Jesus is "Emanuel" (God with us); he was sure that Jesus' was indeed able to do whatever he was asking for Him to do, and that He would actually honor his request.

Our Lord's response to this man's reverence of Him was quite astounding; He says; of this man's attitude and spirit of reverence; "I have not found such great faith; no not even in Israel."

How many millions of other people prior to this man's account of faith, had also applied faith in God and got the results that they had indeed asked for? How many people called upon the Lord and got an answer through faith?

Abel; the son of Adam; believed God; in fact he offered a perfect sacrificial offering, whereas God accepted the offering sacrifice and the smoke went upwards to God; in Heaven. This was indeed done by faith!

Remember faithful Noah; who answered the voice of the Lord calling him, with the world washing assignment of the flood for fourty days and nights? Noah was require to build an ark for the preservation of all of the living kind on the face of the earth! Consider with all that is inside of you, that an Ark had never been built before!

Of course many people of today seem to believe that the only call of God would be for them to do what everyone else is doing; that is traditionalism my friend!

It doesn't take faith to conform to what the churches or what the world is doing. So many people are so carnally washed out and affixed to the happenings of the world; they can't even get a grasp on the slightest comprehension of faith in God; calling

on them to do an extraordinary assignment aside from what is recognized as the norm.

God calls faithful Abram; He tells him to leave his home and family kindred, to go to a place that God did not tell him where he was going but only said to Him in paraphrasing; (I will tell you when you get there)?

Abram relied on the past teachings that had already been imparted to him concerning the God of all of the creation of Heaven and of earth. He had not seen the mighty things that God would indeed do for him as result of his own faithful obedience; yet by faith he obeyed God. *{Genesis 12:; Hebrews 11;}* Whatever God says is right; and He's right the first time...............

Abram takes out on a remarkable journey and did not stop until God told him, this is where you are going; stop here!

Abram; his family; and his band of servants traveled past lots of splenderous land on their way to their final destination; they could have determined on their own, being weary of traveling, that they had gone far enough; not having the patience to wait on God to say to them that they had arrived at the exact place of His provision?

No doubt; there were times that they all were indeed quite weary of traveling; desiring to simply call some place other than on the road traveling, home?

Chances are that they came upon land with extraordinary food supply and what might have appeared to be lots of good wood and lumber for building new homes and fire to keep warm from the cold, but, God; had not yet spoken to say that this is the place that I am sending you to dwell in.

By faith, Abram continued on his journey, waiting on the Fa-

ther in Heaven to speak to him; Abram was not just in motion moving forward in the hopes that faith would be there whenever he arrived; he was indeed moving in faith, walking with faith every step of the way on his journey.

Abraham; now as we know of him to be called of God; he made it to his destination through the same faith with God arriving at the exact same time that God intended for him to make it there.

He moved out on his journey with the Lord; but he also moved continuously with the Lord day by day; hour by hour; minute by minute; every second by the second, with God!

Faith prevents us from moving against the grain of God's divine intended plan for our lives; no matter what we might encounter along the way of our journey; faith stands there allowing us to remain focused on what God has instructed.

Even when we get off the track jumping ahead of the manifested promises of God; we may feel guilty enough to never ever set ourselves to believe God again! But, faith is there opening the door to the way of another chance to walk in the right path with God; should it ever be necessary for another chance to get it right.

Faith was given for every man on the planet so that all could be used to glorify God; that being the real purpose for which we had been created; and formed in the earth. Thank God; faith was created unmovable and totally affixed to the plan of God for all humanity over the face of the earth.

Faith is the missing element and the hidden cause that so many people are daily in question as to what the plan of God is for their own lives.

Only through faith do we pray and communicate with God

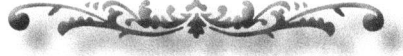

to respond to His will for our lives; God's will for us would be utterly hindered and forever annihilated if faith moved from its place of integrity.

It is such a blessing to have realized that faith itself is indeed sure and accurate; faith has no need of concerns or for apprehensions citing that we may be the wrong persons for the usage and applications of faith in God.

The truth is that we have got to knock at the door of faith before we will have been enabled to stand at the gate to the doorway to the throne in heaven to speak to the father.

Having a desire to avoid actually using the methods of the bible to reach out to God; you are actually attempting to avoid entering into God's presence through the only access; which is only possible through faith.

Negative things and people will find occasion to show up in our lives while we are on our way, but everything that is contrary and not ordained through faith in the spoken directives for our livelihood is simply to be omitted and ignored!

It is important to know the difference in the battles that we have chosen to fight on our own and the spiritual warfare assigned to us for the perfecting of our understanding and for our walk of faith and Love.

Note: God is always in forward progression whereas faith dictates that we move with the motion in the movement of God's forward progression; that which challenges you to turn around and to go another wrought leading you away from faith in God, is not of God; don't follow it, or them!

Faith is so simple that it stands to reason as to why so many people are doubtful and unbelieving that faith is all that it takes to please the Lord.

People; being more evil and ungodly these days; being out-right wicked in their lifestyles on a daily basis, having no shame about it anymore; they question as to whether or not there is a much more complicated methodology to satisfy God in respect of their own determinate will to distance themselves from the presence of God's spirit and from the word of God.

Wickedness and sin requires that we repent; but repentance cannot be fulfilled but accept through faith that God will even hear your prayer and receive you!

We; of our ownselves; according to the way that we have become accustom to think in our minds, we cannot even be changed without having faith in God; first. Only God can change a person and that includes you and me!

Through faith, God is going to work the process of change in our lives. In other words, we will have to set ourselves in agreement with God through faith enabling the power of God to work in our lives to change the things that only He could ever change us in the first place, but through the written word of God.

Faith is always on the scene in the move of God whenever He begins to move in our life. Faith is the reason that God is there and that he has come to the rescue to deliver us from the attack of the enemy in whatever form of attack the enemy may have chosen to use against us.

Coming up in the church as a young boy and up to the time that I began as a young man in the ministry of the gospel, we were taught that prayer is the key, and that faith unlocks the door?

But it has been revealed to me through the spirit of God that prayer indeed is the key and faith reveals the reality of the door

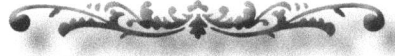

and as to what may actually be the cause that the door may have been locked! Faith was given to let us all enter into the presence of God; faith could never and it will never be allowed to lock us out of the presence of God!

Can we even suppose hypothetically, that it had been faith that failed God back in the garden of Eden? Could you also imagine the condition of utter hopelessness that all of mankind would have been left in, never having had an access to the almighty saving power of God; through our Lord Jesus Christ?

Faith stands as a closed doorway to God to them that refuse to believe by faith; or an open door to access the realistic presence of God; for the benefit of all of our need as we believe God through faith!

We are only shut out from the presence and from the help of the Lord because of sin and iniquity which doesn't have any power to effectively touch faith directly at any time.

Listen, by grace are we saved through faith, from sin and iniquity; and from all unrighteousness. You have never read and you will never read ever that faith was in need of repentence because it failed God!

Understand, that faith was there in the garden seeing Adam and Eve fail the requirement given to mankind by God; in no way was faith a participant voluntary nor involuntarily as a part of the disappointment of disrespecting the direct commandment of God.

Faith still stood erect as the one measure given for mankind to be delivered from sin, faith never sinned against God.

However mankind did indeed sin and fail God losing sight of faith and giving an attentive ear to another voice other than to the voice of God; for which they had already given their ear

to hear the Lord's instruction. My friend they denied the faith when they disobeyed the word of the Lord to them having their relationship with the Father severed; however, their sinful be~ havior could not displace faith!

But, sin and iniquity actually constructed a dividing petition between man; and faith; thus hindering our ability to pleasantly touch the heart of God! That is so that we are able to realize that we have indeed sinned against God!

The very moment that we sin against the will and the word of God, it is at that moment that we have willfully exited the pathway of faith that had actually brought us to the presence of God to be atoned and cleansed from the stains of sin, and from the penalty of death and hell.

Faith; being dedicated and unmovable, unlike our feelings and our emotions that are touch sensitive to the effects of our own personal behavior, it was uneffected knowing it's purpose and it's place among mankind in the earth.

Faith; stood steadfast in it's place ready for our return, in need of being able to touch the Father through faith and repen~ tance; faith stayed on it's job!

As a result of sin, shame, and of fear, we suffered a broken relationship between us and of faith; but we never suffered a broken faith!

I mean for you to know that faith works for us overtime; all of the time! Even as we are in need of acknowledging that through selfish acts of sin, we are allowing a separation between ourselves and God's love which causes faith to work for us; thus repentance is needed to restore us back to the righteousness to allow faith to be able to work for us again.

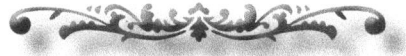

"Integrity of Faith explained"...

Too many questions about faith and of being faithful are looming about the atmospheres of the so-called believers that are almost never addressed nor explored.

The truth may be that many people would never know where to begin the search, and of what to look for whenever they do begin seeking for the answers relative to having faith in God. So in the exposition of my findings, I have determined to share such enlightened truths of the reality of faith itself.

In no way do I mean for anyone to get it twisted and think that I am suggesting that we have no part to play in understanding faith.

How we actually work faith to please God, and how God worked faith in the pleasure of meeting our need as believers are two different aspects of reality to be taken into consideration. Faith works; and is in working order at all times, whether we take out the time to apply faith putting it to work for us, or not.

The allowed questionable platforms of faith and of faithfully believing, and of the only logical originator of faith, which is God; have established intellectual wars of religion, and it has also caused erected walls of doubt so aggressive that the realistic need for faith is even challenged in the life of every individual who walk the face of the earth!

Faith transcends the walls and barriers of scientific reasoning of which whenever the rationale of faith is examined in the laboratory and or classroom settings; it is often found to be unreasonable and quite illogical to the abbreviated usage of the mind through scholastic education and formal instruction.

People, even of the churches have entertained the notion for

many years now, of taking a leap of faith, as if to suggest that one should be prepared for the expected uncertainty of faith itself?

So many people have been led to believe that faith is an instance of an unknown uncertain doubtful desire of the heart in an individual, supposedly as if the faithful are believing and hoping in a psychological or even a mythological image or an idea in the minds of those who choose to think that there is actually something or someone out in space to be reverenced as a higher being?

There has never been the idea of having a limp, a break, or possibly a tear or a rip in faith! These such characteristics are attributed to the flesh or to the natural physical human body and or of tangible things; there is absolutely no form or flesh attached to faith, as faith itself is a very powerful spiritual aspect of God!

Faith is the contributing aspects both of how we look at God as we are interested in getting to know Him; and it is the dimensional sphere of righteousness in how we see God now that we are acquainted with Him; altogether.

By faith we are introduced to God, and then faith is the manner of which we go about getting to know God; through the word of God.

Drop the idea of the possibility of faith being crippled or otherwise disabled, as it is the installed and ingrained integrity of the spirit of the Lord which holds faith seamlessly intact at every instance!

Alike the wedding band which is a symbolic representative of the never ending cycle of commitment of love; faith is the adhesive which continuously holds us securely to the eternal

essence and spirit of God; without end.

The possibility of any such deteriorating happenstances of faith might be apt to suggest that God is not as serious about us as the bible says that He indeed is! Of course you remember John 3:16……

God is ever so serious about humanity as a whole from even before He made us in His own image and in His likeness; before we were formed from the dust of the ground.

Nothing at all fake or playful about God or about the things of God; and of course for sure it is relative to faith! God knows that you and I need Him every step of the way in this life and of the life which is indeed to come.

We were created by God; for His glory and not for the self-gratification of ourselves that we have grown so accustom to; to fail us would be that He; fail Himself also, and more-so Him; than us! Get it in your minds right now, "God don't fail!"

I know that it is rather convenient for people to convince themselves that God is somehow non-existent, or that He is not as serious as the people of the churches and of the religious communities at large, have describe Him as being.

People are further encouraged not to take the bible too seriously; of course you know that it suggested that man wrote the bible and that there is no reality of God to be found in the scripture?

People are totally turned off at the idea of the bible's scriptures being the only truth of the validated reality of God. On the other hand, many people have come to know the truth in the reality and of the actuality of having faith in God.

Though they find it necessary in their own minds and even

in their hearts to move in the opposite direction away from the presence of the Lord according to His word. Without the word of God, there can be no faith in God; at all!

God is invisible and He can't be seen with the naked eyeball, and likewise also faith is invisible and it can neither be visualized with the natural naked eyesight of any man, or should ever be wrapped up in the feelings and the emotions of anyone.

So many people have deduced the reality of God and of having faith in God to what they are able to feel emotionally and to have physically; that usually being reduced to having money!

Being in the presence of God is even more-so than to that of a feeling of some sort and so much more to the fact of knowing that He is the higher being somewhere in the sky above the world in control of all things. True faith prevents us from being deceived as to the realistic presence of God; as He is so much more than the feeling of a touch.

Many people have based their total reasoning for turning away from the truth of God and of faith in God, upon the idea that being unseen means that He is unreal.

How deceived they all are for sure; God; is more clearly seen and is more real than everything seen with our visual ability; only through faith are we enabled to see God, and to know that He is real.

Certain systems of belief are failed and incapable of sustaining those who believe in them. In effort for the methodology of believing to be powerful enough for any people to increase and to manifest the hopeful result of haven believed; that which had been relied upon as a legitimate method, has to be flawless and strong enough to stand on its own, thus being capable to sustain the believer and that of which they have believed for.

Herein is where we truly find the integrity of faith.

Integrity ~ the quality of possessing and steadfastly adhering to High Moral Principles or professional standards; the state of being complete or undivided; the state of being sound or undamaged.......

Then said his wife unto him, dost thou still retain thine integrity? Curse God, and die. {Job 2:9}...

So many people talk of having integrity that have never even had a real clue as to what real true integrity is! I have discovered that a lot of people desire to have integrity because it sounds sociably acceptable and like a great characteristic for being able to consort with the upper class people of the society. Ignorantly, people have even assigned a certain look of appearance with the idea of being a person of integrity.

I have discovered as perhaps as many of you yourselves have also discovered as well, that most people who confess to having integrity, that they never had integrity; period!

Integrity have nothing at all to do with where you shop or of where it is that you bank; or of which neighborhood that you live in; or even of what type of an automobile that you drive; although because of the integrity you have allowed yourselves to be awarded more elevated opportunities of living.

Such definitively weakened distorted views of integrity and of faith itself, totally wipes out the notion of faith having its own encircling shield of integrity; being eternally incapable of failure.

But, it is infinitively capable of producing all that is ordained and established by God. Such slanted viewpoints of faith and of integrity have caused major distractions and all sorts of disruptions in the systems of believing God through faith.

113

Sweetly; we sing of the "Amazing Grace" of God; in Christ Jesus; however, what is even indeed most amazing is the understanding of the actual reality of faith!

The scripture instructs us that we are saved by grace, but that is only to become the reality through faith! The grace of God is unmerited; we could never deserve it, but it cannot and will not work for us without first, the application of faith.

Even though grace is unmerited favor; there is nothing at all that we could ever do to make any special request for grace to be given to us.

Without the ability to see through faith, the viewpoint of grace can be comparable to any manufactured product on the shelf in the store where magic products are sold. To a faithless mind grace may be nothing more than a mythological product of some sort to appease a religious thinking mind?

One of the greater issues of the churches worldwide is that too much of the world's designated influences are allowed into the teachings and into the thought provoking materials that are given to the people of the churches for the sake of having a hand in what the people should be allowed to think about God and of all that matters concerning faith.

The teachings of grace is like the most powerful cars on the showroom floor capable of cross country expeditions, but it cannot even be moved across the city or the country without a driver who purchases the automobile.

On the other hand; the great act of grace itself, may be viewed as the manufacturer which have faith in its product, before ever having it assembled to be passed on forward to the dealerships, for retail sales to the general population?

Grace speaks relative to what faith has to say about us con-

cerning our willingness to receive God. Somehow, we have been deceived into believing that we are able to place demands on faith and of grace; never further from the truth!

We spend so much time attempting to tell grace and faith what to do for us; and we fail drastically at allowing grace and faith to do that which it have been designed to do for us.

Grace and faith have both been so powerfully programmed to make life worth living and to bring the impossible things into the realm of being totally realized possibilities of truth.

Grace; and Faith are reality makers in the realm of humanity! It is such a mistake and a misnomer to the intellectual reasoning of the people to think that we need to make realities of faith and of grace!

As information is exalted above that of the knowledge of faith and grace; the egos of mere men runs wild, causing such thought processes of superior humanness, whereas people are led to believe that they have control even over God and of all that is associative to Him.

The human mind is outstandingly brilliant and superb; but it will never cancel out God; who created the mind and gave it to humanity. The human mind was never created to question everything in the realm of humanity, much rather it was created to receive all of the beauty and splendor of God's creation.

Science and the acquisition of information have taught us to bring all things into question, even though the questions created in the minds of the people are formed, but without relevant answers?

The things that are often being brought into question are clear and precise if not at all self-explanatory? That mindset of questioning everything alone of itself have the ability to stop

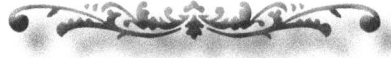

what is to be understood as the eternal flow of grace and faith, from flowing to and through your total being.

We as the believers of faith in God; must come to the point of knowing and respecting the differences between what we think about faith; and the mental limits that we apply to faith determining whether to accept faith as a reality, or to go with the rest of the people of the world who choose to view faith in God as being unrealistic.

Or the God given divine reality of faith in God for truth! We can all be saved by grace through faith; we can all live by faith; we all should walk by faith and not by sight!

As we learn faith and increase in the true knowledge of faith in God, we become enlightened and strongly encouraged to do all that we do on a daily basis through faith in God! All that we have done has been made reality through faith; absolutely no one has been overlooked or denied.

Listen to faith; though faith may not be able to speak audibly, it is never silent, nor unspoken; whereas those who hear are made aware that the words spoken are officially through the aid of the written word of God, by faith!

As it has been ordained to resonate through the vocal chords of the mouths of everyone that embrace faith in God; the sounds of the spoken words of faith will reach out to all of the ends of the earth and fall upon ears that are indeed prepared to hear them, having been taught through the written word of God, and made sensitive to the spirit of God through prayer.

Even though we will never converse with faith itself, it is faith that allows for us to be able to communicate in the spirit realm with the spirit of God; through the powerful reality of the Holy Ghost. Watch out for faith; although it is invisible, the works of

faith will always and forever be clearly seen and visualized with the human sight of both the faithful and the unfaithful; even though many are determined to deny what they have witnessed as result of faith in God; the works of faith won't be denied.

We are often given the credit for being imaginatively creative when reasoning in our thinking capacities, but I assure you that faith is so much more than what we will ever be able to enquire of or to mentally expand upon, as our minds are too finite. Our minds were created to stop at a certain limit, whenever we have reached the allowed boundaries of human reasoning.

Our eyesight is limited to see; as our ears are limited of hearing; but so far away from our immediate vantage points. Sound waves bend and curve disabling us from hearing originated tone generations of sound too far away from where we are.

Faith; through the spirit of the Lord, allows above and beyond the norm according to our intended purpose, for us to hear the distant sounds of where it is that we are destined to be; though it may be yet far in the distance!

The geographical plains are hilly and curved, whereas we are unable to see across the plain; from east to west. After looking so far away in the distance, the plains of the land and of the seas seem to sort of disappear into what is seen as a fog or a blur depending on the strength of the viewing instrument that we may be using at the time to see in the distance.

This is all true in the natural realistic realm of humanity, right here where we live. Truth is parallel in the natural and in the spirit!

Mostly, the people of the religious communities, all across the board, struggle to realize that they have not seen everything that there is to be seen in the realm of the spirit of God! Many,

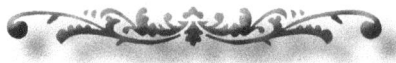

who are seriously donned as the rank sinners of the streets, shy away from God, because they have been informed of the vastness of the reality of God. They have been informed and they believe that God is big, and that He may even be bigger than anyone on the face of the earth is able to describe Him as being!

One of the greatest errors of faith, is the idea that faith suggest? No; faith demands that all who are indeed faithful that we receive all that God is, and all that is because of God! Most people often mistake generosity and kindness for weakness.

Faith is indeed generous and kind in that it doesn't force us to choose God; but it is unmovable and steadfastly standing in its place demanding that whenever we do come, that it is only God in Christ Jesus; that we enquire of and seek through faith. Faith demands that you receive the Holy Ghost in an effort to see God in the fullness of His power!

Faith knows that you can't seek God; denying the total deity of God; and receive all that it is that you desire to receive from God! So many divisions of the churches worldwide say that they believe that have received God; even though they deny Jesus Christ as the only begotten son of God!

Others, who have indeed embraced Jesus Christ, are adamant that they do not believe that they need to receive the baptism; infilling of the Holy Ghost!

Faith demands all or nothing; even though one may be overwhelmed to feel as if they are doing the right thing being a member of a local church body, that they are indeed complete in faith?

Faith; was here even long before your local church organization was formed; much longer than the head of the leadership in your churches.

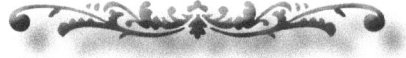

Faith knows what salvation and relationships with God is; what it looks like; what it reveals and produces; and finally, faith knows who is indeed saved and in a faithful relationship with God; the Father; The Son; and the Holy ghost. (Elohim ~ The Triune God) we understand it as God in three persons; better referred to as The Trinity.

Faith and truth stand together almost to the likeness of identical twins; truth is parallel to faith even as faith is also paralleled to truth at all times!

You can never believe in the truth without first having faith and you can never develop in faith without knowing the truth, which is the word of God.

Faith knows why you are so willing to argue what is indeed the truth, allowing for the blockage which disallows you from having faith in God through Jesus Christ.

The true integrity of faith disallows faith from ever relenting, losing its place of strength, relative to its place of reverence to the truth and of God!

Faith; is where it has always been and it will never be removed, as it cannot be removed from the place where God placed it before the beginning was.

Thus we finally resolve that "FAITH IS"; ~ indeed!

Chapter 5

"Faith And God's Permissive Will"

For I know the thoughts that I think toward you, saith the Lord, thoughts of peace, and not of evil, to give you and expected end. {Jeremiah 29:11}

"Broadsided, ~ by what God; Permitted!"

People are crying their eyes out every day, depressed and in despair; walking away from the local churches, disconnecting and dis-fellowshipping the relationships they had forged with the local clergy, all because they are disappointed with what God permitted to happen in their lives, even though they were led to believe that they were under the cover of divine protection haven made such spiritual alliances.

Many of these people had believed that they had secured their faith through the names of the churches, church organizations, and the ministers of the churches and or even in the sociable climate relative to the economic and financial status of the people with whom they have connected.

Many of the spiritual leaders in the churches have led people to believe that their financial contribution to the local churches places them in the positions to manipulate the will of God for their individual lives.

So many have fallen prey to the deception of these con-men that they are sure that everyone else are just haters and jealous because the system of the mammon of this world is working for them in ways that others are yet to even discover?

Although they have been led to believe that they have the money to tell God what to do, unexpected things have broken through their own secured walls of protection; they think that God has failed them!

We understand God's will to be His desire for us in the earth, but for His glory. Although we have the bible which is the written word of God; we have it handy for us to read and to follow daily; but that does not always allow a reader all of their own intelligence, to know and to properly discern the will of God.

Other elements such as much consistent prayer and articles of faith and faith itself; are required that will place us in the proper relationship with the Father in heaven, but even then we will need to prayerfully attune our spirit to His spirit, praising and worshiping Him in spirit and in truth so that His will can be revealed to us, but better and much more clearly discerned.

As it is, we will have to work on ourselves as flesh and blood cannot inherit the kingdom of God; meaning that in the flesh or the in the natural realm of our own earthly experience we will never know the true will of God for the church neither for our own individual lives. We have to work on ourselves to even come to the point of even wanting to know what God wants for us.

Naturally, as the result of our own human experience, we are hard head-ed stubborn self-willed human beings; we want to do what we want to do, whenever we want to do it! We know that God is real and that He has a de-sign with us in mind, but it still doesn't change the fact that we want to see

what's in this earth for ourselves; we want to see the results of what Adam did to us in the garden up close and personal, if possible?

Let me also add that there are so many people who will be responsible for causing us to be displaced relative to taking a stance on staying in faith, in God; if and when we give ear to what they have to say to us about having faith in God.

They see the things that will have come about in our lives that are not so beautifully attractive to anyone who look at those things, or better described as to the things that are happening to us; only, the other people will want to distract you from thinking righteously on the Lord; they will see you as a bit twisted for having a mind to yet be thankful to the Lord; anyway!

No matter what comes into our lives we must continue to be thankful to the Lord; not only because things could be much worse than they are indeed, but because we have a thankful heart; we Love the Lord; our God! *{I Thessalonians 5:18}*

The reason that we find ourselves to be unhappy and feeling as if we had been broad-sided unsuspectingly is because our will is consistently tugging against the will of God! We already had a list of the things that we desired to do that were interrupted and overturned without our permission, and it looked as if the interference slipped through the surveilling security of the all-seeing sight of the Lord!

That's right; things didn't slip by God; this is permitted by God; the tug-of-war between the flesh and of the spirit is necessary in that we will know the difference between what is indeed natural and what is spiritual; and between what is acceptable to God and what is not.

Sometimes the things that we desire to do may not be wrong or sinful; but they may indeed be the types of thing that are weighing us down and even holding us back; they are slowing us down causing us to miss out on being positioned right where the Lord would have for us to be.

We as people of the churches will often be found saying yes out of our

mouths to the Lord's will for our lives, we will choose to do what the Lord wants us to do. But, we have got to put our own spin on it, and do things in a way that doesn't offend the ungodly and make the unsaved people around us and in our churches to feel uncomfortable.

"Yes Lord"; we'll do your will, just as long as you allow us to do it our own way; we know what the bible says about following you; this is the attitude of many people!

As we move forward in this chapter, it is necessary that the understanding be given that God does not allow things to interrupt us because He is mad at us, or even that it might have been a judgmental act against us; He Loves us so much that He will not allow things to remain in our lives that block us from what he desires for us!

For the flesh lusteth against the spirit, and the spirit against the flesh: and these are contrary the one to the other: so that ye cannot do the things that ye would.   {Galatians 5:17}

When left to our own self wills and to the desires of our own un~surrendered hearts; we will find ourselves out of the will of the Lord for our lives every time. The Father in Heaven, He knows that we are excited about the earth and all that has been created within the cosmos.

Putting our human hands to the things that God created doesn't lend to us the defining reality for those things and neither the proper manner for handling them.

If we would only look into the realm of the spirit through the spirit of discernment as result of praying and fasting; we could and will see the posted signs everywhere attached to the things that are indeed detrimental to our spiritual walk of faith in God; which instructs us; "do not touch!" *{Colossians 2:21}*

Although we believe in what is to be respected as the will of God from the broader perspective, better referred to as a corporate or collective mindset of the people who have willfully decided on the necessary acceptance of the

churches, whereas we all are regarded as the replacement worshipers; it is most necessary that in retrospect, we zero in on ourselves as individual worshipers.

You know the story about how Lucifer the Arche angel and the chief worshiper in Heaven, was cast down and dethroned as the worshiper; he was terminated; eternally! A job vacancy that big needed big shoes to fill it, so instead of one personality; the Father; chose the one human race in totality, with all of our personalities to fill the position of worshiping and glorifying God.

While we are now the worshippers, we have situations that will happen in our lives without our own permission that even though they may have come unexpectedly; through our praise and worship we will have built the more resistant sheltering protection against allowing our inward feelings and emotions to cause us to charge God foolishly, accusing Him of mishandling us; or even of allowing us to be mishandled by the cares of this world.

Too often those of us who worship God in spirit and in truth are vulnerable to think of ourselves as having reached the plateau of entitlement to be kept free from hard painful trials and disappointments.

But not all people are worshipping God in the spirit and of truth; such infiltrations of unexpected disastrous occurrences against our understanding of being secure in Jesus will often cause their focus to be spiritually offset to believe that the Father in Heaven doesn't care for them after all?

Whereas they may be insufficient of prayer and a lack of dedication to studying the word of God; they begin to feel that it's got to be the devil causing me all of this unrest and trouble because everything that's happening don't allow for the day to look like the beautiful hues of the flower garden filled with bright sunshine.

We will explore the flip side and even the more positive side of the permissive will of God.........

Permissive ~ allowing the freedom of behavior; giving permission; grant-

ing permission…

As people of the churches; who are often passively donned as faith-filled believers; we are often quoted as suggesting that certain things which may have happened in our lives are the results of God's permissive will; perhaps the reasons for giving it the much lesser value in comparison to that of what we will regard as God's Perfect will in command?

We simply did not want to embrace the fact that our God could be responsible for allowing some hideous and degrading unsightly things to happen in our lives, that never really happened to our lives!

That's right; many things can happen in our lives that will never be permitted to happen to our lives! Many people have wrecked their automobiles who never even suffered a scratch nor any physical debilitations from the wreckage!

Great storms have shattered all of the possessions of a family household and their businesses, but it was never permitted to shatter the family! Many people have testimonies that their bodies were stricken with sudden illnesses out of the blue, they never expected to become ill; but the illness being as deadly as it was could not kill them and take them down to their graves.

Even though God permitted certain things to attack and to happen in our lives, we are not at all to be found basking in the fact that it happened, rather we should lose ourselves in the fact that God permitted for us to live on in spite of the attacks!

It is more than just a cliché for me to say to you that; "you went through it to get to it!" How often is it that we take traveling expeditions having to go through one city or state in effort to get to the next, on the way to our destinations? So it is in the spiritual realm; everything that we go through has not been designated to be our concluding final rest or the intended destination!

We used the term; ["permissive will of God;"] as if to suggest that there are some things that are able to intrude upon our lives both in the natural and in the spiritual realms that never have to bow to God's command, but

that is deceptive thinking!

No matter how perfect a thing may appear to be; it had to come by the way of our God first before being released into our own personal space and time! As important as faith is to our God; so are we who are purposed indeed to be the faithful saints of God! As we have been led to think of allowing faith to get on the inside of us, we need to walk our whole body soul and spirit into faith!

Many people of today are not even as strong in the faith as they perhaps ought to be based on the fact that they have shifted the purposeful meaning of the things that occur, they never think that those things should have happened to them.

As result of not being truly knowledgeable as to why it happen to them, so many things that have happened in their lives as having been to the left on the lesser applied list of things that somehow or another escaped and got by the perfected protection of God's hand and made it to touch them, but only most undesirably, those things are disdained and rejected as being a possible tool for God to either teach them or simply to even reach them?

They even spend a greater bulk of their time pondering in their own minds on how much better their lives might have been had certain things gone differently for them in the past, whereas if God hadn't permitted those things to happen to them, their lives might have had a much better outcome.

Painfully; I likewise brood over the idea very deeply within my own sober mind of just how many people have been unsuspectingly caught by surprise.

In all fairness and truth, we are aware that many things that have happen to most of the people of faith and trust in the Lord have been very painful, and sometimes almost shattering to them. But, I will tell you that the constant reflection of those things have been even the most painful than even to that of the actual incident itself.

The initial visitation of the thing took us by surprise, we weren't ready for it to happen to us, but to keep looking back over the thing continuously, sort

of re-ignites the pains of the condition that were produced, as a result!

How many times in a conversation have we uttered and have had the phrase uttered to us; "seems like, just yesterday?" The more we tend to remember that it happen to us, the more it appear that a certain occurrence of our lives remains, still; closely upon us, right on our backs.

Some people that we talk to on occasions; they talk to us as if that thing that happen to them had been the only surprisingly unexpected thing to ever happen to them in their entire lives, since they had been alive on the earth?

Please; don't receive me as being insensitive to the pains and to the heart-aches that others have experienced which caused them pain and at times may have caused them uncertainty; my point in fact is to cause us to think on the fact that we have been perhaps taught erroneously concerning what we have considered to be God's permissive will?

In truth I think that our teachers were more-so thinking that at those certain times of our lives that we were in what might have been God's [passive will]; instead?

Being the teacher did not constitute the fact that they had indeed become faithful to our God; whereas they could discern and even comprehend what is to be better understood as to the permissive will of God!

We have been led to believe that a permissive will or of having to ask for permission to do most things in life as to that of being cowardly, or not as authoritative, not as to having the power to do so at the volition of our own will and discretion.

Clearly these are the times that we as people might have been guilty of suggesting that God may be just like as unto mankind; maybe for some reason that we cannot even find written in the word of God; perhaps He had to allow some things to bypass His command to happen in our lives, but against His will for our lives? We had indeed missed the truth about the powerfully permissive will of God!

"God Permitted it Indeed!"

Because of self-gratification and of confusion; and more than most of us would like to permit others to know about us, because of outright pride; many people of faith in God are often found shouting and dancing over the things that they believed that God blocked concerning them, refusing to allow threatening things to happen to them; in other words we are over joyed that God did not permit certain things to happen to us!

Of course I have said; that out of sheer embarrassment we assign what we believe to be a permissive act of God when it seemed that He didn't block certain ugly things from happening to us!

We speak these words about God's permission but in total disagreement to the encounter; deep down on the inside we feel that we were so much better than to have had such a thing as to that which came so unexpectedly, to happen to us!

In truth, we as people in general have a tendency to fight against the commanded will of God; like as when we have had our loved ones to pass away. Lots of people have spent years arguing with the reality of God's will in those instances citing that they just don't understand it; they weren't ready for them to leave?

I have witnessed a few people who literally lost their minds and ended up in insane asylums wanting to rebuttal the plan of God in the death of their loved one; they thought that God should have or at least He could asked for their permission to take them?

It is only because we as people are so prone to look to the negative side of the equations, that we are often found to miss the meaningful relevance in the realistic movement of God in our lives, in spite of the fact that we're so hopeful that things are getting better by the moment for us now that we are saved!

Especially, when it doesn't look like what we might have been led to believe or are taught to respect as being something that would appear as that

which only God would do to us, or could do for us?

Most people of the churches worldwide are found rebuking the devil and casting out evil spirits when in fact it has been the Lord permitting a certain thing for our making and definitely for our good! *{Romans 8:28}*

On the professions of our newly found faith in God, and of the desires of our hearts to be used of the Lord for the purpose of His own glory; God begins to work on us! He knows where and how we are to be used of Him; only He knows how to build us and to make us usable for the purpose of the kingdom of God.

Just because we refuse to acknowledge that it is God working in our lives, even though we don't like the way that it feels to us, it doesn't erase that fact that it is God indeed!

The moment that we got saved and sanctified, God set some things in order to begin finishing the final profile and spiritual scope of our lives, so as to ensure that we would never be the same again.

The types of things that we begin to experience will cause us to have even greater desires to look to the Lord for the answers to our questions and the solutions to our problems instead of going back into the secular realms of what had been indeed familiar to us, before being saved.

The church has omitted to tell the new converts that learning to live holy and righteous is made a reality through a process of change; it doesn't come over night.

However; detrimentally, many people of today have determined that they are going to bring the past lifestyle of their own secular world of living with them now that they have been saved?

They refuse to believe that it is any longer necessary to be separated from their old ways of living; suggesting that people of the churches that have been with the church the longest, that they are outdated and old fogy in their ways of thinking?

They feel that the church need to be upgraded to the more modern times of living; people like to drink and to party like never before; so why not allow the new converts to bring the party with them in their lifestyle? It's out with the old; in with the new; else what is new about it?

The people of the world that have always been in rejection to the present reality of the churches in the communities worldwide; they are now wondering what happened to the churches?

The ungodly people of the society are now thinking that God must have allowed for the churches to change for the sake of the people of the society who never believed in the message of the bible?

However, I do believe that many people who never came to the church are looking in disappointment, in that they had a hope that if or whenever they might have decided to come in out of the world that the church would still be there steadfast and unchanged; even unmoved by the resistance from the world! The true church is still standing strong in the power of the Holy Ghost!

My friend; it is God indeed who permit a sinner to remain in their sin when they truly choose to do so. It's amazing that the discussion of the permissive will of God is most heard among the people of the churches who confess to having been save and washed in the blood of Jesus Christ!

God will even permit a sinner to die in their sins if they refuse to hear the message of repentance and of salvation! You and I alike have been the witness to this truth over and over again as we have watched young and older gang members shot down in the streets, dying for a cause that they themselves are not completely sure of!

An outrageous number of the people of the gay communities have died HIV POSITIVE; and with full-blown AIDS; they were most determined to live against the natural grain of their own genders, having same-sex relationships against God's word!

God permitted for them to die so dishonorably, leaving their families and

their close friends embarrassed and ashamed at them; though some would even vow allegiance to their dead friends as a way of resisting the truth of God's word; they promised their now dead friends that they would never change!

They have even now convinced themselves that their lifestyles are impossible for God to change them; as a matter of the fact they blame God for being homosexual.

Learning to lean and to depend upon God through faith is a process which requires for some things that we are not necessarily familiar with to take place in ur lives; it is necessary to know whether or not we were indeed serious and forever determined to remain saved sanctified and holy for the rest of our lives?

Only God knows what it really takes to test us to see what is in our hearts! There may be times when even we ourselves have not come to terms with what is in our heart towards God; so it is necessary for the Lord to permit some things to infiltrate our peaceful lives.

To shake up the established platforms of living that we had already built for ourselves that are not at all conducive for the benefit of faith, and the kingdom of God.

Never forget the fact that people have come to be saved from all walks of life, whereas, they were notorious for running things and for being large and in charge! Only Jesus Christ, is Lord; and master of all of our lives; God is in control, so you can't be!

God; permitted for you to grow great big in your own eyes and in the eyes of your peers; but be advised that every high thing must come down before the presence of the Lord. The greats must decrease in the presence of the Lord; "God is Great; and Greatly to Be Praised!"

Just because the leadership of the churches have been allowed to bring secular artist and Movie stars into the fellowship of the churches, to give them elevated platforms based on the popularity of their secular statuses,

doesn't mean that God approves of them also being in the highest platforms of the churches.

People of the churches are permitted to do a lot of things in which they are determined to do, but that does not mean that they will not have to give an account for their deeds.

Simply because it is public knowledge that they have amassed great financial wealth and have acquired great gain; so many of these people at times are pushed right past the necessary processes of God's calling first of all; and the process of being made usable for God's purpose.

They are permitted to believe their success have made them all that they will ever need to be. Their egos have cause them to believe that they are better people than the average people of the churches anyway; even though they are only professional pretenders; they are better at acting the part at best!

They are not all willing to acknowledge that they have sinned and have done more wickedly than many of the people in the churches simply because they had the money to do so! Too often they are more cewlebrated than any people of the churches, which give them the signal that they are alright just as they are.

Some leaders in the churches fear that if they should tell these professional sinners the actual truth about themselves, that the possible expected financial support just may be compromised!

A large percentage of the people from the wealthier statuses of living among us only come into the churches for the sake of portraying the part of a changed life; they still maintain the contacts and the lifestyles of their past social connection.

Those who come into the churches having great finances and wealth; they also come in having great desires to run things; even if that means displacing the leaders and replacing them with themselves?

They may often even think themselves to be smarter and more intelligent

than the preachers who stand before the congregation every Sunday to declare the truth of God's anointed word; they have the audacity to sneer and to turn their noses up at them in grave disrespect.

Although it is the church that they have come to citing the need for a change in their lives; somehow, simultaneously they have been convinced that they need to change what they see in the church!

So many people are in schools and Theological seminaries trying to become knowledgeable and usable for the Lord; but if that were possible, things in the churches around the world would definitely show forth the glory of God by a much greater standard percentages; much more than what it is that we are seeing.

No matter what you may learn in school and Theological seminaries; you will never know what God knows, especially what He knows about you! God permits us to get into trouble at times just for the sake of allowing us to know firsthand that no matter what we get ourselves into, that He is able to get us out of it when we ask Him to get us out of it in faith!

My late pastor taught me that even if preaching the gospel of God get me into trouble; staying with God faithfully continuing to preach the word of God would also get me out of trouble.

Other people; can neither make faith, nor make you to be; or to become; faithful! We must return to the understanding that there are some things that only God can do for us, and then allow for God to do it for us!

Not even finances and great wealth have the powerful ability to make one faithful to the Lord; it often does the very opposite in that it builds a false sense of security, making people to believe that they have got it all together now; they can handle it from this point on; they think anyway!

But in the very hour and times of our lives when things seem to occur that might have put us at the lowest places of our existence, or when a solution to what has indeed taken place in our lives is out of our reach; to our surprise, those are the times when God was indeed needed to work in our lives!

It didn't feel good to us and it didn't look good to our families and to our friends for certain! But in the supernatural omnipotent sovereignty of His will; God will dumbfound all of us at the very same time. It is only afterwards when all the dust and the chaos settles, that we are better informed at just what the Lord was up to all of the time.

Firstly; by revelation of the permissive will of God; we are made aware of the surgical like corrective procedures made in certain areas of our lives, by God's own hand.

As we will have already begun to walk in the newness of the altered changes of our lives, others will eventually be made aware that we have indeed accepted the changes and have altered certain mannerism of our personal lifestyle and behavior towards God! It is at these certain times in our lives that we know that we are being perfected and fashioned for the master's use.

God; permitted for us to be changed through the working power in the shed blood of Jesus Christ, on the cross at Calvary on Golgotha's hill! Have you ever thought to think about the fact that God could have left us in the sinful state of the flesh?

God could have even annihilated every trace of mankind all over the face of the earth; He could have even totally disintegrated the earth without a trace to be remembered no more. Suppose God had decided to start over from a new beginning for mankind destroying the present human race?

He didn't because God permitted a finish before He ever got started with mankind and the finished work of the Kingdom of God in the earth. It is about time that we as people begin to think more on the purpose of our lives and why it is that things have been permitted to take place in our lives, even without our permission.

God is indeed finished; but by many principles of His own purpose and plan, He is not necessarily through with us. We are what God had intended for us to be as human beings; yet it is consistently revealed to us as individuals, of the exact need for our existence here in the earth as children of the

Lord to bring every man woman boy and girl to the present atonement, and to the perfected will of God!

Chapter 6

"Not Until" Faith Is Fulfilled!"

Till we all come in the unity of the faith, and of the knowledge of the son of God, unto a perfect man, unto the measure of the stature of the fullness of Christ; That we henceforth be no more children, tossed to and fro, and carried about with every wind and doctrine, by the sleight of men, and cunning craftiness, whereby they lie in wait to deceive; But speaking the truth in love, may grow up into him in all things, which is the head, even Christ: Peace be to the brethren, and love with faith, from God the father and the Lord Jesus Christ. Grace be with all them that love our Lord Jesus Christ in sincerity. Amen. {Ephesians 4:13-16; 6:23-24}

"Christ; is waiting on us!"

We often wonder what it is and even why it is that God hasn't showed up; that He has not come to our aid as of yet even though we have prayed; even though we have preached the gospel of God in Christ Jesus? Even though we had been kind to our fellowman, and had done so many wonderful things in the name of the Lord?

Doesn't matter what things that we undertake to do in the name of the Lord or of what activities that we concur to involve ourselves where other

people can see our involvement; these things don't make faith and neither are they always capable of showing forth that we are faithful people of the Lord!

There are so many charitable organizations in the world which have nothing at all to do with God in Christ Jesus; but they do almost everything that the churches are doing and even more at times? While they have the powerful ability to make people to feel extremely grateful at times as result of the charitable deed; they cannot make unfaithful unbelieving people to become otherwise faithful in believing God in Christ Jesus.

Many rich people will at times do things for certain selected people without desiring to be recognized publically; but not even they themselves even desire to be recognized as being people of faith in God.

Many people have even settled in their hearts that faith is never what they are going to need as result of being financially well off, to the point in fact that it would take several life spans to spend all of the money that they have amassed. Whatever it takes money to do for us in the earth, they have it already and then some.

Most people have been deceived to think and to believe that the only real true need for faith is to bring God down to humanity to open up financial possibilities in that we can live more comfortably in the earth among the others who are indeed rich and wealthy.

I am not at all ashamed to inform you that in most instances, the true authentic faith of God in Christ Jesus; is being over-looked and totally left out; the true scheme of faith in God has been redirected to be the prosperity claim that many ministries have now embraced.

The scripture informs of that faith comes by hearing and hearing by the word of God. Faith is already made and already complete in the total essence of its existence. What we don't hear or read in the word of God; is that faith is made while hearing or reading the word of God.

As we are instructed that faith comes by hearing from a sent preacher, we don't make nor produce the faith that comes as result of our obedience of

preaching God's word. Consider the reality of those who are in the pulpits preaching that will not even preach truth on purpose by design of their own volition.

Many preachers have determined that they should satisfy their own desires for faith teaching, so that it will be more acceptable to the people in their congregations. They need for the people to be more comfortable supporting what has been purported to be the financial need of the ministry; so they choose not to put pressure on the people to satisfy their ideas of faith from the pulpits.

Many of the former spiritual leaders would teach us of the necessity to meet the conditions of faith in effort to move God. Others came along who were determined that it doesn't take all of that to get a blessing from the Lord. My friend but it does take all of that to be a blessing to the Lord; for the Lord!

We simply hear about faith, and read about faith in and through the word of God. It is rather bewildering to me that many people would even have the nerve to think within themselves that they have been given whatever it takes to make faith; it took faith for them to even be saved in the first place! We need faith in our lives every step of the way; but faith is not to be thought of in the same light as money. We need money so we go to work and do a job to receive a pay check; we earn the money that we need!

God; is the reason that we need faith, being that He created us to be faithful individuals; God has the wisdom and all of the reasons of why it is that we will always need faith; God; believed in Himself; so He made the faith that we would need to please Him!

Never again would God ever take a chance on mankind knowing that man could be influenced to rethink Gods commandment to man in the earth, and totally miss Him; and lose out for all eternity, and end up in Hell. This is the reason that so many people seek desperately to humanize Christ; they refuse to align their lifestyles with faith in God.

Common sense gives us to know and to realize that faith had already been here before we were put here! No man, woman, boy, or girl knew about faith

on their own since having been born here in this world of which we are living; as it had been ordained of God for us all to be taught about the faith of God, but by someone who had already been taught themselves?

Alike breath, all we had to do was to breathe; of which no one would have to teach us to inhale. Faith had already been given for us to approach God; all we would need to do is just to believe in faith and begin to exercise faith in God!

It was initially intended of God for the atmosphere of the earth to have been a spirit filled reality of living whereas faith would have been normally regarded respectively as the sense of touch in our skin; as the seeing of our eyesight; as the sensitivity of sound in our hearing; as the recognition of flavors in our taste buds; as the various scents of our sense of smell!

Faith should have been the normal characteristic of every human being. It is now necessary, as a result of sin separating us from the Father in heaven that others teach us about faith in God, allowing us the opportunity to make the choice to adhere to the teachings of faith in God.

The desirable acceptance of faith in God; is what indeed allows for the knowledge of faith to increase in us, even opening us up to the more elevated possibilities of greater faith, placing us in faithful platforms of living according to the written word of God.

In other words, it is because we want the faith of God in our lives, acceptably and desire to have it even more than to what we have already believed and have understood faith to be and to work in our behalf; that faith is unlimitedly released into our understanding and into our spirit being.

Faith; being to the likes of an elevator, allows for us to get inside of the elevator which takes us up to the more elevated levels of the buildings that we are in. The elevator itself as the mechanical instrument that it is constructed to be, is not constructed to stop us as we are walking bye to get on the inside of us to go wherever we are purposing to go; being too big and designed for the benefit of serving many others at once, we have to take the action to move the elevator!

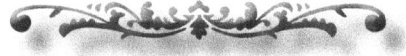

Whenever we have pushed to button to alert the elevator of our need of its service, the elevator responds to the request of our need already prepared to get us to the next level of the building?

Faith can actually take you to places; having already been created with the preparatory connections to God, through Christ Jesus; to get us to the next levels and or even to the next dimensions in God, of which we will never get to on our own!

Contrary to the teachings of many of the religious organizations concerning faith, you could never take faith to places in God so stop trying to do so! You don't need to take faith to God; you need to have faith in God! God knows exactly what faith is and what faith can and will do or allow to be done for you; with you; and even through you!

Too often in the scripture we miss the messages of faith that are being released in the scripture; we know of the instance in the scripture when Jesus and His disciples are walking by a particular Fig tree, He reaches into the tree to take fruit from this tree which was in full bloom; but there was nothing but leaves on the tree.

There were no fruit on the tree; Jesus cursed the tree, and said that no fruit would ever again grow on that tree! *[St. Matthew 21:19]* Within 24 hours; the tree was wither and dried up; the apostles were amazed at how fast the tree responded to the words spoken to it by Christ Jesus.

Jesus; responds to their amazement; *[Mark 11:22]* passing back by the tree Mark reports the admonishment of the Lord to them saying; "Have Faith in God!"

Jesus is showing us the error of our ways many times; as we strive to prove to God that we have faith, we miss out on the manifestations of faith to our detriment. Rather, God is assured that you have adhered to faith when you have spoken through faith to Him! Even you will know when you have spoken in faith to God through the rapid response of the manifestations as result of faith in God!

There is to be a great falling away from the faith in God; this is because so many people are determined to get and to maintain a controlling touch and a grasp on faith!

The expository preaching argument from many of the pulpits nowadays, is that you need to prove yourselves to God through your faith? As a result; many are coming to the churches and walking down the aisles of the churches, responding to the altar call in the church; thinking that they are bringing faith with them to the presence of God?

A very sad commentary to humanity is that faith is what it takes to even turn to God's direction of which is provided to us by God. Faith is the reason that they have even come to seek God at the altar, in the first place! They have missed the fact that God has proven Himself to humanity through His faith, which has been given freely to every man on the face of the earth! People are there in the face of the Lord attempting to show Him that we now possess what He has given to us to even enter into His presence?

We had been taught that it is necessary to possess faith; we need to work through faith! Allow faith to work for us; faith knows right well how to work for us on our behalf to get us to the presence of the Lord, even so that God can give to us the things that we are asking of Him according to His will.

Faith is as awesome as God is Himself; being created by God, faith has the ability to allow for us to see the greater things of the spirit that are indeed hidden from what we as mankind have always known to be realistic to our human existence. Faith doesn't need the gadgets and control mechanisms; faith so excellently reveals the hidden things of the spirit to us in effort for us to retrieve them and to have them for our benefit in the earth.

God; being so wise and so smart; has not released everything to mankind for our own desires; He knows that we would destroy those things of the spirit realm just as mankind have destroyed most things in the earth that they have been allowed to get their hands on.

We wonder why it is that even though we have used the name of the Lord, we're still waiting on the manifested presence of the Lord to change things

and to prove to all of the onlookers who knew that we were waiting on the Lord, that we really had a connection with the Father in Heaven.

It has only been a recognition kind of thing that has been the motivation for doing the work of the ministry in the first place. So many people had received word of true prophetic utterances, which they had never mixed the spoken word received, with faith.

Perhaps there may be some truth to about 40% of those spoken words as result of the people who are indeed hyped up on media exposure, and name recognition? Had it been a person of much lessor recognition; perhaps they might have been more apt to seek the Lord concerning the word and even to test the word according to faith and the written word of God.

Often, others have accused the prophetically spoken words as having been untimely released against the will of the Lord's timing and even spoken out of turn? Most people who had been prophesied unto, they had set themselves to readily receive that word based on who the purported prophetic messenger was supposed to be?

So many people have done all of those things for many years and have now become discouraged and disappointed of the fact that God had not thrust them into utter prosperity of needless; issue-less; lack-less living? The teachings of the scripture and the instructions that they had received have all but failed them and had left them hanging in the balance; so to speak!

The words of which they speak have now taken on a different tone, whereas, they are soured and embittered at the thought of faithfulness; when all along the problem had never been faith itself; the problem was that the motives for doing all of the things of which they did were never of faith!

The things that were indeed done were never for the sake of satisfying the fulfillment of faith; but more so for the sake of self-gratification; to establish a well-recognized name for themselves in the communities, and even across the country.

According to the scripture, I would have to file these people away into the

high stacked file of glory seekers? While everyone now recognize them by their names, and their big churches; faith has not recognized them as being dedicated children of the Lord Jesus Christ; whereas God-like manifestations are the normal occurrences of their ministries!

In the presence of the true ministers of faith; there we experience the flow of the spirit of the Lord, as He fills the atmosphere; unquestionable and undeniable, God is there! Be advised that faith would never turn its back to look away from a sincere obedient lover of Jesus Christ.

It is paramount that we as people understand that we can never disappoint and disobey Jesus Christ, and satisfy faith simultaneously! *[Numbers 14:]* So many glory seeking leaders of the churches, who also desire to have all of the people to love them, even if they don't really love the Lord; they are leading the people down a path that is headed straight for hell and eternal destruction.

From the pulpits they are giving suggested freedom to the people to go forward with disobeying the word of God. The deception here is in the fact that they don't even have the authority to give you the freedom to go ahead and live sinfully.

Faith is of God; it cannot be active to produce the things of God to those who refuse to believe God and to believe and to obey His word. For too many years and decades and centuries, people have been allowed to think of faith as being stupid, blind, and ignorant?

They think within themselves that faith will just do it anyway! Doesn't matter if they hate the church and everyone who attend church services; they can get the exact same benefits of faith in God; anyway? People have been allowed to believe that they can trick faith into bamboozling God to fill the request of a need, even though in their own hearts, faith is despised!

Oh yes; people have some very twisted ideas of faith in God; only according to their ideas and the word of God, their twisted imagination of God and of His word disallows for any faith in God to reside on the inside of them. Some people prefer to reach right into the heart of the spirit of the Lord if

it were possible, and to rip the authority of the spirit away from the truth of God!

They don't want faith to work according to the word of the Holy Bible; they want to take faith into the classroom, laboratory, and even into the workshops of their own opinions of faith in God; tearing it into pieces, to rearrange it so that it works for them the way that they desire for it to work.

The only problem is that there is no other book other than the bible that can give the only God ordained definition of faith; instruction on the usage and the application of faith. Perhaps others have added faith to other literary works, but the ownership of faith and its know-how; wisdom of instruction belongs to God.

Looking unto Jesus the author and the finisher of our faith;
who for the joy that was set before him endured the cross,
despising the shame, and is set down at the right hand of the
throne of God.   *{Hebrews 12:2}*

God created faith from the beginning of time; when He knew that man would fall prey to the satanic scheme of the devil; whereas sin would be allowed to creep into humanity; grace and faith would be most necessary to bring mankind back into a harmonious relationship of oneness with the Father through the sacrifice of the only begotten son of God; Jesus Christ. As result, we have been accepted into the beloved of God; as dear children of the Father in Heaven.

Through History the plan in the heart of man has been to satisfy the requiem for religion. Even to this very day it is the more common practice for people to satisfy religious regimen; having a form of godliness but denying the power thereof!

Many people please themselves while they listen to the teachings of faith, but they never truly hear the intended message of truth concerning faith. Faith pleases God; it is our duty to please faith to the point of fulfillment, in effort for faith to know that it is the proper moment and time to address the father on our behalf.

145

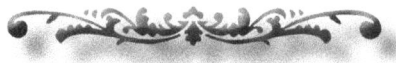

As it stands, the Father could have left us out of the kingdom of His own dear son; but by grace it was the Father's intention not to allow the purpose of faith itself to be dissatisfied and left unfulfilled.

Faith has been created to work for you and for me; but it has been instructed as pertaining to what elements would be required before making any movement on the behalf of mankind.

I stated earlier that most people have the idea that faith just ought to do it for them anyway! But you need desperately to understand that faith itself cannot disobey the Father in heaven!

Faith will never make an unsatisfactory approach to the Father on the throne because of the fact that you as a believer failed to apply knowledge, virtue, brotherly love, kindness to your understanding of faith.{II Peter 1:5-7}

The most important thing about having knowledge as it pertains to faith, is to gain the comprehensive wherewithal, to know what faith itself knows about God and the word of God and how it is that the two are so eternally intertwined to creatively allow the manifested honor of God's presence to provide answers to prayer; to release blessings in the earth as result of true faith in the word of God, and even to produce miraculous interventions for the sake of the limited extremities of mankind in the earth.

It is neither surprising to God nor is it disappointing to Him that we as people are always at our limit! But it is displeasing to Him that people are indeed faithless, to the point in fact that it hinders God from being able to bless us and to meet our need. God has always intended that we would depend and rely upon Him. However, His plan includes the acquisition and the true dependence of faith, to receive whatever it is that we desire of Him.

"Unzipping Us; To Release what's On the Inside of Us!"

As a result of utter failure in the teachings of faith in God; we are as a sent package shipped to our destinations, now needing to be unpackaged, opened to release the inner hidden contents of the arrived package. We are

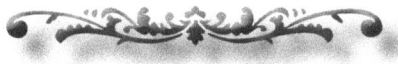

just as a downloaded computer program; which has been zipped to make it easier to ship the program from the seller to the buyer over the computer network; in order to get to the product it has to be unzipped.

We are sent here to the earth to produce a product that is pleasing to the Father in heaven; that will pass the inspection of the judgement, having been already tested and tried in the earth.

Our carnal minds allow for us only to focus on what comes out of the manufacture; we never even have the mind to think on the products that shipped into the manufacture to produce the products that are eventually shipped out as a result of the manufacturer haven successfully produced and packaged for delivery.

Living in such a land of make-believe, and of fantasy as we live here on the earth; somehow we allow ourselves to believe those things about living and getting those make-believe things of fantasy out of life that are totally impossible for us to ever have; because they are not even real to begin with.

Just to talk to the average person of the country, and you really don't have to travel far away at all to find people who are of the description that I am about to give; people are dizzy in their minds with the farce of "what if this could be real?"

"Disney World" and "Disney Films" continue to be one of the most productive companies of the entertainment industry, for their ability to take the minds and the imagination of the people to the unlimited entertainment heights unknown!

They have been masters at getting the people to agree with and to believe in the never possible unrealistic even the unimaginative worlds of animated living on other planets; or Islands out in the middle of the ocean somewhere uninhabitable?

In other words; people are hyped and dizzy on the possibilities of doing the impossible that is also the biblically forbidden for us as mankind to ever do! For an instance; such films for years have been created to suggest that

there just might be alien life forms on other planets? They keep on trying to suggest how we might get along to exist as alternative life forms to each planet and learn from each other as neighbors.

In general, as people we fail to even get along with the other people that we know for sure are in our land that may live across the street, in another city, another state, or perhaps in another country even!

The entertainment industry moved in a hurry to take the control of the minds of the people who watched their films, starting with the children in the cartoon industry?

Jack and the Bean Stalk; and the Giant who lives above the clouds somewhere, who vows to "grind the bones of man to make his bread", distorts the idea of us moving out of this world to live with the Father in Heaven! After once being made aware of this fictitious fable, the children decide at very early ages that they don't want to leave this world because of the issues of safety in this world! Why; because of fear of the unknown!

Disney; have also been instrumental in leading the parents to believe that they are entertaining their children; harmlessly? Because it is probable that most adults/parents will leave the television to entertain the children while they attend unto the chores of the household.

The cartoon industry has taken it upon them to also teach that fear is also healthy for our minds. As the children progress through life they are found to be fearless of Horror movies filled with gore and unthinkable violence to the normal individual; the deeper the industry goes with the films when allowed they are found putting the ideas into their films. Only a tip of the issues……..

We are often concerned as to why it is that so many people struggle with faith; we see where the struggles may began as suggested; through early childhood entertainment? The television industry from the very secular perspectives take it upon themselves to get their opinions of faith in through commercials; movies; weekly shows; news broadcast and etc……

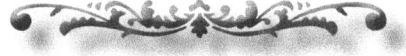

The truth is that many people are simply truly confused before ever going into the church to be taught about faith in God. The greater deception about faith is that the preachers are often led to believe that through the messages that they preach that they are putting faith into the people?

People have already been negatively informed about faith in God, before they ever decide on coming into the church. But their reasons for coming into the church; is often for the purpose of testing the theories of the secular industries? It had already been suggested to them that faith is neither necessary nor real, and that it doesn't really amount to anything worth wasting time on!

We see people by the scores gather to sing hymns, read scriptures, and to even recite a prayer corporately but also they are a group of people noted as having no root of faith in God whereas they are successful at even getting a prayer through to God for themselves, or for anyone else for that matter.

They are people who have read the bible from cover to cover; however er the word of God have been stopped at their limit of being able to retain written scripture. The God of the bible have never succeeded to prick their hearts, as they leave their chosen churches of choice, they feel they are finished with the bible until the next service.

The real detriment is that these certain people, although bye the scores of Tens of Thousands; have never even gotten started with faith! They are satisfied to only do whatever everyone else is doing; they are often forbidden through the teachings of their churches to never explore any depths of faith; nor of faith in God! Some churches are very adamant that they are teaching you enough about faith which alleviates any need for any of the people to seek anything more than to that of which they have been taught.

We see that many churches are indeed satisfied; in that they are able to get the people to respond to their own teachings of their own specific brand of faith, whereas they have been able to build large monuments; and to amass great funds for the bank accounts, having been successful at attracting people from far and near to attend their services.

149

However, most of their parishioners are very limited to having none transformative exploits of faithful manifestations of which their lives are showing forth the glory of God in their changed lifestyles which totally reflect the presence of God's Love.

"Only Love Can Satisfy Faith!"

For in Jesus Christ neither circumcision availeth any-thing, nor uncircumcision; but faith which worketh by love.
{Galatian 5:6}

There are a lot of things that are taught and heralded as the important things of any particular church; relative to the denomination or of the religious practice; itself. People have now for years become practicing agent of the teachings of the particular church in which they choose to attend.

We see people standing on street corners handing out pamphlets of information that highlights the teachings of their churches. The people are dedicated to stand in the hot sun, the cold, the wind, and when allowed they would even stand in the rain, were it not for the people who refuse to stop to give them their attention in the wet weather?

We know that the people are being influenced by the churches that they attend because of the dedicated activities that they show forth in public view despite of the ridicule and the criticism from other people who reject their views.

We see many ministries nowadays; who give out to the homeless and to the needy, but they do so having their media teams all over the place to catch the charitable activities on camera, so that the people can see that they are doing ministry?

It is clear that their outreach ministries are truly trained and catered to the homeless people who really need it; but they take for granted and miss the fact that many other people can see that they are indeed fishing for more people to come and to join their churches; which appear to be more import-

150

ant than the ministry to the needs of the people that are indeed homeless!

They want people to come into their churches that have been duped and deceived by them, to further obstruct the message of faith and trust in the Lord to them? Faith; must be seen in order to be taught!

The real true dangers of deception; is that you never know that it is deception until you realize that you have been deceived! The signs of deception all read as something other than what it really is until the blinds have been pulled revealing what's truly behind it all.

The deception of many of these types of churches and charitable organizations is in the fact that they really do perform many charitable deeds and go out of their ways to serve humanity; but what is indeed lost are the inabilities to focus on faith in God as the motives for which the deeds are done.

Such deeds are done to cushion the blows of society and of living, and even to offer a sense of human touch for the fact that the people of the lesser more destitute angles of living are in need of feeling a healing touch; often faith is suggested as being the manner in which those who have been allowed to participate in coming to the aid of those in need, is done?

Many will come to the need of the homeless and to those who are in poverty, out of pity and or sometimes even out of pure utter disgust. Faith is often turned upside down and inside out, for the sake of a more easily acceptable method of becoming faithful in the eyes of the people.

Faith is whatever God says that it is indeed; what we do as result of faith is what is seen; so many people are looking for faith in the land, who are often disappointed to see that the things that people are calling faith in no way show forth the power of the presence of God.

People are quick to highlight the fact that what has just been done was the type of thing that any human being could do? So while many of the religions and the churches and charitable organizations are feeling that they are sending people on blind expositions of faith, simply for the fact that faith had already been installed as the method of pleasing God; even the faithless can't

always be fooled!

For a truth, whenever we begin the dialogue about faith, the minds of any people automatically turns to the direction of God! Everyone with good sensible reasoning, automatically think of God as being the only reason that faith would ever really be needed.

We already have ideas and knowledgeable skills to acquire most everything in the earth; but simultaneously we also know that the same available skills and knowledge are incapable of getting the things that we need from God. Whenever we even begin dealing with God; the word of God; and the things of God in Christ Jesus; through the Holy Ghost; we already know that it involves faith first!

To deceive people is definitely one of the greater strategies to block and to hinder the people from being able to properly approach faith having the right understanding that leads them and allows for them to please the Lord.

The bigger picture of religious aspects of faith shows the average person that no one anywhere, appear to be getting everything that they want from the Lord; so we all just have to do things according to faith in the particular manner taught to everybody that will keep us all from losing our minds and from turning our backs on the idea of faith.

Many religious leaders have allowed for the ideas of faith to be floated into many different directions; faith have been given many different reasons for being in existence, even though it cannot be seen directly as a physical thing to be manipulated and handled!

As a rule, faith itself is checked at the front door, meaning that whatever is posted on the front door or out on the marquee out in the front of the building is the total representation of the faith that is taught and represented at that particular place of religion, or denomination.

Many months and years are gone by whereas the only teachings on faith are relative to the association to the ministry. What has indeed been the deceptive act of teaching is that the bible is opened and interpreted to be

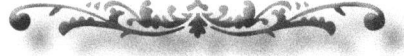

relative to the teachings of the standing religion of the denomination where the people are presently seated. The very comprehensive definitive value of the knowledge of faith is often cheated and devalued as result of erroneous teachings.

Since faith in God cannot and will not be denied; many of the people nowadays are taught that God doesn't work in a particular manner of the scripture, as He had done in the past? They want you to believe that the ever unchanging God; that He has changed!

Faith is given a bad rap as people who attempt to apply what they have been taught is faith; when they seek to get that from God that only faith in God can deliver, they come up short of receiving what they expect. We see this happening often throughout many aspects of the churches, and relative to every area of humanistic welfare and need.

God promised to be there for humanity and even that if and when we ask of Him in faith, that we would never be denied! Deception shows up in the fact that many people think that they are asking God when in fact they never had the right angle of faith to even proposition the help of the Lord.

We serve a God of Love; God's love demands us to care and to share with mankind of all walks of life; however, we as people are often pushed into a corner by those who demand Love! People by the scores are angry with the preachers and the entire spectrum of the clergy, because they sought to demand a show of Love for their own benefit, but were eventually denied the aspect of love to which they were seeking.

Love; demands excellence and perfection which in its clearest of definitions means that we finish to the highest level of completion being careful of the manner of which we achieve excellence, and certain of the fact that God is our destination.

We ask for what we want having sought to the greatest level of receiving; in other words we ask having no doubt of the request, we know and are sure of what it is that we want from the Lord; we ask knowing that the Lord is able

to do whatever we ask of Him in faith; and finally we ask of the Lord knowing that our request is coming to pass!

I'm in love with fact that God; is God; He is able to do everything but fail, and I know and respect the fact that everything that I need from the Lord He is able to do, and that because I have come to Him in faith, he is going to do it!

I am sure that it is faith that has allowed me into the presence of the Lord; the need to have God move for me is too serious and important for me to error in faith when approaching the throne of Grace.

God; my friends, is looking for the faithful, as He already know where faith is; so whenever we come in and through faith; it is faith that is pleased which speaks up on our behalf agreeing to the possible response to our request.

Erroneously we expect for Jesus to do all of the work for us, for which His greatest work for us has indeed already been done. Through the atonement of the shed blood of Jesus; it has been made possible for us to even approach the throne of God on our behalf.

As we move in the direction of the Lord, our ascent to the throne speaks for us in that it either alert faith that we are coming, or it silences everything about our arrival as result of the fact that we are void of connecting through faith.

Under the guise of certain said instances of approach, through correct teaching and instructions we know whether to expect anything or to just keep on moving right past stopping to enquire of the Father at the throne. Up to about 85% of the people who claim to be faith believers need to be sent back to faith 101; for a lesson on true faith and faithful application.

Chapter 7

"God; Is Faithful "

Know therefore that the Lord thy God, he is God, the faithful God, which keepeth covenant and mercy with them that love him and keep his commandments to a thousand generations;   {Deuteronomy 7:9}
Thus saith the Lord, the redeemer of Israel, and his Holy One, to him whom man despiseth, to him whom the nation abhorreth, to a servant of rulers, Kings shall see and arise, princes all shall worship, because of the Lord that is faithful, and the Holy One of Israel, and he shall choose thee.   {Isaiah 49:7}
God is faithful, by whom ye were called unto the fellowship of his son Jesus Christ our Lord.
                    {I Corinthians 1:9}
There hath no temptation taken you but such as is common to man: but God is faithful, who will not suffer you to be tempted above that ye are able; but will with the temptation also make a way to escape, that ye may be able to bear it.   {I Corinthians 10:13}
Faithful is he that calleth you, who also will do it.
                    {I Thessalonians 5:24}
But the Lord is faithful, who shall stablish you, and keep you from evil.   {II Thessalonians 3:3}
Let us hold fast to the profession of our faith without wavering; (for he is faithful that promised); Through faith also Sa'ra herself received strength to conceive seed, and was delivered of a child when she was past age, because she judged him faithful who had promised.   {Hebrews 10:23; 11:11}
If we confess our sins, he is faithful and just to forgive

155

us our sins, and to cleanse us from all unrighteousness.
{I John 1:9}

"Be Not Deceived; God Knows Faith!"

Opening this chapter of discussion, I feel more than impressed in my own spirit to offer apologies to those of you who have been misled and erroneously instructed concerning the actuality of faith in God, and God's active response to you as a faithful believing, and trusting individual of faith in God; and to the written compiled scripture of the canonized bible!

God is eternally committed to respond to faith of the trusting and believing people of the earth; God being faithful means that He is in forward progression to act upon His word!

From Genesis to Revelation; we see and are able to understand that God is God; from the beginning to the end of the bible. There are answers to the incomprehensible phenomenon and the unforeseen disasters alike written in the scripture; of which it doesn't take a rocket science to comprehend it as the truth.

We see years and decades, even millenniums of data compiled, relative to the accounts of the move of God; the creation of the world; the earth and the heavens, along with the creation of mankind and all that is in the world to this very day, written in the scriptures.

I realize that such instructive reasoning causes an inferiority of confidence and total assurance; leaving an individual weary of the actuality of faith, distrusting that faith alone could ever be the reason that we as people could ever learn the unknown.

Receive that which had not been given to us as of yet; and or to touch that which is indeed intangible to the natural human sense of touch. To say it best, on a general principle, people are not encour-

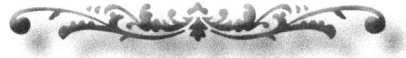

aged to believe; more than often they are admonished not to spend time believing anything.

I have been assigned to write about faith from the standpoint of knowing and not just believing only!

To believe only also leaves the dismantling option to disbelieve; to doubt; the platforms are laid out for people in general to question or even rather to bring in to question the things of God and ultimately faith; whereas faith itself is never questionable; such mindsets renders an individual as questionable themselves; apprehensible.

In other words, the empowered actuality of faith is more than often rendered inoperable and powerless, thus disabled and deactivated to close the gap between what has been hoped for and to be eventually manifested received results of faith in God.

And to alleviate the sin-forged distance between man and God to produce atonement for the benefit and for the need of a relationship to maintain a life of righteousness in Christ Jesus!

Many have been led to believe that God in some way or another is in search of faith; as if to suggest that He; Himself might have given to all mankind a faith that He is not even familiar with. Even my friend such a mindset, erroneously suggests that there may be some form of a deficiency in the all Omnipotent God.

He is ever infallible and all knowing beyond our greatest I.Q.; even outside the bounds of our wildest imagination. There is no thinking capacity in all the created realm of the earth that has the ability to match or to stand up to the mind of God.

We are instructed in the book of Proverbs; to get understanding! But, don't get it twisted; the things which God knows, understanding itself can't comprehend! Inflated egos and arrogant minds think and believe that they are just as knowledgeable as the creator of all knowledge?

Some would go even further to acknowledge that even if they are not as knowledgeable as the all Omnipotent God; that it doesn't matter to them because they are still not going to trust and believe in Him.

Such thought process is assassination to any ability to acquire even the slightest inquisition of faith; and it certainly blocks the mind of an individual to view God as anything more than just a fleeting possibility of thought more wonderful than the human can actually afford itself to ponder or to even grasp?

The splenderous diety of His own reality is far greater than our minds are able to even imagine; though we have been given minds that are quite creatively imaginable to design beautiful structures in the earth for the sake of producing the more elevated things of value.

We've come to the understanding of why it is that so many people are easily swayed from believing the bible, even though they may have read it from cover to cover?

I have personally discovered that many of the people who have spent time in scholastic settings for the sake of studying the bible, have often come away failing to believe and to see the connection between the spirit of God and the natural tangible written word of the bible as being one and the same.

Even though they have first believed before entering the scholastic studies for higher learning and study of the bible. Somehow or another their scientific thinking have brought about a disconnection between earth and heaven; between God and man.

The truth has begun to unfold as to why it is that many students and the instructors alike, of so-called Theology have deduced the bible as to being really nothing more than an earthly book of religious historical occurrences that are left to the imagination and to

the thought process of mere men, to decide whether they choose to believe that what has been written in the bible is actually real and authentic; or someones inflated imaginary thoughts?

From the beginning; God decided to make us in His own image and in His likeness; and He did do so according to His own will and desire! God decided to make us alive, living capacitor conduits of faith, as He is faithful; Himself!

God trust no one but Himself with the people of His own creation; He would never ask us to be something other than what He is. We that come to God must believe that He is; simply because we are being transformed into to being exactly what He is! We will never be who He is; and God is not apologizing for that; but we must become what He is!

God takes no other chances on us coming to Him except through faith; as faith is that system of God's that allows us to intertwine and to connect with who He has always been, who He is; and with who God will always be!

The word of God is therefore necessary to help us and to enable us to receive God; for He has always been; not just a new idea of what we might desire for God to be! God; in no way has He been forged and formed as an idea of thought from any new aged mental configurement.

Faith says to us that if we can receive who God always is from the past up until this very present time, then we can be received of God; for always! Somehow the minds of many ungodly people have been led to believe that God has to accept us even if and when we fail and refuse to accept Him as God!

It is utter insanity to believe that we can hold God to a particular standard, while at the very same instance in our minds we are pushing Him away from us in every way possible.

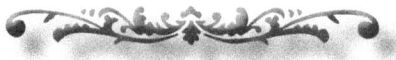

Faith enables us as the people of the earth to be received of God; as sin passed on all humanity, it was sin which separated us from the God who made us just like Him!

Faith is God's method of examination which ex-rays our total being, revealing to God that we are indeed ready to be received of Him. Too often our mouths can be speaking a multitude of things that never reached faith being so filled with question and doubt?

Hebrews 11:6; tells us that; *without faith, it is impossible to please God;* in other words it is faith that must be satisfied so that it can indeed please God who loves faith! Faith answers to God yes when we have indeed met the required condition for faithful satisfaction, to move God on our behalf.

Faith stands in the presence of God with the angels and all the host of heaven. God is overwhelmed and totally pleased with faith at all times to the point in fact that we have never read and we never will read that God has ever been disappointed with faith.

The very heartbeat of God is the pulse of faith; in other words, faith lives because God is alive at the very core center of faith! Faith is not something that showed up on the face of the earth one day for the sake of the pitiful need of humanity, all on its own; saying, "I will go and tell God for you!"

There has never been a moment in time that God did not have his hand on faith; God tells faith; faith answers to God; like as unto all of creation.

"Faithful; to The Finish!"

Better is the end of a thing than the beginning thereof:
{Ecclesiastes 7:8A}
For I know the thoughts that I think towards you,
saith the Lord, thoughts of peace, and not of evil, to
give you an expected end.   *{Jeremiah 29:11}*

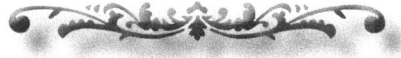

But I have a greater witness than that of John: for the works which the Father hath given me to finish, the same works that I do, bear witness of me, that the Father hath sent me.   {St. John 5:36}
When Jesus therefore had received the vinegar, he said, IT IS FINISHED: and he bowed his head, and gave up the ghost.   {St. John 19:30}
Being confident of this very thing, that he which hath begun a good work in you will perform it until the day of Jesus Christ;   {Philippians 1:6}
Looking unto Jesus the author and the finisher of our faith; who for the joy that was set before him endured the cross, despising the shame, and is set down at the right hand of the throne of God.   {Hebrews 12:2 }

Consistently we are being taught, as many others have been taught that the Lord leads us; however we have also been left to believe that the destinations of the Lord's leading will be based on our individually acquired faith?

As if to suggest that our manipulation of faith have the ability to suggest and or to dictate to God, just where it is that He ought to be leading us.

Erroneously; we have been left to our own understanding of faith to believe that as the scripture states that as we delight ourselves in the Lord; that He would give us the desires of our own heart; we have taken that to mean that we will be given the benefiting favor of placing faith as we have been led to believe in faith as being our own personal possession!

Wherever it is that is most comfortable for us is where most of us would often choose to be led, not even realizing that we will have left off from following the leading of the Lord? It is believed that God will show respect for our personal preferences relative to having faith in God; which is a lie straight from Satan.

We see the fronted image of the local churches all in disarray,

segmented, though disjointed and separated; as result of thinking that we have the right to believe that our faith is better served if and when we are alienated from certain other people?

Even, it is believed that certain ones of the faith (so-called); are more effective being boxed in, put on open display to be viewed and observed as the more faithful and deserving of the favor and of the provisions of God?

I have personally set in the congregation of some churches whereas the pastor of those churches were advising the people from their pulpits to believe that they were better informed than other churches having a greater grasp on the understanding of faith in God?

As a result, they were also led to believe that they were indeed in better position to be respected and desired as being more favorable as a group of people to worship the Lord God with?

To smooth things over a bit, the teaching in many of those said churches is that through their own walk of faith in God; that they are creating a possible lifestyle that invites God to come in and to finish what we have started through our own religious motivations?

Only; the truth is that we are to walk the walk of Faith and to live the lifestyle of Faithfulness in God that has already been established and completely finished; from the end; back to the starting point of the beginning!

In most of our churches people are encouraged to follow after certain people of the congregation, citing that they might have developed the more pleasing lifestyle of faith that better pleases the Lord?

Those people themselves are very proud and think a great deal of themselves; being supported from the leadership of the churches and of the community, their heads are held high, and their attitudes reek of arrogance; though many times they may not even be aware

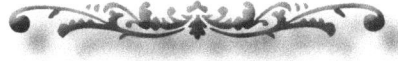

of the fact!

Today's self-serving ideas of faith and of God have caused so many people to think and to believe that they have indeed made it; whatever making it is all about here in the earth!

Some way or another, people are led to believe that having received great financial statuses, and great possessions, that it is indication that their images as people of the churches serves the meaning and the messages of the bible concerning faith and believing in God.

These messages of the today are referred to as; Prosperity gospel messages? People are led to believe that when the stuff starts to come in to them, that they have arrived to the place of faithful pleasure whereas God is now pleased with them as they support the churches financially.

However; the same people are often also found to be laid up in the hospital after a while of being sure that they had made it to graduated places of faith in God, but are unable to get a prayer through to God in faith for their healing!

Without going to deeply into these purported ideas of faith in God, my purpose is simply to show how it is that so many people have arrogantly believed that they have not only shaped faith for so many others, they also believe that they have finished the replica for what everybody else ought to follow and to adhere to as the working order of faith.

I hear too many from the clergy and the theologians stating that we should never exegete nor isogee too much from the bible, as if to suggest that we are apt as people to get too much out of the understanding of the word of God or to actually see too much into the word of God?

According to the 1ˢᵗ chapter of St. John; God is the word; I hear

such teachings and or admonishments as suggesting to people not to think too much of God?

People need to think everything of God and allow their imagination to soar above and beyond all that they are able to ask or to think; because God is above and beyond all that we can ask or think! {Ephesians 3:20} We wonder why and of course how it is that so many people are indigent to rely upon faith in God?

We know that God is here and available to all mankind that believe on Him, but it is often puzzling that people who have been in the churches for decades, haven been born in the church, in the natural and in the spirit of God; yet they have not the spiritual connectivity to God that allows for them to bring God into their own personal atmospheres of living.

Too often, where God is needed; those who have been in the churches being taught to be the faithful people of God, they are confused and perplexed when trouble arises in their lives.

The pastors are too often heralded as super heroes of the faith in the churches, whereas the people need only to get in touch with the pastor to get him to pray for them to fix and or to repair the situations of their lives?

People are falling away from the churches now by the thousands all over the world, for the simple fact that they are finding the pastors and the members of the clergy to be more humanistic and much less spiritual, impeding that that would make them to be super in any manner of their beings, unable to effect any type of a change to alter the things that are indeed unfavorable to their lives.

God is faithful to the preordained completed finish of faith! Faith in and of itself was finished before it was ever introduced to humanity. The God given assignment of faith has already been completed to fulfill all of the need of humanity in the earth.

Whatever it is that we are in need of from the Father in heaven, it is only necessary to connect through faith, making the necessary opening within us to receive God's provisions.

In the natural we start at the beginning to see the end of the thing; God started from the end of the thing in an effort to establish a beginning for us. We struggle to begin our journey through life's plans for us in an effort to see and to realize that it is indeed a beginning for our own human experience!

The finish is always in expectation of our arrival the moment that we begin whatever it is that has been assigned for us to undertake.

Ignorantly unlearned, many people are struggling through their ministries and through their lives; not able to even realize that God stays with us in the processes of our lives because He is faithful to our preordained, predetermined finish!

Just because we are struggling our way through, it is in no way an indication that the Father is struggling with us as well! Neither does it suggest that we are some sort of a broken problem for the Lord!

Our struggles can often be the defining point of determining that we are exactly where the Lord wants us to be, it is only that we are not settled being where God wants us to be, so we fight and like fish caught on a fishing hook, or to the likes of animals caught in a trap trying to free ourselves.

Our struggles don't send God the message that He should change His mind for our destinations because we don't agree with what He has chosen for us! If we could see the finish as God sees the finish of our lives, we would be more agreeable to what God has planned for our lives.

This is the reason that we need to adhere to faith and never waiver from the faith; we can never realize our true given destinies of

success in life to fulfill the God given purposes for humanity that give glory to God in the earth.

Broadly, across the spectrums of believing in God, we are seeing that too many people are struggling against the even flow of faith in God, whereas the unbelievers are not seeing enough to witness the true power and presence of God in the midst of the people who claim to be His.

In the past Five decades, the leaders in the churches have been teaching and preaching messages that cause the people to think that they can dictate how and where God is to be faithful to them as the people of God.

Listen, God is faithful through all that is happening in and all around the world in the midst of His people, but it is never to be assumed that we as a people have bullied and or manipulated God through faith.

Through all that is happening in the world, as the people of the Lord we had better believe and understand that we better follow the Lord our God through Faith and the word of God.

Even as we purport to follow the spirit of the Lord closely; it is only through the word of God that we are assured that it is the spirit of that Lord that we are following for truth! The people of faith are off the track as result of following erroneous teaching and the teachers themselves.

Chapter 8

"Faith "As" A ~ Grain of Mustard Seed"

And Jesus said unto them, Because of your unbelief: for verily I say unto you, if ye have faith as a grain of mustard seed, ye shall say unto this mountain, remove hence to yonder place; and nothing shall be impossible to you. Howbeit this kind goeth not out but by praying and fasting. {Matthew 17:20-21}

"Preface ~ Understanding the Mustard Seed principle"

As ~ a grammatical word; indicating simultaneity; (two or more things happening at the very same time, season, or span), causality; (interconnectivity, fate, destiny, or chance), comparison; <u>or the identity or function of somebody or something.</u>

That he might sanctify it and cleanse it with the washing of water by the word. {Ephesians 5:26}

Connotation ~ implied or additional meaning; an additional sense or senses associated with or suggested by a word or phrase. Conno-

tations are sometimes, but not always, fixed, and are often subjec-
tive. In logic, the characteristic or set of characteristics that makes
up the meaning of a term and thus defines the objects to which a
term can be applied.

Mustard ~ the powdered seeds of a brassica plant, or a hot spicy
paste made from these, or sometimes whole seeds, water, and other
ingredients, eaten in small quantities as a condiment; enthusiasm
or zest; to be up to the desired standard of performance, ability, or
quality.

Seed ~ a plant part produced by sexual reproduction that contains
the embryo and gives rise to a new individual. In flowering plants
it is enclosed within the fruit.

But without faith it is impossible to please Him: for
he that cometh to God must believe that He is, and
that He is a rewarder to them that diligently seek Him
{Hebrews 11:6}

"There Is No Failure In Faith" Faith Won't Fail You!

God is not pacifying us with the gifts of our unfaithful
request while allowing us to continually get it wrong as it
relates to faith, just to keep us as His own. Realizing why it
is that those who often claim to believe by faith fail to receive the expected desires of even their continuous heartful
prayers.....

Even as the embryotic genus of a seed determines the product of the expected growth out of the ground; so likewise
faith is infused with the knowledge and the word of God; assured to produce the expected results desired from the Lord.

The great mega-ton tree which sprouts out of the Mustard
seed as result of having been planted underneath the soil
in the ground, or in a planting pot ~ is exactly as the great
mega-multifaceted you which comes forth as result of you

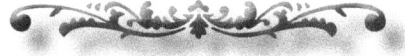

being deeply enbedded in God through the word of faith!

Just to believe in God is never going to be enough, as it is to the likes of having the knowledge of the connectivity of the ground and of the seed, you drop your seed on top of the ground never burying the seed, which will never produce the mega-ton Mustard tree; which is indeed in the seed!

But, you must <u>Be</u> in God! Your whole body, soul, and spirit covered and totally immersed in the shed blood of Jesus! Being in Christ enables us to realize and to experience the promise of the scripture assuring us of the new life in Christ as result of now being in Christ.

Not just being as of many people who hang around the local churches or someone who attend church services but have absolutely no faithful productivity of growth. They have not the word of God in them which produces growth in the light of the Son of God; Jesus Christ (The Light of the world).

Therefore if any man be in Christ Jesus, he is a new creature; old things are passed away; behold all things are become new. {II Corinthians 5:17}

Confluence ~ a coming or flowing together, meeting, or gathering at one point; a flowing together of two or more streams, rivers,   ~

The discussion of the mustard seed and of Faith; are two streaming trains of thought flowing both together to create a sence of reasonable comparison for the sake of understanding and then out of the same sentence as the benefit of comprehending the meaning of what had been spoken from the mouth of Jesus on the subject of having the things of which we desire from the Lord as result of faith in God. [Confluence of Thought]

My purpose is to show you how the analogical com-

parrison of the mustard seed and of faith come together and meet at the exact point of meaningful relevent flow of thought to cause one to think and to develop the acceptable understanding that will produce all of the promises of God found in the written word of God.

I have attended many services and or conferences and even revivals where people were given the tiny little Mustard Seeds, as a comparative means of possession to what should be their own personal possessions of faith.

The meaningful gesture of the gift of the seed was to encourage those persons who may have been feeling as if their level of having faith was low to very minimum; almost to the point in fact of having none faith at all.

Most always, the metaphor of tiny little seeds is misunderstood to mean that it only takes a very miniscule amount of faith to get a whole lot in return; as to the like manner in which many people go about playing the lottery. Whereas they put in a little money; much less than they expect to receive as the reward of the win; they truly expect to get a whole lot in return for their chance, as result in believing that they have a lucky winning hand.

Thus; faith and luck are put into the very same category, of which I must inform you that that is of the greatest misunderstanding ever gleaned from the teaching of Jesus Christ concerning faith.

Many never put in the prayerful effort or the biblical work study to acquire the necessary understanding of faith that empowers those of us who are born again children of God; activating their faith/or faithful adherence according to the written word of God.

I am a witness that people have placed those tiny seeds in their purses; wallets; billfolds; they have even been somehow affixed to the inside of their bibles; and also the seeds are also attached to their eyeglass cases?

People have taken the ownership of such little seeds as if to be building their actual mental fortitude to open up their thinking concerning either faith or the seed; and spiritual strength to receive enlightening concerning their faith.

Receiving the seeds as a means of building faith, people have been duped as result of having no definitive knowledge that should support such analogous reasoning for having the seed in their possession.

(In other words; nowhere in the bible is it stated that to take hold and possession of the mustard seed, would indeed cause their faith to increase!)

Somehow the study of that little seed has placed the mental statuses of many people's understanding of faith into utter chaotic confusion of falsified security in the the acquisition of faith in God; they think within themselves that their ability to take hold of faith must and should grow greatly into something other than what it is already ordained to be initially from the creator of faith.

The mustard seed grows when placed in the right soil conditions, under the guise of the rays of the sunlight, into a megaton tree; of which is already in the tiny seed.

Our handling of the seed; manipulating it in any manner doesn't have any bearing of what comes from the seed. That which comes from the seed is what is already imputed into the seed, initially.

The seed being natural; has great spiritual connotations,

and biblical references. Being a natural thing of nature, even the seed itself cannot be left to the natural elements never being placed in the ground, having no authority of its own to take its strength and power to grow and to deliver that which it had been initially intended to produce.

The seed can't absorb its nutrients from other trees or other seeds, or from any other source in the air or from the water alone. Water alone will drown the seed and allow for it to begin deteriorating its way to disentigration. Seeds must depend on God in the ground for the increase, no matter who plants it or who comes behind the planter/sower; to water the seed....

The seed itself must be planted, or otherwise injected, dropped or planted into the actual fertile and intelligible impute of the ground; so as to be deciphered and assorted into the naturally planned process of nature from the ground, to begin moving its way through the growth process, to fulfill its many purposes; while reaching upwards from the ground to receive the blessing to produce from the sun.

God has forever programmed the ground to compute the given program in the formula of each and every individual seed; it is therefore perpetually dependent upon the word, the original plan, and the provided nourishment from God who gave the seed the germinating process to produce after its own kind.

The rain the sleet and the snow on the other hand, will not drown out the purpose of the seeds natural growth process; and neither will it hamper or dilute the elementary power of the product rendering it too weak or impotent to produce growth and benefits, as long as the seed has the assurance of the ground to apply and to absorb the moisture from the rain, sleet, and the snow to water the seed.

However, the seed must be planted in the proper timing and season for the sake of the production which has been imputed into the soil of the ground.

Planting seeds in the ground in the improper timing of the seasons, assures the failure of the growth process of the seed. The right thing can be done with the seeds but at the wrong time and it will kill the product of the seed.

The right plot of the ground can be chosen to plant the seed, but the right conditions for planting and for sowing seeds is highly dependent upon the exact seasons for the activity of sowing seeds. Sowing seeds at the time of harvesting the products of seeds sown earlier will be futile to the harvester.

The mustard tree grows big and tall and its branches reach far and wide; both upwards towards the sky reaching for the sun and it grows outwards, as if to be reaching out to adjoin itself to the surrounding splenderous array of God's creation.

Left in the hands of mere people having no planned purpose for the seed to be planted into the fertile ground, the seed is of absolutely no benefit at all to humanity; or to the birds of the air neither to the animals in the wild; with of course the mere percentile exception of the edible seeds.

The very detriment of many people of the churches is that we have been left to accept faith as only a mere system of belief, rather than to take hold and to firmly grip the controlling grasp of faith to handle the gift of knowing that God truly is; for ourselves!

Faith itself should swallow our will and the plethora of choices and choosing that living on this earth presents to us on a daily basis. However, as a result of seeing faith as an option, our wills have swallowed up what we have believed to be faith denying us the access of knowing; only letting our faith up for air to be activated to live and to breathe for us in a crisis.

Otherwise many people have benched their faith alike a player in a game whose position on the playing field of the game is no longer needed to win the game; one might think anyway!

Whenever people get into trouble, they tend to develop the desirable knowledge of what it is that they feel that they can allow themselves to believe that faith is, in that God can or will do for us? This particular mindset of the people in the churches worldwide, have crippled the desire of many to be faithful, and to trust God totally as a general rule of living with God.

It is otherwise suggested, that calling everything into question rather than to believe with the heart, unto sure faith; as science proposes that it produces a more level scope of living for the given free willed reasoning of every man.

The secular people of the world who adhere to science; they are teaching people to question everything to the point of utter~most doubt and even the possibility of rejection to disprove the actuality of a thing?

I have come to realize that the ungodly and even the unbe~ lievers along with the devil and all of the fallen angelic host from heaven know something about God that most people of the churches who claim faith as true believers only choose to ponder in their minds, though never settling within the very spirit~man on the inside of themselves to accept as truth.

Unless God is allowed to give life and increase to the seed, life cannot spring forth from the root system that enables the

root system to nourish the plant life of the product in the seed.

A plant in the ground without roots is just a plant dead in the dirt! Many people have swallowed the seeds of knowledge on every occasion that they have been allowed to do so, but those seeds have not been able to take root down on the inside of them.

I planted cactus in my landscaping several years ago, which grew to be about Seven feet tall. This winter in the very cold season I open my front door and looked outside only to see that the top of the cactus had broken apart on its large extended stem from the trunk base of the plant and had fallen to the ground.

I took the part that had broken off and planted it in the ground hoping that it would take root and spring into life again. Putting it back into the dirt I actually put it on life support? But because it had not root; each day I could see signs of the plant withering away.

Sincerely, I had hoped that it would live and continue to share the splendor of its beauty to my landscape, but the truth of the matter is that it had also fallen away from the root system which gave it the nourishment to continue growing and increasing in its size.

Hoping for the cactus to live though un-rooted, having no ability to communicate with the intelligence of the ground, the hope for the cactus was dead itself from the beginning, even before I began to see that the cactus was indeed dying in the ground. The seed itself need so much more than just to be a seed owned and possessed by an individual.

Knowledge on the inside of many people is as the cactus which was dead in the dirt; as there have been no faithful

germinating of the seeds of knowledge!

God formed us from the dust of the ground, therefore we are yet dirt creations destined to return to the dirt when the living part of life expires and leaves the body form.

Too often knowledge in our minds is simply on life support being on the inside of many people; and of course there are those people who allow the seeds of knowledge to rest atop of their ground, so to speak; never allowing the knowledge to be implanted into the fertile soil of their spirit and intellect in their minds.

There is no place for the seeds to even take root to grow up and out sprouting its branches in the living order of those individuals.

Some might even ask the question; well why didn't your faith activate the root system of the cactus so that it could have life and live again?

The truth is that the cactus had indeed reached its number of alloted days of living just like all living things on the face of the earth, no matter of whatever could be cited as the causation of its demise.

Have we not realized that God has not given to us to turn the dials of nature to control the climates and the conditions for which plant and animal life fair in the weather condition, and to regulate the timing of their life's span on the earth?

I will say to those who would ask such questions of my acquisition of faith in God; that that kind of thinking is at its best hocus-pocus, magic; or some type of black arts which seeks to control things outside of the will and the natural order of God the creator!

The greater nucleus in the genus of that kind of problem-

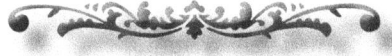

atic idealism is that faith is severely taken for granted, supposing that it can do and that it is something other than what it is really ordained to be.

I know that we have been taught that we can through faith speak those things that be not as though they were, of course on our own natural abilities to speak out of our mouths; which is an error to what that the scripture really is actually teaching us concerning our ability to speak forth things out of our mouths according to the faith in God.

Our mouths must line up with speaking those things which are written in the word of God; as the increase of our mouths speaking must come from God who gave us faith initially!

The scripture actually reads; {Romans 4:17 D......
and calleth those things that be not as though they were.}

This reference is given in recognition to our God; the faithful maker and creator of all things. We like to play the part of being the most powerful among most men; but no man actually have the power to speak out into space and to call things forth that never existed in the beginning! Only God can do that!

Wherefore let him that thinketh he standeth take heed
lest he fall.   {I Corinthians 10:12}

Faith never attemps at moving into the stead of being God, and neither does it ever allow or encourage any man to move God aside to become themselves in the stead of God; neither to become a god?

For the lack of study and knowledge of the word of God, people are often found taking the word of God out of the necessarily, needed context of understanding, over thinking in their minds, believing that the authentic power of the word of God should step aside for our own desire to take authority of the word to cause faith to perform

other than what it was and has been forever designed to do.

Death and life are in the power of the tongue; and they
that love it shall eat the fruit thereof. {Proverbs 18:21}

While faith does do the impossible, faith respects the word and the ordained divine principle order of God according to the written word of God. I can speak death and life with my own tongue, out of my own mouth; but when doing so I am speaking to me and to my own situation; the cactus being plant life of nature, and not of human life; was and is not a part of me!

Therefore, you and I can speak and talk until we change color, and reduce in size (figuratively speaking); it will have no bearing on the status and the condition of the cactus being alienated from the root system down in the ground.

Being as tall as it was, the cactus had fallen too far away from the root system, being broken off from the nourishment of the plant? The seed of the cactus had already produced what it had been designated to produce, and it was well nurtured and cared for as it matured into a splenderous array of the landscaping on my lawn.

Even though I put the plant back into the ground, I never returned it to the original nourishment of the plant, being that it was impossible to reattach it to the roots in the ground! I must admit that it was indeed a smart move to put it back into the groud in hopes that it would indeed live and not die; however my friend smart don't always mean intelligence! I believe that intelligence might mean the completeness of the knowledge that we possess.

Thou fool. that which thou sowest is not quickened,
except it die. And that which thou sowest , thou
sowest not that body that shall be, but bare grain,
it may chance of wheat, or of some other grain: But

God giveth it a body as it has pleased him, and to every seed its own body. {I Corinthians 15:36-38;}

"Exactly What Jesus Meant"

And Jesus said unto them, Because of your unbelief: for verily I say unto you, if ye have faith as a grain of mustard seed, ye shall say unto this mountain, remove hence to yonder place; and nothing shall be impossible to you. Howbeit this kind goeth not out but by praying and fasting. {Matthew 17:20-21}

Grain ~ a small hard seed; a tiny individual piece of something such as sand or salt; a tiny amount of something; the arrangement, direction, or pattern of the fibers in wood, leather, stone, or paper, typically aligned along a single axis... the basic quality or characteristic of something or somebody; the smallest unit of weight; natural inclinations, wishes, or feelings.

The actual true message of the mustard seed and of faith is often lost in the last verse of the statement of this particular scripture. Praying and fasting appear to lend a much greater sence of power and authority than faith in God; most people are led to think and to believe anyway?

But my friends people are also led to misunderstand the fact that without true faith, praying and fasting is of noneffect to those who choose to pray and to fast. Without faith, prayer is no more than that of a monologue in the woods where there is no one present to hear the conversation but one's self.

Many who believe that they are indeed fasting are only dieting and obstaining from food for a span of time. Faith opens the period of obstaining from food and drink for a period of fasting to allow God into your personal atmosphere

and space and the discipline to allow God to do as He will with you in your surrendered state.

It takes faith to continue on afflicting ones body and soul for the benefit of receiving more of God's manifested presence and power, to operate as a spirit filled child of the kingdom of God.

I hear Jesus saying to the apostles and to the people gathered in the crowd; the error of your understanding is in the manner of which you have contrived your own unreasonable thinking relative to faith and of what you ought to be able to do with faith.

Your own reasoning is indeed the causible failure in your ministry of delivering the young boy from the demonic possession of the enemy. Thinking alone that you either have faith or that you know what to do with faith will never be enough! Faith requires so much more than your head knowledge, and even of your high level of intelligence.

As we search the scripture more assuredly, we discover that the analogous reasoning of the parable set forth to these people was never intended to slight their acquisition of faith! Jesus was not at all suggesting to them that they needed not to go hard after acquiring the God kind of faith.

Although we are victoriously on the winning side being with the Lord; it is utter failure to maintain in your thinking that Jesus; has done it all, therefore, if He wants certain things done in your life that He will do it Himself?

You must see the erroneous comprehension of the understanding of what Jesus was indeed saying relative to faith; know that Jesus is the author and the finisher of our faith; he is not the author of confusion! But, mere men have caused the confusing definitions of faith, causing people to miss the

mark indeed!

Faith had already been measured from the beginning as God meted it out to every man; Jesus, is God; in the flesh talking to the people! Just why would you reason in your own mind that God had given a reference to us to suggest that the acquisition of faith can be so much more narrower than the originally alloted measure which has been given to every man?

To look upon the mustard seed as a meager measured amount of faith is a blatant error in the heart and in the mind of any person. Absolutely, faith is immeasurably more in size and subsistence in power to produce than anyone could ever imagine or measure in a balance of any kind.

It is a waste of time to attempt at measuring just how much faith is present at the time of any request or of any need. Only faith knows that God has indeed been pleased and satisfied so much that your own individual request has been granted.

Of our own humaness, we are incapable of measuring faith! We are often stomped at the miracles and the blessing that are awarded to certain people that we were perhaps sure that they had little to no faith in God at all?

Too often the people who are indeed dedicated church attendees on a regularly consistent basis, we take it upon ourselves to deem them as being worthy of the entitlement as faithful. The people who refuse to attend services on a regulated basis, it seems to be bewildering to many of us of the churches whenever they get in touch with God and receive true miracles and blessing from the Lord!

It's time that we as the children of the Kingdom of God come to the realization that the average people of the king-

dom or at least of the churches have not at all been operating in true faith!

People are in the churches standing on the threshold waiting at the gateway to the entrance of the mystery and of the presence of God, but because of the lack of true faith they are also forever unable to enter into the joy of the Lord.

So many people are baffled and bewildered from Sunday to Sunday; from service to service, wondering why they appear to be hindered and stopped at a certain place since a long time ago, for as far back as they can remember?

For I am a man under authority, having soldiers under me: and I say to this man, go and he goeth, and to another, come, and he cometh; and to my servant, do this and he doeth it. When Jesus heard it, he marvelled, and said to them that followed, Verily I say unto you, I have not found so great faith, no, not in Israel. And I say unto you, that many shall come from the east and west, and shall sit down with Abraham, and Isaiac, and Jacob, in the Kingdom of heaven. But the children of the kingdom shall be cast out into outer darkness: there shall be weeping and gnashing of teeth. And Jesus said unto the Centurion, Go thy way; and as thou hast believed, so be it done unto thee. And his servant was healed in the selfsame hour.   {St Matthew 8:9-13}

Jesus; verbally announces to the crowd that this man's adherence to faith in God through Jesus Christ; was indeed more remarkable than even to that of all that had been experienced from God's own chosen people; the Isrealites who were the first to receive the covenant of God from the initial messanger to the people being Moses.

God instructed Moses in how to teach the people of Israel; teaching them how to believe God and how to know that it was indeed God who answered their prayers.

Moses; taught the people of Israel how to worship God in the beauty of holiness and of truth. It is then expected of those people who have been taught in righteousness to be about the faith of God whenever they were to enquire and to seek God for all of their need.

The Messiah; Himself; had experienced that they had fallen short of both faith and of being faithful! People still take it for granted that the Lord knows whenever we are in the faith, and whether or not we have indeed been faithful to the word of God.

Many people are indeed dedicated to church attendance and community service, who are also gravely unfaithful to the word of God! Our Lord also cites that many who are presently in the kingdon will be cast into outer darkness away from the presence of God in heaven! You know what; THE BIBLE IS CORRECT! Every thing that the Lord said is right; and He is right the first time!

The reality is that the leadership in the churches have become more determined to passively instruct the people in their churches, teaching secular scientific inflated ideas of faith that are non-biblically based teachings of meta-physical questioning of faith; which are not teachings of faith in God!

Jesus admonishes to the people through this particular moment of recognition and discernment of the centurions latch to faith, not just to recognize that that is only at best an idea of what he might have been told that faith was; but just as the centurion soldier, we should know what faith is.

The centurion knew what to expect as a result of asking the Lord; presenting the need of his servant in faith believing that the Lord would grant his request. The heart of the Centurion leader was indeed right in his desire to see his servant healed and delivered from the sickness that was indeed threatening his time of living on the earth.

His desire was that he might live and not die; as he peered into the life-line of all living kind upon the face of the earth, he asked; master can my servant have more of the living that you bear in your own body?

It is not just that we are able to recognize the shell covering of the seed supposing that we know what to expect from the seed; it is the heart of what is indeed on the inside of the seed itself that we are indeed aware of!

It would be devastating to plant a seed expecting one product of the seed but actually get another product all together not really knowing what the seed was initially supposed to produce!

What is on the inside at the core of the seed is what has to please God so that a body can be given to the expected product of the seed. Just as what is in the heart of the individual applying faith must be accurate haven taken hold of faith in God.

If the internal heart of the seed is rotten and otherwise damaged in any way, there is absolutely nothing to expect from planting the seed. It is futile to expect for God to participate in supplying what is to be refered to as a lying manifestation from your false idea, and wrongful grasp to faith.

Everwhere that we turn nowadays, people apply what they have determined to be faith to almost everything and to every

subject. Amazingly they are turned off at the idea of having true faith in God. The people of the world want everyone of us to have a sense of faith, just not faith in God!

Without true faith it is impossible to please God! God is not moved by anything other than true faith! It is seriously paramount that we check the core of the matters that we are presenting to God, seeking His approval and desiring that He honor our request with the favor of His manifested blessings.

So much of the information that have been planted into the minds of the people of the churches and the kingdom, have been proven to be comparable to garbage and trash in need of being thrown out and forever discarded!

There have been times that seeds were planted into the ground, that to the surprise of the sower, the seeds were dead and incapable of producing any product.

The heart of the seed has to be in the proper necessary condition being able to communicate with God in truth; who gave the seed in the beginning of creation. Anything else that would be trying to spring up from the seed is indeed miscommunication and total disconnection from the creative process of the seed thus being nothing more than a lie.

So, as Jesus is teaching us that if we indeed have faith as a grain of mustard seed, that even as the tiny seed knows what it is going to produce without a doubt; whenever we apply faith to what ever it is that we desire from the Lord, we are faithfully required to know without a doubt exactly to expect what we have asked for, settling for nothing less than what we have petitioned through the application of faith in God.

Too many are requesting of the Lord in prayer according to what they indeed believe is faith, though doubting the

truth about God and of the actuality of faith in God, all of the way!

Whether they were taught to believe or they developed the ideas of faith all on their own, in error they are on their own thinking that just maybe God might have mercy on their inability and outright refusal to believe that He is indeed God; and just do it for them anyway?

So, then faith cometh by hearing, and hearing by the word of God. {Romans 10:17}.....

Know assuredly that Jesus being the only flesh form of the word; and the word to all flesh on the face of the earth; He would never teach us to disregard the word of God; Jesus knows that we can never hear when we refuse to discipline ourselves to sit in the presence of the preaching and the teaching of the word of God.

My people are destroyed for lack of knowledge: because thou hast rejected knowledge, I will also reject thee, that thou shalt be no priest to me: seeing thou hast forgotten the law of God, I will also forget thy children.   {Hosea 4:6}
And beside this, giving all diligence, add to your faith virtue; and to virtue knowledge; {II Peter 1:5}

He wasn't telling us to choose the very miniscule acquisition and activity of faith, so that we would have the power to move all of heaven and earth. If such were the case, they would have never been in the coversation as to why they were incapable of delivering this young boy from demon oppression!

Faith delives to us the power to move heaven and earth;

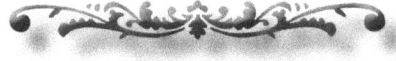

but then there are those times that we need to move the forces of hell that may have come against us! The greater detriment of many people of the kingdom is that they have power through faith, but they have not the comprehensive skill knowledge to use the power that they indeed have; by faith!

This father would not have caught Jesus on the way to tell him how that His Apostles were asked to cure his son of the daily consistent demonic attack, but they could not cure him? Remember, the Apostles walked with Jesus; they believed in Him and they followed after His teachings. But, there was a deficiency in their level of understanding faith.

In Jesus' teaching about faith and of the mustard seed; He is trying to get us to understand the installed explosive power of faith. Just as we don't make the seed or put the mega-ton mustard tree in the seed; nothing that we do has the power to make faith capable of producing whatever we ask God for.

Faith has the exact combination to get the job of reaching God on our behalf; done! We are later taught by the teaching and writing of the Apostle Paul;

But, without faith it is impossible to please Him;   {Hebrews 11:6 A}........

Faith already knows what it takes to please the Lord whenever we are in need of getting the Lord's attention for whatever we are in need of whenever we pray.

Faith knows God like you and I could never know except through faith itself. Without faith we are totally shut out from the presence of the Lord; even from the selfless powerful sacrifice of our Lord and savior Jesus Christ.

Faith and the Seed both know the powerful eternal dependence on God to bring forth expected manifestation. Nothing

else have the power to work the seed or to work faith on our behalf. The true understanding is that we don't work faith ourselves; we work with faith and God will then give us the increase, in signification that faith had pleased Him!

Faith is not some kind of a magical combination of unknown ingredients that just might produce a product which resembles what we have desired from the Lord.

God knows also what He has put inside of faith; God knows exactly what is coming out of faith for every individual on the earth.

If God could ever be surprised concerning faith, it would only be that He was surprised that you finally applied real true faith for a change in your life.

God; is never seated on the throne shocked at the behavior of mankind, or their inability to take fast hold of His word through faith.

Without faith it is impossible to satisfy the system of God's attentiveness to those who call upon Him; causing Him to not only look in our direction or to hear the prayers that we pray, but to move favorably in our direction on our behalf, to aid us in our need!

Only God will answer faith; as He alone only can even see faith for a truth! Others think that they see your faithfulness as result of the manifested things that have come to pass in your life?

People are quick to believe that another individual might have strong powerful faith in God; they think that you must have great faith according to the things that they are seeing in your life?

**Things don't determine faith or that one might have

faith! Faith; determines that one might definitely have those things; anything that is not contrary to the word and to the will of God for your individual life!

Faith itself doesn't determine who God is; God through His willingness to respond to any faithful application, determines what faith is, indeed!

The principle order of the seed and of faith can't be omitted, tricked or otherwise remonstrated, as there is no way of getting around it! It is a predetermined demand which mandates that we pay attention to know and to recognize exactly what it is that we are dealing and working with.

Hast thou faith? have it to thyself before God. Happy is he that condemneth not himself in that thing which he alloweth. And he that doubteth is damned if he eat, because he eateth not of faith: for whatsoever is not of faith is sin. {Romans 14:22-23}

Chapter 9

"Wavering In Faith"

But let him ask in faith, nothing wavering. For he that wavereth is like a wave of the sea driven with the wind and tossed.   {James 1:6;}

This discussion is for the benefit of faithful people; as there are enormously tolerated issues that give consent for maintaining human inconsistencies and a frail weekened grasp to the written word of God; above and beyond the need for having faith in God.

Faith that is needed at the most serious instances of an individual's desperate requirement of the help of the Lord, the people are instead found to place feelings and emotions of anger and un-forgiveness; and so many other elements as viable reasons to reject faith in God.

In this day and age, those who are determined to stay with the gathering of the local church on Sundays and for other weekly meetings, they are not

willing to obey the mandated laws of God; written in the bible. They are encouraged by others members of the congregations to walk on the edges of the teachings of the church, if not to teeter in the middle on the line between what is righteousness and sinfulness.

People go out of their way to show you with proof to support their claim, that everybody in the church is not all saved and washed in the blood of Jesus; as if to get us straightly informed that everybody have not chosen to believe the teachings of the bible.

Most dangerously, people have distorted viewpoints on the purpose of faith in God; they have chosen to follow after churches that use the teachings of faith in God to show them how to prosper financially, and to amass great wealth and to create sociable acclaim and national recognition.

They believe that faith is all about getting things to define who they are to the society they live in; their neighborhoods, and communities.

It is no wonder that the media and of the government agencies and the IRS; are closely scrutinizing the churches nowadays. The governmental regulations are in observation of the churches worldwide; closely watching the financial activity of the churches and the clergy.

It's not good that the Judicial System outside of faith in God; have to step in to pull the coatails of some in leadership to tell them that they are openly out of control! Faith in God will never allow for us to stray away from the word of God.

The church should never be put on a platform of open embarrassment and shame! It's obvious to me and it should be obvious to you that the teachings of faith in God has been deminished by certain ones who themselves had never even been "Born Again"; washed in the blood of the savior, Jesus Christ.

As the teachings of faith in God are taught and misconstrued as being not much more than a system of beliefs and personal choices, the people of the churches are left to themselves to believe that they have the right to change

their minds as it relates to having faith in God right in the middle of choosing and or making a request of the Lord, finding other directions that they'd rather go.

In my own opinion, most people never attend bible studies and Sunday school settings because the teachings of faith are so washed out as being not so necessarily important to the people of the churches; anymore.

The very moment that people are saved, the battle is ensued against them, in their minds; that is designed for an entanglement of their souls. Let's make people more aware that they are now the people of faith; indeed!

Being people of faith is the ultimate inviting announcement that the enemy needs to engage a battle against you to hinder your ability to grasp and to hold on to the faith as a living member of the church, and a warring entity of faith in God against that same enemy.   You will never be successful at applying faith when your mind is confused, and divided into multiple directions.

For instance: At first you're in with the Lord, then you're out with Him; as soon as the enemy begins to start fighting against you, your household, your finances, your job stability, and with the friends that you have known for many years, you allow the enemy to cause you to believe that you have made the wrong decision in choosing to be saved and sanctified; washed and redeemed in the precious blood of Jesus Christ; and to be filled with the Holy Ghost; the total assurance and the complete fulfillment of God in Christ Jesus.

There is a real struggle to go to the church for a worship service; but the same people put on their best dress clothes to attend the Symphony; Ballet; Opera; Matinee, Casino, Race Track, Football Stadium, Basketball Arena, and the Concert Halls.

They visit regularly, the palm readers and advisors, mediums and witches, warlocks, wizards, soothsayers, Tarot Cards readers; and on and on and on. I have found that the very people who are indeed afraid and terrified of faith in God; they have no fear of sinning!

People are spooked and allow for the smallest things to drive them away

from the churches. But you and I alike have seen people who are dying of Alcoholism and Drug addictions; who have had major over doses and have over drank themselves into a stoopper!

But they have not allow the negative life threatening situations to even bring them close to walking away from their addictions and sin. They have a lot of support for their addictions; paid professionals inform them that they can't help themselves, they will always be addicts, just as they are right now.

Once you truly become faithful to God; according to His word; you will forever be in the condition of being faithfully rewarded and blessed to overcome all that arises against you.

You will forever be recognized and known in all the realm of righteousness and of God; accepted as the beloved of God. Being faithful to God; you are now a worthy opponent to fight against the entire kingdom of darkness and of Satan?

It's reasonable that many people are in desperate need of understanding the things that are happening to them since having been saved by grace; but by faith.

The world; Satan; and your own self have got you flipping and flopping like a fish out of the water; you need to remain aware that fish never lose the desire to be in the water, as it is flopping to find its way right back to the safety of the water.

When you have noticed that you are being pulled away from the safety of the church and you are flipping and flopping around trying not to lose your way, just know that you belong to the church.

Fish know that they belong in the water; people of faith belong in God! Alike fish that are born of the water, we that are born of God need to understand that living in God, is just as important as it is for the fish to live in the water after being born in the water.

The divine creator of the soveriengty of His own infinite wisdom, He cre-

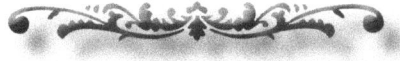

ated the fish to breathe in the water and to gain all of its nutrients and energy from the sun as well as to those of us who walk on dry land of the earth, upright breathing from the atmosphere.

Whether the fish are in an aquarium or in the Ocean, feeding and nourishment has already been provided. All the fish need to do is to feed on the supplied nourishment and they will grow uninhibited to sizes and lengths that often dwarf the growth and the sizes of most land mammals.

There are too many things of the aquatic world that we will not glean any comprehensive likenesses to faith, as the natural nature of the fish and the water of which they live and thrive, is too vast and of course much less solidarity to that of faith in God.

Fish automatically know when to ride the currents and when to dive beneath the flow. There are challenges to the fish swimming in the water just as there are challenges for those of us who are immersed and walking in the word of God by faith, living in righteousness and the peace of God.

The trials of faith, and the spiritual warfare waged against the faithful people of the Lord, have caused so many to turn away from following the faith.

What would be the fate of the Ocean and the Seas is the fish that were being preyed upon by the predators in the water; if all of a sudden the fish begin to swim to the banks finding ways to leave the water?

In all truth and fairness the fish are going to die if they are out of the water for extended periods of time, the air would really began to smell disgustingly fishy. Everything that they were created to do, they were created to do it in the water.

Born again believers need to understand that everything they have been born again to do, must be done in the will of God. Perhaps the stink that has been caused by the people of faith who have walked away from the vastness of the safety of God can be better understood.

"Wavering in Faith; Albeit; Unaware!"

The book of James admonishes us not to be like the waves of the sea; or of any aquatic body of water for that matter. The instability of the water and of the waves is not a picture of the faith that God has dealt to every man.

Through erroneous teaching and the lost comprehension of the failed translations, the pictorial representation of wavering in faith has been misrepresented.

Those who are of authority in leadership roles are suggesting that they understand what the people are feeling, and are offering support for their instability.

So many of the leaders don't want to be viewed as being too stern or as a mean leader for not being flexible when adhering to the word of God concerning faith and trusting in Him; where there is no flexibility at all!

Unqualified leaders are leading the churches everywhere but to the presence of the Lord! Not necessarily mindful that they are required to watch for the souls of the people who follow their leadership.

They are more apt to tell the people of the churches to get a life jacket and a paddle to row the boat for themselves, because every man has got to look out for his own soul!

The leaders are looking to surround them with like people to support their weaknesses and their willful refusal to obey the word and the will of God for leading the people in truth and righteousness.

They prefer to be recognized as leaders who are yet leading while bleeding all over the sheep; Note: they are apt to defend and to fight when called out over the fact that they

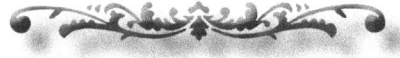

have just bled all over the people of the church! They no longer maintain lives unspotted from the world.

As the leaders are indeed cognizant not to allow anything of spiritual danger and of a detriment to the faith of God; to be taught to the people of their churches, they do allow people who are not at all qualified or skilled in the scripture to teach the people creating a more chaotic atmosphere of confusion, in their congregations. As those types of ministers pose no threat to their leadership positions.

The people who fit into their cliques and private littles clubs and groups are preferred to teach doctrines that are of the devil to the people which annihilate faith rather than to build and to increase an adherence to faith in the churches.

People are allowed to teach questionable ideas relative to faith and to teach scientific compositions and formulas of faith applications disregarding the scripture which is the only authority to be taught on faith.

The word of God states; *"let not that man think that he shall receive anything from the Lord!"*

Is that the state that you want to be in; a place spiritually where you have forced the hand of God to move away from you rather than to move upon you and in your life because you have not believed in total faith?

There is no good or godly reason to go light or to go along with the people and half teach the word of God; as they will never become disciples.

While you are slowly but surely displaced, moving further and further away from faith in God, you need to know that only the truth will be able to restore you back to faith in God.

You will never get a grip on knowing and receiving the truth of the word of God for the sake of settling you and stabilizing your stance and your walk of faith through the word of God, as long as you waver. *{Romans 1:18}*

People are rather fascinated with waves, or rather even of surfing the waves of the ocean and the seas around the world?

It is reported that some of the waves are more dangerous than others, depending on the body of the water and or of the cause of which they are developed and formed.

The excitement of the surfer is definitely in the raise of the height of the waves. Although the waves are raised on top of the water, some 10 – 100 feet in height elevation, the wave doesn't have the power to bring all of the water with it as it rolls across the surface of the water.

Waves are a bit deceiving in that they have the ability to take your mind off of the normal water level and even of the original depths in the water.

As it is, whenever we look to the raise of the waves on the water unwittingly we are allowed to forget the depths underneath the waves and the possibilities of the other life forms which may also be riding just underneath the surface of the wave.

There is always more riding with the waves and underneath the waves than are able to meet the vision of our eyesight.

Everything of our lives is raised to the extreme limit; blood pressure; heart rate; adreneline; blood sugar; and all of our emotions as we are fearfully increased to worry about how things are going to turn out for us?

It is not possible to raise every concern to the top of the list as a priority as we begin to waver in our faith before God. It is necessary for us to maintain our adherence to faith on a balanced level of knowing and trusting that God's got us, no matter what!

Our attentiveness to the development and the outcome causes our concern to go through the roof with raised uncertainty.

Wavering, and fear terrifies us in that momentarily we can do absolutely nothing about our situations, seeing that in that instance we have lost all reason and sight of faith in God!

We allow ourselves to believe that our newly arised issues have the right to be more damanding of the need for God to move on our behalf, simply because the new issues are more centered in our focus.

The new issues may also have been over exaggerated down on the inside of us, suggesting that we place a greater demand on God(if such a thing could ever be possible); to change the urgency in how He responds to our need, we're in a hurry?

We're actually experiencing a wave of fear and doubt, much more than it could ever be a wave issue concerning our need.

Waves of the oceans and the of the seas are indeed fascinating and interesting, the bigger the wave, the higher they raise the more the adrenaline flows on the inside of those of who witness to the phenomenon on the surface of the water.

The excitement is in the fact that the water has risen up and is in motion moving forward towards the shoreline.

We have a certain amount of finances in our bank accounts alloted for a specific bill to be paid at a set time of the month; but then we get a demanding notice for another unexpected expense which may indeed be important, and in need of our attention?

We think to ourselves that we should push the red button of God's divine line.

Because we allow that new notice to bother us, we think that God should also move our previous request aside to answer to the request of the newly demanding issue? See the rise of the wave here?

Because of the now impending demand for our attention, wavering causes us to feel as if God ought to be afraid for us; or maybe even with us? There is no fear in God; and neither is there any fear in faith!

Just be mindful to remember that the waves will settle right back down to rest at the surface of the water; even after a disastrous washing over the land, flooding the planes and drowning out the beauty of the splenderous array of the landscape scenery.

The water is still commanded to recede back into the oceanic rest. God placed the water just where He intended for it to rest on the earth.

Never disregard the truthful fact that waves were never designed to remain up high and elevated above the norm of the water level; it doesn't have the ability to remain risen, as there is no such supporting system or structure to maintain the destructive balance of its height elevation.

No matter where the water finally levels out, so will the waves! The waves will go with the water, wherever it goes!

Likewise, those things in our lives which cause an up rise in our emotions and cause us to think that perhaps we are dealing with issues that require a greater demand for God's attention, they are not designed to stay in the position of high demand either. Soon everything in our lives is designed to settle right back down to the place of peace and tranquility.

The older saints of the church taught to sing; "I'm So Glad that Trouble don't last always!"

If we can but always remember that things are not going to always be this way, and stay in trust, knowing that God is going to bring it to pass, we will begin to see things getting better right before our very eyes.

Miraculously, we will see the hand of God working on our behalf; everything will instantaneously take on a new dimension and shift into our desired expectations.

Faith is so much more important now that we have been saved, set free and delivered from a life of sin and shame, and filled with the Holy Ghost.

Faith is to be understood and regarded as the engine in the wheel house of the kingdom of the body of Christ which drives the people. It is the transmission that accentuates the movement of our forward progress whenever we are in the right gear.

The churches are making attempts at moving out in forward progress, but they are in neutral not understanding why it is that they can make no progress?

It is the responsibility of the messengers of God to teach and to inform the people of the kingdom of God; how to faithfully behave themselves; as people by the scores are wavering to the point that they have become totally unstable

and non-dependable relative to having faith in God.

They really do have a desire to move out for the kingdom of the Lord; but while they have been preoccupied with where to go; how to go about getting to their intended destination have been overlooked and totally wiped out as the motivation of the inner-drive of the spirit and faith is compromised.

Nothing; will have the power to move the line, to get between us, since faith is always first priority for us as it relates to our relationship with God, as long as we never waver!

Wavering; suggest; that for some reason or another, God had left us and had moved away from us, leaving us to handle our own need? Thus we are in need of getting God's attention all over again?

The real truth of wavering in faith is so much more involved than asking for something of a desire or of a need, it has a bit more to do with struggling in our minds to stay with God since we have come to Him, and of being postured to stand in adversity when the attack of the enemy has come at us.

It has a great deal of truth to be reckoned with as the people say amen to the church when they are in the service with the people of the churches,

But then change and flip flop in their position to the word of God in the presence of the people who are non-churched and unsaved people who oppose the teachings of the bible by way of the church.

So many people will shake the hand of the minister, who ministers the word of God in a service, and leave the service and begin to share thoughts from the message delivered, only to be met with very stern opposition and alternative ideology and outright rejection to the bible.

202

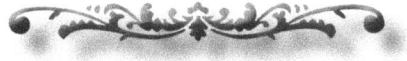

But just because they refuse to accept the knowledge of the preached word of God, should never create a platform for the hearers of the message to change their minds and to now reject the message that they had earlier accepted and received.

Far too many of the bible teachers and instructors have been made skillful when being indoctrinated to pastor churches of their particular denomination, they have learned to make people who are unfamiliar to the messages that they preach to feel convicted and ashamed, allowing themselves to be manipulated to make an on the spot decision for which they were never prepared to make.

They will walk the aisles of that particular church to become a member, but after a short while when either the warfare arises, or a controversial teaching is levied upon the congregants, many of the new comers to the faith look for and find the exit.

Such behavior causes them to be labeled as people who church hop from one church to the other, from one denomination to another; or even from one religion to another seeking to selfishly define faith in its most successful working order suitable for their own desired understanding.

After a while, having itching ears they find churches that cater to their desired brand of faith and of God; or rather to find a faith that works according to what they think within themselves that they expect to receive as a result of faith.

So, our discussion of wavering in faith is most necessary for the sake of helping some to get a grip of holding fast to their acquisition and intentional choice of faith in God.

Too often our determination to understand wavering in faith is left to our ability to select; as when we might visit a dealership to purchase an automobile.

We may look at one car and even decide that is the car that we

want to spend our money on. Only we are made aware of a better deal for our money, better car, better financing with the greatest Annual Percentage Rate for the interest of financing the note.

The change of making the better selection is not to be viewed as the same as wavering in the faith! No, not at all! It is more so the reality to the likes of being a good steward over the provisions that had been given to us.

Many who think that they are struggling with faith are actually suffering the consequences of being a very poor steward.

You are indeed a poor steward when the money that is needed all month long to handle the financial obligations and the needs for the household is coming in but as quick as it comes you are wastefully spending it on recreation and fun.

So you think that God is hiding from you, or that He doesn't care for you, when all along God has been watching you as you squander all of the finances initially given to you by way of your employment.

You continue to prove to God that you are not going to be trusted to handle finances wisely and intelligently. You will do nothing to learn how to manage your money, or to create a plan for saving your money for the future.

Didn't you hear the scripture; *"let not that man think he shall receive anything from the Lord." {James 1:7}*

While you are thinking that you see God and how that He is not helping you; take under consideration that God sees you in that how you will do absolutely nothing to help Him help you!

Those who waver in faith are found to have grave disrespect for faith in God without even knowing that they are of the spirit of disrespect. More teaching to respect the faith of God needs to be taught in the churches to enable a much better understanding for

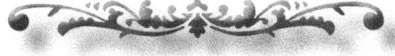

us and of our God.

Doesn't matter how many fits and tantrums that you may throw; God is in control and He has the final say so on faith, what is received through faith to Him, and what is given as result of faith by Him. We need what he has for us; I know that many of us have been taught to work faith according to the desires of our own hearts and of our need, but we have been taught wrong.

You need to sit down and to take a closer look at you, but in the mirror of the written word of God, to determine whether or not you are sound in the faith.

"Who's Faith Are You Applying?"

People are not even sure of the faith they think they are using to live to walk with God; or even to pray for others and to pray for themselves for that matter.

People are allowing others to influence the thought that they are receiving faith from the minister of their churches, but faith is given by God.

Faith is yours from the standpoint of being given to mankind as a whole creation of God's. He gave us His faith to work with to exercise and to apply as we approach the throne of grace to find help in the time of need.

You have got to go back to the bible and search the scripture for the answer that you need for the reasons that you are not being answered according to faith in God.

As we stand in the way and the word of the Lord, faith is there to keep us standing and growing in the grace and the strength of the Lord. Even my most faithful brothers and sisters in the Lord can't give me faith.

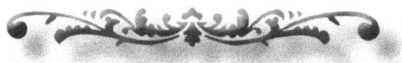

Some have frustrated the grace of God in the event that they have determined to tamper with the faith that only God has given.

God has given us so many gifts freely, that we never need to tamper with the gift of faith desiring to take control of faith and the faithful. Many have entered into the spirit of witchcraft seeking to control the faithful people of the churches of God.

God has ordained that each and every one of us should stay in faith; in an effort we have to stay in the spirit of God through praying and fasting, constantly being in the word of God.

Faith in God is not meant to be temporary, something that we use every now and then whenever we decide that we need it.

We live in faith and breathe in faith; inhaling faith with every breath that we take. We have to allow faith to see through our eyes and surrender our hearing to faith so that we will hear what the spirit is saying to us.

That that I have been given, if it be mine for sure depending on what is it that was given to me, I can use it at will even at my own discretion.

Some people that are questionable relative to faith are not at all wavering in the faith, and neither are they using faith illegally outside of the will of God; simply because what they are working is not the faith of God! You will hear me say this often in this book.

Although they have started with the wording of the scriptures from the bible, they have converted the understanding of faith relative to their own rejection of what the scripture have to say about faith; and they have perverted the usage and the purpose for which faith had initially been given to man.

The devil have deceived many into believing that they are able to cast spells and work wicked schemes through faith enabling them

to succeed at entangling the lives and spirits of other people denying their access to the throne of God in the time of their need.

They believe that they have the faith to block the faith of others, creating hardships for them.

It is indeed Satan who answers in such a time as that, as he is the motivator for such ungodly behavior, and the very evil in the heart of an individual.

Just because Satan is at work; doesn't let a person go free of responsibility who agrees with his evil plot to hinder the lives of the faithful people of God; those who allow Satan to use them must be judged!

Faith is not to be used to try and to bring others to Satan, and all other sorts of other doctrines, devils, and of men.

So many people refuse to go to the churches bible study, but they have someone else that they have met, that may even be a member of the church, where they have chosen to attend, teaching them in their homes instead.

Don't be so quick to trust in other people denying the fact that they just may have a demonic plot to destroy any desire that you might have to be closer to the Lord through faith in God.

Not everyone teaching in their homes is teaching wrong and intentionally erroneous on purpose; that is not what I am saying or is it anything that I am suggesting.

Many ministries start from the homes of many ministers who are indeed called and ordained of God; who are filled with the Holy Ghost; so don't miss my meaning here.

However, many of the members of the churches will not attend the churches to be taught by the pastors whose leadership they are supposed to submit to.

However there are some people who are demonically possess and influenced to wreak havoc among the people of God who are indeed people of faith in God.

They know how to meander in and throughout the churches, they know how to mix in, and they know the right things to say to get the attention of the believers to make them to believe that they are also just as believing as they are themselves. They know the skill of gaining the confidence of other people; they're just like Satan.

Their agenda is to kill your confidence in the faith of God that you have embraced and have begun to walk in.

There is an applied wisdom that is needed when giving your ear to listen to certain people, by which a keen discernment is needed.

No wonder that you vacillate back and forth trusting and then distrusting in the power of God; demonically influenced people will set you up for the most devastating failures of your life!

No need to fear; but the greatest need for solid faith is needed and required of you, so that you will not fail the faith that is forever designed never to fail you!

We can no longer just sit in and throughout the churches thinking that wavering in the faith is simply a minor infraction that can simply be rectified at a moment's glance.

By the time that many people have realized that they have wavered in the faith, they also discover that they have also drifted far away from God! How far; is too far away to forever prevent a possible return?

When you have gone so far away from the reality and the prayers of the churches, speaking that which could only come from Satan; that you have allowed to fill your heart, you've gone too far.

The danger of wavering is that you will also become a drifter on

the surface of the troubled waters of doubt and unbelief that challenged your faith in God.

Now you're in imminent danger of the depths in the unknown just beneath you. The enemy has designed that you drift out over the depths too deep for you to swim back to the surface once you begin to sink.

Certain waves of the water have the power to cause you to drift out in the middle of the ocean before you know it. Wavering will cause you to be left alone out in the ocean all by your selves.

Doesn't even matter how strong of a swimmer that you are there are some conditions in the water where you are no match for the waves or of the current of the water.

The schematic danger underneath the truth of wavering in the faith is dangerously designed to drag you straight to hell.

No man can pluck you out of the hand of the Lord; but wavering in the faith can allow for you to sink and to drift away from the safety and the security of the Lord's all powerful hand.

Search the scripture for yourselves; you tell me whenever you find in the scripture that God has kept anyone who through wavering and eventually denying the faith, didn't want to even be kept by the Lord!

I digress; there are some certain situations and warfare that are indeed challenging and focusing on the situation and not faith can cause you to entertain the idea of leaving and walking away while you're in the midst of it.

But then the victory comes and the truth is revealed of the strength that is within you, and the glory of the praise that comes from you as a result, and you know the blessing of staying in the fight.

You know now that you are gifted and anointed with divine pur-

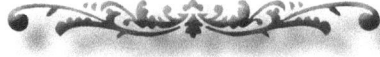

pose to win the fight and the war.

I encourage you to stay with the Lord; just as the Lord has stayed with you through all of your frailties and your weaknesses, and through all of your inconsistencies.

Stand right there where you are standing in the Lord; don't be moved or removed from where you are in the faith.

Genesis chapter one tells us that we shall be like a tree that is planted by the rivers of water. That that you need to grow and to flourish in the faith is right under your feet; this is the reason that self and Satan continue to keep you wavering and moving from place to place.

Remember the Lord says that you should never expect to believe that you are going to get anything from the Lord! Even the older people from the past generations used to teach us that a rolling stone don't gather any moss.

It is not ordained of God for us to move around like a planet among the stars in the galaxies and in space. Nourishment will finds the roots of the tree and the roots dig deeper to find the nourishment.

Trees that have no roots are dead in the ground just standing there until the right force of wind or forest fire comes along to remove it.

Encouragement strengthens your faith in God; we used to sing songs of such sweet melodies that kept us thinking on the goodness of the Lord and the Love of God. You need to stay with the ship; the church; so that you have a solid foundation and a system of support to help you to retain you stability in the Lord.

We used to sing; "I Shall Not Be Moved!" "Just like a tree that's planted by the water, I shall not be moved." It is just now at all of

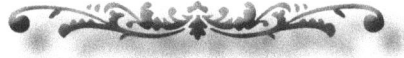

these years later on in my life that I am able to get the meaning of the message in that song.

As the Lord has been speaking to me relative to wavering in the faith; now I get it. It is not about somebody having the power or the ability to move us from the faith that we have in God; but our determination to stand regardless of the person, place or thing; is what it's all about!

Everything that God have for us is right here where we are in the faith that we have in God! Nowhere to go, nowhere to search for that that God has for us; faith would have us to know and to accept that God's blessing are right here, right now!

What you need to believe in is the question that you have asked; but you need only to trust that God will do it, because you know that He is God.

Believe in your request; examine it to be sure that you are abiding in the word of God; align your request to the written mandate of the scripture, then apply it to faith in God and trust the process of God to get it to you.

God is real, there is no Hocus~Pocus, or tricks involved with God. He will do just what He says; and He will do what no other power, or manner other than the Holy Ghost power can do!

Chapter 10

"But, Let Him Ask ~ In Faith; ! "

Ask and it shall be given, seek and ye shall find, knock, and it shall be opened unto you: for everyone that asketh receiveth; and he that seeketh findeth; and to him that knocketh it shall be opened.   *{Matthew 7:7-8;}*

If any of you lack wisdom, let him ask of God, that giveth to all men liberally, and upbraideth not; and it shall be given him. But let him ask in faith, nothing wavering. For he that wavereth is like a wave of the sea driven with the wind and tossed.   *{James 1:5-6;}*

"It Is Most Necessary To Ask!"

This chapter is centered on the fact that you have to ask God for whatever you need from Him; even though He knows what you need and want before you even have the opportunity to ask!

The blessings, the answers, the solutions and whatever else that we could ever think of that we are going to ask of the Lord are already provided and prepared to be given unto us; but, by faith.

The real approach to understanding what has been writ-

ten in this book; ("Faith Knows God") is founded within the acceptance that God has already circumscribed faith to us, being the creative originator of the spiritual regulatory ability to access His presence!

The true revelation of the unveiled gift of "Faith" has been awarded for the benefit of all mankind. Ignorantly, many are searching for faith; which has already been given and set before us in plain view.

Available in place is the faith that you will always need for you to make your request known to God. Don't make the mistake of thinking that you need to ask for more faith to make a certain request; faith itself is always enough for you to ask of the almighty God; who is always and forever more than enough; Himself!

What we need of Him, is all in Him, faith avails us to the greatness of Him! {II Corithians 1:20; Hebrews 11:6;}

It is imparative that we learn to decifer the vernacular in the historical coloquialism in the living dilogue of the scripture; it will allow for the multi~onion like layers of erroneous teachings intended to either positively edify or to negatively denigrate the meaning of faith; to be pealed back to reveal the glorious God given truth about faith in the scripture.

People are being taught that you have to ask God; for faith? But, you tell me; how is it that you have to ask God for faith when God requires that we ask of Him; in faith?

Such teachings suggest that you've never had the faith to ask God for anything; including forgiveness of sins and for salvation to enable a life changed from all the power of sin?

Simply, you need to take hold and step into trusting the entry way to reach God for whatever it may be that you need

214

to request of Him; the only methodology is asking in faith. The awesome power of faith is God's originated method of success for reaching out to Him.

Be very watchful not to bask in or to become caught away in the mysterious wonder of why it is that faith can do what nothing and no-one else can; God ordained it that way.

One of the greater spiritual disabilities is that as people have decided to exit the church and the teaching of the bible, they think that they can take the awesomeness of faith and apply it to the world's idealogy and force faith to work!

They crippled their own ability to think of faith; too carried away with questioning questions, and the answers! This is so on both sides of the spectrums in the natural and even more so in the spirit realm when seeking the Lord.

Applying faith has become utterly impossible for the average common thinkers because people want effortless blessings that require absolutely nothing on their part!

It became rather chaotic for the judicial court system of America to put a magician on trial; forcing the magician to admit in open court that magic isn't real! Imagine the devastation for some people who thought that they would substitute magic for faith?

People; are now inconsiderate about putting the time in to connect with God through prayer and studying the bible on scriptures that give understanding and directives to having faith in God.

They never suspected that the frontal image of the churches across the board would come to the ruin that it has indeed come to as result of false teachings of faith, relative to just name it and claim it; write that $10,000 seed and watch God

move for you?

You don't have to get into the prayer line to pay for faith, or for using faith; faith has been freely given to you, just know that from now on.

Faith; and believing in God have proven to be too costly just to receive a blessing from the Lord; through the teachings of many of the churches, but that is deception, try asking seeking and knocking!

You can have the money to sow the seed, but being a disobedient rebellious ungodly giver of that seed, you have just sowed a corrupt seed that was as good as being dead already when you sowed it!

Although a seed has to die in the ground before God can give it life and a body, it must be at first a living, alive seed! You will not get a single thing from the Lord, because your double mindedness has already crucified the productivity of your seed!

The image of the church has taken on an attack as result of the faithlessness and the merchandising of faith to the parishioners. But, the church is untouchable being that it is yet God's house of prayer and peace.

The church is built upon the solid rock foundation of Jesus; Jesus promised that the gates of Hell would not prevaile against the church.

Naturally; no sane human being would ever show up on payday to receive a check who had never been employed; neither would they go to the mail box expecting a paycheck knowing that they had not worked!

Something would definitely have gone wrong in the minds

of those who would be expecting electronic tranfer of funds, knowing that they had done nothing to cause those funds to be deposited into their accounts.

They would be gravely disappointed and in the very same financial condition they were in originally!

However, people are encouraged and allowed to believed that they could just show up before the Lord looking to re- ceive the same blessing and the anointing as to those peo- ple who have been obedient and have stayed with the Lord through the trials and tribulation, faithful to praying and fasting!

So many have been allowed to think on faith as not being necessarily designed for them to receive anything from the Lord, mainly because they have often asked for some certain things from the Lord but they are not able to comprehend what the issue is that is preventing them from connecting to the Father in Heaven?

The real and the only true problem actually begins with the lack of teaching and the inability to enact, or to interact with Faith according to the written word of God.

The pictorialization in the utter huminazation of faith, is hazardously compounded with being comparable in respect to pagan holidays such as Christmas.

People come before God wondering whether they had been too bad or if they had been good enough to receive from Him; questioning whether faith would even work for them?

This has caused a darkening of the understanding of faith in the minds of many people?

People who need to hear the teachings of faith in God;

they can't learn how to apply faith to their lives on a daily basis for the sake of utter doubt and disbelief. They have disdained the need for having faith because of what they have laid their eyes on as the failed examples put forth in the lives of the so-called people of faith?

True faith in God has the power to paralyze whatever you see with your own eyes; you may have actually witnessed the things that you purport to have visualized, faith doesn't take away the true reality of the thing!

But it does disallow the powerful effect of what has been seen to destructively rest upon your heart! Inspite of what you might have just seen, you can still break through in faith to touch God concerning your issue!

While it is become acceptable to doubt and to disbelieve in the power of faith in God; it is seen almost as a criminal act to speak out against Santa Clause, his sleigh and eight tiny raindeer.

Who fly through the air at Christmas to drop gifts down the chimney; which is a total lie for the sake of making money by the truckloads, and for creating and sustaining mystery and make believe to bolster youthful imagination.

It appears to me that most people have convinced themselves never to be satisfied with an answer, a solution, or most assuredly with the findings of a search.

Something on the inside of their minds is consistently telling them that there is either more to the equation or something more altogether underneath the matter or behind the scene? Anyway they seem to feel that it is better for them if they are never made aware of the truth.

The world's systems have managed to distort that which

had been factually proven, and sound; spinning, around and around in circles, dizzy with insecurity and doubt; disbelieving as it relates to faith in God.

Many enquiring of the Lord, are often mystified at the manifested results because they never really considered whether or not to expect anything from their prayer?

I pity those who fall to their knees to pray but on their way to position themselves to pray, because they refuse to trust the truth about faith, they are questioning, but confused as to whether it makes any sense to engage in a conversation with someone that they can't even see and may not even hear any response in answer to their prayer.

Most people allow themselves to engage in what I will refer to as a test dialogue; it may often begin with the words which form sentences like; "they told me that you are real and that I should try talking to you about my life; if you're real; if you really exist?"

You know it's like throwing bunch of things up into the air just to see where they all fall and land? Let the chips lie wherever they fall?

You and I alike have had conversations with people who are not very skilled at expressing themselves; they say things as best as they are able to and then say to us; "you know what I mean?"

The success of the conversation is hinged on our ability to decipher through the shredded grammar and failed dialogue; if and when we as the listener can make it through the moment and come up with an understanding, then we can say that we have talked with those people.

However, I'm not really sure that that form of verbiage

in speaking to the Lord is acceptable dialogue or even suitable when we need one thing but ask for another because we failed to say exactly what we want from the Lord?

The only way to ensure that we are praying faith filled prayers to the Lord is to say what the written word of God says back to the Lord. God needs for us to know and to believe His word to the point in fact that we become users of His word, by faith.

We learn to speak well and to maintain grammatical skills, being able to form sentences, in an effort to clearly and to adequately express ourselves plainly for the sake of being able to mix well with the other people.

Even we learn to read being literarily skilled to know the difference between the writing on the labels and signs.

But how we speak to other people and how we communicate with God are diametrically opposed in that we speak the common vernacular to one another but we need to speak the word of the bible whenever we speak to God.

It is important that we never waver when speaking to God in prayer vacillating between the common language of the earth and speaking according to the written word of God; that's confusion.

What people say and the ways that they choose to say the things they say are often contrary to the way God says things and to the manner of which He would prefer that we say them.

God's ways are not our ways and His thoughts are not our thoughts; I would admonish getting acquainted with God's word which reveals His ways and His thoughts.

The gravitational grounding systems resulting from the support of close friends and family members unite towards utter faith-less-ness for those who are unsure and leaning away from faith in God and His word; have tipped the scale to the imbalance of about 75-25% percentage rate in faith decline, pulling strongly in opposition to what should have been the spiritual elevation of faith to lift people to the higher standards of holiness and of righteousness.

As result of being so carnal, the support teams often refuse to see that they themselves are even being dragged downwards to the much lowered grounded understanding to be manipulated and controlled by utter humanism.

Unintentionally, they have conformed to the people of which they had empathetically given their hearts to understanding their sinful and disrespectful behavior?

While omitting to tell the people to dig deeper into the understanding that will lead them to greater faith in God, some ministers are suggesting over the pulpits that people are too stressed.

Almost everybody confesses to being stressed out; or at least everyone is being told that they are stressed out, by their job psychologist, or even their physicians.

It really doesn't help the dilemma that many of the senior pastors are committing suicide; leaving their churches and backsliding.

Now they are divorcing their wives, the mothers of their children and leaving their families for perverted relationships with same-sex relationships, after many years of marriage and children; turning away from the faith stating publically that it was all a waste of time?

Hast thou faith? Have it to thyself before God. Happy is he that comdemneth not himself in that thing which he alloweth. And he that doubteth is damned if he eat, because he eateth not of faith: for whatsoever is not of faith is sin

.   *{Romans 14:22-23;}*

"*For whatsoever is not of faith is sin;* ignorance of the law is not an excuse." Please, take notice of the fact that the scripture doesn't say; whatsoever is not of your local church; or of church is sin; the scripture says; whatsoever is not of faith; is sin!

While being passionately instructed to appreciate the things that are natural, firstly; what is missed or possibly overlooked is the fact that people are being led into confortable platforms to sin fearlessly!

Respecting the natural; but avoiding the realm of faith and the spirit; lacking the spiritual introduction by way of the parents and teachers disregarding the need to take hold of the matters of the faithful spiritual realm, at least 85-95% of the people in the world are living in sin, as result of denying faith in God. *{I Corinthians 15:46}*

In the very spiritual atmospheres of what is better referred to as the Holiness/Pentecostal churches, during highly spirited services when we were in the presence of God; through the intrusive demonic manifestation of those who might have been demon possessed.

We were taught and made aware of their detrimental conditions of being possessed with demon spirits, of which is a truthful reality indeed.

On the contrary, we are not often taught the compara-

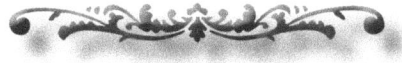

ble likeness that is of the people who are sinfully possessive among us; they are people who are willfully given over to the gullibleness of sinning at every opportunity.

They are driven with the desire to experience everything that rebels against the knowledge of faith and of God, according to the scripture! They've heard about it now they need to try it!

The people who are becoming Entrepreneurs and business owners, are often celebrated in the churches and rightfully so.

But, as many of the leaders are no longer servants of faith; they are now become taskmasters, demanding offerings and gifts from the people in the congregations; telling the to employ other methods of getting things regardless to God's will for them to have the things or not.

Many of the pastors who celebrate their likewise secular influences outside of their churches, are deceptively dual in that they will encourage the people to hold on to faith in God.

On the other hand they will give high-praises to the people who show up bearing gifts as result of having found other methods of getting what they wanted rather than waiting on the Lord through faith.

Many leaders, having always been rebellious to the practice of living according to righteousness of faith in God; themselves; they don't possess the true where-withall of the spirit of faith in righteousness to properly instruct, teaching biblical mannerisms of how to approach the throne of God through faith in prayer, asking the Lord to meet their needs.

Adamantly, they teach thankfulness to God; but only while they omit to teach the true righteousness of living holy ac-

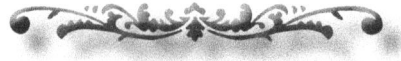

cording to the written word of God!

Unaware, they are teaching the people of the churches to be thankful to God for the applied wickedness of the streets, and the evil undermining schemes of deception used to get the stuff that they have?

They have no desire to assist the people in their congregations; because they have realized that the people in their churches are more alike themselves, whereas they are not as faithfully dependent upon God as people of the churches used to be.

It is outright sinfull to agree with the people who are adamant about the refusal to apply faith in God to get the things that they want; they know that people want stuff, they don't want God!

I have talked with people who are members of a church, that are totally disconnected from the idea of asking the Lord for anything; they don't ask, they take or steal and manipulate others to get whatever they want.

Many of the leaders have admitted that they believe that people spend too much time on their knees praying; they believe that once you've finished praying, just get up off of your knees, and do what you've wanted to do in the first place.

The teaching is often, that there is so many other opportunities that no longer require waiting on the Lord? But my question to you is; why would you even ask the Lord knowing that you never really wanted His answer?

"Trust in the Lord with all thine heart, and lean not to thine own understanding; in all thy ways acknowledge Him, and He shall direct thy

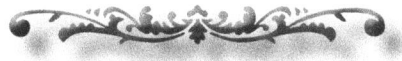

path."   *{Proverbs 3:5-6;}*

It's a very sad commentary against the leadership of the churches, to admit that they have grown rather weary of the sufferings of the people of faith, who are struggling in their own daily applications of faith and righteous living.

It's sad because the scripture admonishes us of the trying of our faith in God; in that it brings persecution, trials, tribulation and some painful experiences that will in essence strengthen us as it relates to latching on and holding on tight to faith in God; unmovable and unwavering.

Each time that the people are applauded for doing things in their own signatured manner, they are also being spiritually weakened and encouraged further to refrain from asking the Lord; waiting before the Lord; receiving the answer from the Lord, and finally from learning to hear and to obey the voice of the Lord.

As result, we are seeing so many who are utterly on the floor at their lowest when troubles heartaches and pains have ripped through their lives.

They have never been ones who practiced going to the throne of Grace to obtain favor in their time of need, through faith! *{Hebrews 4:16}*

It's been their practice rather to skip going to the Lord in faith as long as they think that they have a grip on things, and can get it done without bothering to pray in faith believing that God will do it for them.

Others have allowed themselves to believe that faithfully seeking the Lord is so unnecessary in these modern times of which we are now living.

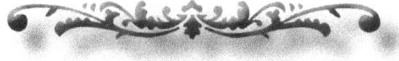

Having to ask, or to enquire of the Lord is not at all predicated upon how you might feel about what the Lord is going to tell you as a result of what you will have asked!

People who are hesitant about asking the Lord for certain things are feeling that way as result of knowing for a surety that they going to ask for the wrong things and they doubt if they are qualified to receive what they have asked for.

Oh yes; people have the nerve to ask the Lord for the things they already know they can't have!

Learning to ask of the Lord is a course of study which needs desperately to be taught in the churches worldwide, all over again, as the people even in the churches have been sinking down in faith for a long time now.

"The True Faith Formula"

As I began studying Matthew 7:7; I noticed that the words of each beginning phrase of the scripture; Ask; Seek; and Knock; the beginning letters of the word are; A.S.K. The initial letters all come back to the word; "ASK!"

The assurance is that we are going to get what we want from the Lord depending on how determined we are to receive what we have asked for. Should we apply the necessary due diligence of the scripture according to faith, we are going to receive without a doubt!

The three key words of Matthew 7:7; are each itself principles; methodologies of enquiring of the Lord. There are times when they must all be applied simultaneously, while at other times they are individually to be applied as the schematic technique of our enquirery.

To "Ask"; being the simplest method of enquiring of the

Lord, only requires that we open our mouths in faith speaking to the Lord for the things that we need; it's that simple. In the times of asking, what matters most is that we are indeed sound in faith, according to the written word of God.

We need to "Seek" the Lord for guidance and for the wisdom to get the things done. When we need direction for a decision; we need to know which way to go; we need to know whether or not to move or to act upon a particular situation?

These are indeed the times that we have to diligently search to be assured that we will not get off track or stray from the assigned pathway to get to where the Lord is requiring us to go.

When we truly don't know a thing we are in the dark concerning it; we either come to the light or we have to shine the light in that particular situation.

We should "Knock"; pounding upon the enquirery through faith and prayer; understanding that the enquiries for which we would be knocking were most likely closed and or locked doors having blocked or otherwise hindered our entrances, notwithstanding that we may be locked out, the scripture never suggests that we break in and enter without the doors first being open unto us.

People never realized that as a result of being so impatient, that they are indeed acting out in the spirit like thieves, burglars and robbers; as they have got to have the answer right now and they can't; or rather they refuse to wait!

The scripture assures that we will be granted entrance through asking in faith, in God. Receiving from the Lord as a result that we have asked in faith, is a process of which the principle order cannot and will not be over-ridden.

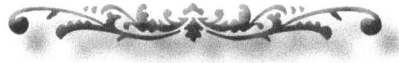

Whenever we show up at the mall just ahead of the time of its doors opening and they are still locked; the average persons will not get an object, and break into the mall because they just can't wait.

The laws of the land are there in the back of most of our minds preventing us from perpetrating a foolish crime, keeping us in mind that we will suffer the penalty of the law.

Likewise, the mandated laws in the principles of the scripture are in place; I say to you respect the laws of the scripture. It doesn't matter how painful a reality it may be for some folk to have to ask of the Lord, no matter how you may pout and throw a fit, you still have got to ask and wait for the answer!

Everything is not given to you in this book by design intention; some things you will not even respect and cherish as truth and important until you search the scripture for yourselves and find those truths; search the scriptures.

I love and respect the fact that James says to those of us who ask of the Lord; *"but, let him ask in faith."* Asking; itself is the proper order of things; but, *"Asking IN Faith"* is the proper manner in which the method of asking must be applied.

Lots of people don't mind asking the Lord, they just cant wrap their minds around the idea of asking through faith; they have to mind the ascribed manner of the scripture.

Remember that faith already knows the revelation of what the answer will be as God reveals the answer through faith, so align yourself with the truth and a pure heart to receive the manifested results of faith in God!

Many people have bought into the ideas of blind faith? That, which is indeed considered to be blind faith, paralyzes

any movement in the spirit of the Lord; being that it is not the proper representation of faith in God.

However, be advised that such thinking about faith in God; also puts blinders in the minds of those people who also believe that that is the order of the faith they are to use to get whatever they want from the Lord or even to do anything required of them to do for the benefit of the kingdom of God.

When blinded concerning faith; we are blinded firstly not being able to see our own instability relative to having faith in God.

Many people come running to God in the times of what might be deemed as serious trouble to get attention from the Lord; as if God had not been there to see the conditions all of the time?

We are blinded to the fact that such wavering disrupts the flow of our faith and perhaps the trust that we have had in the Lord already! In a sense we are asking the Lord to disregard the previous request and look at this one now?

As if God should just send the provision for the first request back to heaven's storehouse, and get what we need for the sake of the resources that we need now!

This is not to be understood as the meaning of what now faith is?

Now faith does not suggest that God should address this that is now my concern instead of that which I have already been waiting for in faith, having asked Him to meet that need already.

We need most definitely to discern when that which might have showed up in our lives as a now incident; that it may

indeed be only a major distraction to that which has been intended to establish the movement of God; as a result of true faith!

Now faith, {Hebrews 11:1} simply means that faith is ever presently available right now for us, enabling that we may touch God at any time!

Not at any moment in time is God depending on us to manufacture faith; to go and to retrieve faith from a closet of from a warehouse of some kind; and neither is God demanding for us to wait in a certain place for faith to come to us wherever we might be?

Because of the provisions of faith firstly, that in which we believe God for in faith is coming to us! The only things of which we will find ourselves waiting for are the manifestations of our faithful request.

Faith's been there since the beginning, the same faith is standing in the presence of the same God who have also been there for us all of the time.

"Block Out All of your Faith Blockers!"

In light of the fact that it had been brought to our attention that we have wavered in the faith; the highlight of the notation to us is in the fact that we had to be made aware that it is we, ourselves; who had left God!

God is not in the business of leaving us knowing that we can never make it on our own! The Apostle Paul says it like so to Galatians;

Ye did run well; who hath hindered you that you should not obey the truth? This persuasion cometh not from Him that calleth you.

{Galatian5:7-8}

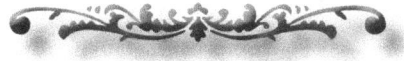

The leaders of the churches used to teach us to be very aware of the people that we hung around as everybody were not all people of Faith in God!

Many times we may have to extrapolate back over our lives reflecting on the people that we have spent time with, to see where we learned to lessen our grip on faith.

Wavering in faith comes as a disruption to the faithful adherence to trusting in God. You started out right but in the middle somewhere you had been influenced to question as to whether God would do it for you by faith this time?

The things that we ought to bring into question, are often the things that we leave unquestioned and unchecked.

Daily, we may encounter people who have rejected Jesus Christ as Lord and savior of the world, who ask for just a few moments of our time to share their systems of belief with us?

Satan knows that these people don't have a system strong enough to erase the truth of God in Christ Jesus; but the designed encounter was to weaken our grasp on the faith that we have in the Lord.

Even their encounter with us might have only been designed to raise the wave of concern in your thinking as to why it is that God would even allow such people to be here disrupting the teachings of the churches worldwide, raising questions as to whether if any of the things that they are saying are true?

All of a sudden mentally you are now in a boat out on a shifty sea, with waves up and down, being tossed and driven in every direction, but to God.

You used to think of yourselves as being stable and sound

in faith, but now you are not sure at all if what you have been taught from the Holy Bible is true at all?

Many are fallen prey to the subtle schemes of the wicked through the collegiate classroom professors; television Media, alternative religious practices, and books?

The outright enemies of faith in God also write books to discourage faith, and to suggest that all of the noise of the churches of God in Christ Jesus; that it is all nonsense!

Angry people may have tendency to cause you to question all that you have believed in the Lord since birth! Not everyone had been born into a faith teaching environment; whereas Jesus Christ is the center of the teaching.

As we have been taught to receive Him, many are taught to reject Him and to stay away from churches that teach about Him!

While many people of the church and of the world now suggest that you just take it easy and relax a bit; they're suggestions are that you don't be too concerned with how everybody is living now because there is no penalty for what we are calling sin anymore?

Of course the greater struggles in and around the churches now is definitely all because of sin; the attitude is that the churches ought to lighten up and leave the people alone and allow them to live their own lives as they are pleased to do so.

The real questions ought to be; "why is it that the people of the world are reaching for my convictions as it relates to sinning and living against the will of God's word?"

The church; is being beat down by the secular communi-

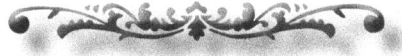

ties! Used to be a time when the power of the churches was felt all over the place! You knew that the church buildings weren't standing and erected in the communities for the sake of beautification?

You could ride bye or even walk by the churches at high-noon any day of the week, and sense the power of God there. Even the worldly people who never attended church because of their uninterest, never allowed you to feel as if there was nothing at all to the church!

Even though many people would not come to faith in totality; they wanted the church to be held in solidarity, so as even should they die, they wanted to have a funeral and burial through the church; they demanded that the preacher or even that a priest would exercise the last rites; over their dead body.

Not that such a desire would have any bearing over the fact that they had denied the faith in their living and of their lifestyles; but they desired that the landmark of the churches in the community and of the world all together to never be removed.

Many people who would almost never miss going to church, as of late, they are now just as comfortable staying at home on the couch looking at television.

Wickedness have reached the behavior of the members of the clergy in many of the pulpits of the churches and the wickedness has been exposed for the truth that it is, but many of those who are responsible in the churches refuse to leave as the leaders.

So many people have taken it upon themselves to blame God as being the one responsible for the wrong people being

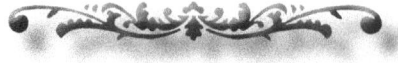

at the helm of the leadership of the churches!

Such occurrences has had an effect on some people but it will never have an effect on God; being God! The behavior of mankind throughout history, has never been able to affect the reality of God!

In the final analysis, when all has been said and done, we will have to admit that man has been wrong all by his own will and desire.

So it is to this very day and time, people are disobedient towards God and to the word of God. God's got better judgement than you and I; watchout to never be misplaced from the truth of the word of God; whatever you need, God; indeed has got everything that you need.

Most people want to go to heaven; but, how to get there other than dying and leaving the presence of this world is not quite available to their understanding, as many of the people are allowed to doubt and to question the authentic truth of the word of God, they do a lot of stuff in the hope that it will be satisfactory?

We are going to die and leave this world; but not always are people truthfully and faithfully prepared to enter into the presence of God in Heaven according to the written word of God; for the simple reason that they had never become faithful people of the kingdom of God.

The manifested power of the Holy Ghost was never allowed to work from a personal perspective in their own lives.

Question: ~ Would you bless you knowing who you are; the you that nobody else knows?

One of the songs of the church that has stayed with me

for all of my life has been; "Hold to His hand; God's unchanging Hand; Build your Hope on things Eternal; Hold to
God's Unchanging Hand!"

Chapter 11

"Faith; and The Prophetic!"

What? Came the word of God out from you? Or came it unto you only? If any man think of himself to be a prophet, or spiritual, let him acknowledge the things that I write unto you are the commandments of the Lord. But if any man be ignorant, let him be ignorant. Wherefore, brethren, covet to prophesy, and forbid not to speak with tongues. Let all things be done decently and in order.
{I Corinthians 14:36-40}

"Empowering Prophet's Confidence; Through Faith;"

Here is a promise for your mind: We will explore what the scripture and the spirit of the Lord has to say about the office of the order of the prophetic.

There is an extreme vast difference between what is to be known and understood as the gift of prophecy and the order in the Office of the Prophet.

Honestly, many people both in and of the outside of the churches worldwide lack the complete understanding in the differences of the two.

There should be no scisms and competition among them who prophesy and the prophets; and of the people of the churches in general.

Neither the gift nor the title of the gift to which you might have been endowed, is more important than the purpose and the ability of the gift to meet the need of the people of God; through faith and love!

Being called indeed is extremely important to the actuality of the spiritual endowment that come upon an individual as a result; as God anoints what He calls; not what we desire to be called!

It is never ordained of God, neither is it allowed in the presence of God, that we operate out of order contrary to the word of God and cause confusion among the people of the Lord; ever!

We, who are of the Prophetic Order, must always walk by faith and never by sight! As a prophet of the Lord I am ordained to see things in the spirit that may evade even the discernment of an Holy Ghost filled believer because they cannot and will not be able to see!

It requires what I will refer to as "straight faith" and surrendered lives; the extremely powerful presence of God stands up tall and erect in our spirit moving us aside to work as He will do so, and other times, He; the spirit of the Lord will actually stand in the midst of our spiritual vision allowing for us to see exactly as He sees in the earth simply because we are called.

We must operate in total faith and humility; as God hates pride; pride will produce injustice and cause anyone to operate irregularly and out of order in the spirit, without even being aware sometimes.

If only for a few moments, an individual may have open themselves up for the devil to exploit the usage of their gift with the intent to distort their testimony that they have indeed been called of

238

God; and that the endowment of the Holy Ghost is in operation in their lives.

Pride, is always the devil's ability to play in the minds of people; it is to be understood that the very moment that we allow ourselves to get into pride, we have simultaneously stepped away from following after the will and of the power of God!

We stand in faith in the prophetic because hearing in the spirit is internal; we do not rely upon hearing in the natural realm as there are too many spiritual hindrances, and too much noise pollution in the airways.

God trains us in how to hear the Lord through faith as He may wake us up in the early hours of the morning or in the middle of the night, instantaneously speaking to us, and commanding us to go and pray because He needs to show us something in the spirit.

The Lord may often need to relay a direct message for the healing or deliverance for an individual; the quieter atmosphere can produce a greater clarity for hearing the Lord speaking.

The Order of the Prophetic requires faith; people are going to label you as being weird and strange simply because being surrendered to the Lord altars our lifestyle and our behavior.

Doesn't really matter what stage of living we may be in of our lives, there are noticeable differences that often prevent us from melting into the common sociable activities with our families and friends; and of course of those who are in the community.

As a prophet of the Lord, you have to be very careful not to allow others to influence you to have need of getting away to entertainment and letting go of the leading of the spirit, to gather in the crowds of outright secular gatherings of people that are not even seeking the Lord.

Even when they are totally opposed to our change and of our spiritual endowment, people always know there is difference, they just know that you are not like everybody else!

You may be forced very soon to realize why it is that people would prefer that you mixed with the more common people of your surroundings; they just may desire to silence the voice of the prophetic operating on the inside of you.

Faith itself is confidently empowering concerning the Office Order of the Prophetic; in that it actually reveals the true authenticity of the prophetic realm. It is so powerful and giving, releasing the otherwise hidden and unspoken reality that is God; among men.

Faith releases God's presence when we could never see Him, nor feel Him, and it releases His voice through the written word into the entire realm of humanistic hearing when we had been unable to hear Him speaking initially!

The very sound of His presence had been drowned out and silenced in our atmospheric surroundings, as result of the entrance of sin. Adam; reported that in the cool of the day; that they could hear the "voice of God" walking through the Garden!

The presence of His voice accompanied the inhabitants of the earth in Eden; whereas having those who would speak as of the oracles of God in the earth had not as of yet been found as being needed among men in the earth.

It is paramount that we understand that even the silence of God is vibrantly powerful enough to the point that it could cause everything in existence to crumble and to blow away to oblivion! Yet God gently speaks to us; in us; and through us; by His love for us.

Understanding His silence; it enables us to realize that He is God; indeed! We are driven to hear Him speaking to us in an audible

voice; so much so that we are often blown away at the fact that He has chosen not to speak or rather to be silent; though He is yet speaking simultaneously through the absence of His audible voice!

Most believe that He is indeed the God of every nation, creed, and tongue speaking language ability of every man on the face of the earth; in essence that as many people can't seem to intrigue a conversation dialogue with God the Father; in Heaven, acceptably they have resorted to turn to the voice of the prophetic in the earth, in an effort to hear from God.

In the book of I Samuel; of the Old Testament writings of the bible, King Saul had grown accustomed to hearing the voice of the Lord speaking to Him directly; by what has been referred to as "Urim or Thumim"(practice similar to rolling the dice; casting lots); and by the voice of the prophet.

Only, to one day realize that there was absolutely no word of communication from God available for the King; at all. It was quite common for the prophet to have a direct answer to the inquiry of the king. Even, it was commonly expected for the prophet to bring word from the Lord to the King.

However, alike most people of today's modern generations, it is sin and iniquity that has dulled our hearing as men, preventing us from being able to hear the voice of God; and it even blinds us as people from being able to see the move of God in the atmosphere of our own immediate surroundings.

Get this! ~ God; doesn't communicate with sin; God does communicate with men, but they must be people that believe through faith and trust in the finished work of the cross of Calvary.

Faith will show us that the spirit of the Lord rests in the presence of mankind through the office of the Order of the Prophetic; (male

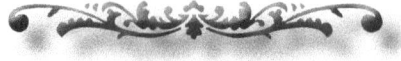

and female).

Saul; unlike many leaders of the people of today, sought hard after hearing the favorable voice of God, speaking to him, giving him the direction for the battle of which had been set in array.

The days of the kings in the bible, were for sure the days when men were most acceptable and accustomed to hearing the prophets telling them which way that God wanted them to go, and of what it was that God intended for them to do.

Saul had willfully disobeyed the instruction from the Lord, given to him by the Prophet Samuel; even in his disobedient state he was assured that hearing from God would mean that God hadn't cut him off.

We see much of this behavior even in today's churches; people show up at the church to hear a word from the prophet?

When in fact it appear that the prophet just might indeed have a word for them from the Lord, people take the assurance that God has not totally cast them away from His presence; as a result of their own sinful and iniquitous behavior and lifestyle.

It is our expectation according to the scripture that anyone who speaks as a prophet of the Lord, that they are directly in connection with the voice of the Lord.

If any man speak, let him speak as the oracles of God;
if any man minister, let him do it as of the ability
which God giveth: that God in all thing may be glori-
fied through Jesus Christ, to whom be praise and do-
minion for ever and ever. A-men, For prophecy came
not in old time by the will of man; but holy men of
God spake as they were moved by the Holy Ghost.
                    {I Peter 4:11; II Peter 1:21}

"Since the Beginning; Faith Has Been Applied"

Confident prophets are often accused of being very heady or arrogant individuals; usually based on how they manage to handle the message that they have received from the Lord to give to the people in the body of Christ.

Although it is the expectation of those who come to the prophet to receive a word from the Lord; that the word be without error or that it not be a word, amiss!

As humility is right and required of those who serve the Lord Jesus Christ; we want to know that the prophets are prayed up and that they are sure of the word of the Lord and of the voice of the Lord speaking through them, to them!

In my experience, many of the pastors in the churches seem to prefer a much less confident individual to stand and to declare what thus saith the Lord to the church?

Inferior prophets are much more easily resisted and denied; as they will accept that they might have missed it as result of your refusing to receive the spoken word of the Lord from them; especially when a word of correction or judgment has been given.

Every person who stand as a prophet to declare what thus says the Lord; they will give an account for every word spoken from their mouths; whether God told them to say or not! *{I Peter 4:11}*

Confident; mature prophets are dangerous to the agendas of the non-spiritual and the ungodly leaders in the churches, in that they have no fear or apprehension as it relates to being who they have been called of the Lord to be, neither of telling anyone what the Lord is saying to them, in reference to them, and or even on the behalf of them.

As long as the prophets abide in faith; the fire of the Holy Ghost accompanies them in whatever the assignment may be. The mouth of the prophets speaks forth with power to move things and to cause change and effect in the lives of the people of which they will have spoken into.

It is disastrous and totally disappointing that so many people who adamantly claim that they have been called to the Order of the Prophetic; they are always attempting to be up in the front of the ministries with the microphone in their hands, purporting that they have a word for those who are in their presence.

They are consistently out of order thinking that the anointing on their lives trumps that of the shepherds of the house, and to that of any overseer who have been ordained of God to set the order and to maintain the order of that particular ministry.

Mature confident prophets are not in a hurry to give a word of prophecy knowing of the accountability and the judgment associated to the word spoken from them.

Even when others are in opposition to the fact that you have been called, and are disagreeable to what God has to say about you; God is still Right about you!

Many people are acting out and behaving erratically all up front in the churches because other ministers have rejected them and have mistreated them in the presence of the people with the intent to discredit them and to keep the people from believing in them as the mouth-piece of God, to speak to them and to show them their wrong; not discerning the grace of God, and His mercy.

I have been acquainted with many prophets who were outright nasty and didn't care to be bothered with the people during the service and after the service had ended? True enough; the more that

the eminent flow of the presence of the Lord becomes, to increase the anointing on the prophet, tolerance levels decrease as it is necessary to maintain clear channels for the spirit of the Lord for many reasons.

Everybody that might have come to the building may not have come for the sake of the ministry that God has intended to take place during that particular service?

Yet being cordial and respectful, kind in the manner that we entreat the people of God is always necessary, and of the extreme importance!

Before an enemy can even show his presence or reveal its plan in the congregation of the people of God in the church; God sends an alert by way of the discernment of the spirit to inform the people in the church that the enemy is indeed there.

Though, as of late, many tragedies have happened in some of the churches whereas the people of the churches never even knew that the enemy had crept in; I am of the opinion that the people were not relying on the spirit of the Lord through discernment of faith, to show them the enemy. They chose to give every one that enters into their churches the benefit of the doubt?

Allow me to say it like so; the prophets of God are always plugged into the anointing of the Holy Ghost; we know that God see and know all things at all times.

There is absolutely nothing that can ever slip up on God or the people of God who are filled with the Holy Ghost; even when you never really wanted to know about an enemy!

As a prophet of the Lord, I know that there is no such thing as the benefit of the doubt when the information that I am receiving about another individual is coming from the Holy Ghost! To give the ben-

efit of the doubt to that information is to call the Holy Ghost a liar!

Through faith; God reveals the intent and the plan of the enemy for carrying out his wicked scheme, all for the purpose of attempting to steal the glory which only belong to God; the Holy Ghost will then expose the culprit who is being used of the enemy, for which God also gives the Prophet the methodology of handling the situation whereas God will get the glory, anyhow!

Faith keeps us mindful of the fact that it is always about God and never about us; I Am; You Are; We Are; indeed called and gifted, but we're endowed with God's gifts, and God's anointing; atop of God's calling upon our' lives. We have nothing and we are nothing of our own, as the power, and the glory, and all of the honor, it all belongs to God!

God gets the glory even when we get absolutely none! By faith we accept the fact that we are only conduits by and through which the spirit of the Lord flows and works.

The disturbing behavior and demeanor of a supposed anointed individual is often released into our midst to block the focus on faith, whereas the move of the spirit of the Lord will be hindered, as God will never work outside of faith.

The enemy will always make sure that certain people of the churches see and recognize the nasty and foul behavior of the people; only by faith are we made aware through the power of discernment, whereas we are often led to begin to intercede that God may be glorified, being able to work through the anointed vessel of the Lord; anyway!

As we look to the behavior of those said individuals who come to share with the body in attendance; we are urged among ourselves in the churches to faithfully embrace them as God's prophets? Even-

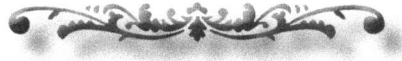

tually during the service as they are released to publically address the congregation, it is then revealed to the attending audience as to whether or not they are who they say that they are indeed; whether they are true or false prophets?

Although, many will remain in question of the leadership of the ministry that invited them; through their presentation some have been recognized as being out of order and even better yet they are out of control!

What they show to us as the people of the Kingdom of God is not at all the faith of the Kingdom of the most-high God that will aid to cause others to come to a total rest in faith and trust; to stay with the Lord.

Faith is heavily required if we are going to be equipped to properly discern whether or not we are indeed in the presence of a true prophet of God; as truth is to be preferred.

Bear in mind of the fact that a false prophet at times may be able to share true information about an individual or of an event which may have taken place in a person's life.

As a result of erroneous teaching or the lack of any teaching that would lend to the comprehensive knowledge of what is a true prophet of God; many people have been allowed to reduce the actual prophetic profile as to that of being one that can give an accurate word of prophecy!

Reluctantly we are forced to consider the fact that many people who are now in the churches as an adult were raised in otherwise occultist practices whereas they are most familiar to psychic reading of palms; turning Tarot cards; mixing potions; candle burning and chanting curses and all of the sort.

Unintentionally; they are often found comparing the ministry of

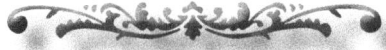

the prophet to that of the psychics. They have not been taught correctly in the churches to recognize a true prophet of God from that of a demonically influenced palm reader, or fortune teller?

Shame on those people of the churches who don't see a problem or have a concern with the magic show! They have not as of yet realized that they have allowed for themselves to be taught that the gift of prophecy and the working of miracles in the churches is comparable to that of the secular show under the tent or in the large auditorium.

There is a danger; in opening up in the churches to prophesy to the people in attendance when there have not been teaching from the bible; the word of God is what establishes the proper atmospheric platform to differentiate between what is ungodly and what is the spirit of true holiness indeed!

I say to you; and to everyone else that I may come into contact with as a Prophet of God; much of what I might tell you from the Lord you probably will not want to pay for it?

I am going to tell you the truth as spoken to me from the Lord, regardless of your feelings and your emotions.

Most people give money to the churches when they are inspired to do so; unless you have been inspired of the truth to give; I will never put myself on the same platform as the psychics; or witchcraft; charging large sums of money for a word of prophecy; God Forbid!

The prophet need faith to give a prophetic word to the people of the Lord just as the people of the Lord need faith to receive the word spoken to them from the prophet!

True prophets have no points to prove; a prayed up fasted prophet of the Lord need but only to open their mouths, and allow God to

come leaping out!

All people; everywhere that you will ever go will know that you are indeed The Lord's Prophet; and that without question! Through faith the prophet is connected to the calling and to the order of working the gift and walking as the called servant of the Lord!

Faith; will keep you as a prophet when others will have been made aware for sure that you are indeed anointed, a sure prophet of the Lord; they will begin to avoid you, refusing to talk with you in the presence of others, as if there is something foul about you.

In truth; people don't have any fear of what they have determined to be a false prophet; however lacking proper faith and trust in the Lord; they allow a certain sense of terror and of fear to grip them causing them to believe that they can flee the presence of the Lord!

True Prophets of God; people really do fear you, because they know that you see them for who they really are! They realize that they can't hide in your presence; the calling on your life unmasked their disguise and it undresses them while they are yet in their costumes.

By faith; we are who God says that we are simply because He says so! Rely upon faith in God and stop trying to convince people who will never be convinced even after you will have spoken undeniable truth to them.

I have spoken prophetically to so many people in the churches who afterwards ask me; 'Now How Did You Know That?"

Many were the pastors in the churches that I visited, and had been inspired to minister even to the pastors themselves. They proved to have been unfaithful and ignorant to the working order of the true prophets of God.

Sometimes after I had finished ministering in some of the church-es the pastors would get up behind me and say; "He Told All of Us Our Fortunes Tonight!" Those words are truly a mockery to the powerful presence of the Lord manifested through the Order of the Prophetic!

As prophets of the Lord; many have been deceived as a result of their determination for people to know who they are in the spirit of the Lord, according to their calling, as they may often be recognized across the country as a prophet of the Lord.

They have not even surrendered to the love of God being of the most importance to the people of God everywhere! They have not learned of the Holy Ghost how to entreat the people of God and how to maneuver them once they have gotten their attention to hear what they have to say of the Lord.

I have spoken with so many people who have so much more of a secular, occultist; demonically influenced idea of what is believed to be a prophet or a prophetess; but even as I am writing this chapter, I recall that I have never had a discussion with any of them relative to the office of the Prophetic Order.

Here is a note for your mind: True prophets of God move and walk in total Love and the victory of Jesus Christ our Lord and sav-ior. God's prophets are not at all ashamed to love you beyond your own comprehension, as they are determined for you to receive the blessing of the Lord.

As adamant as they are and as assured that as a confessed proph-et of the Lord they are in their demeanor; many people are still yet determinately convinced that there is no difference between those persons who operate from the order of witchcraft, Black Magic; Voo Doo; and all other sorts of the works of darkness, other than the fact that some attend churches and the others probably do not?

It is our job and our place to make sure that even the devil knows that there is a noticeable difference in us and the workers of darkness!

On countless occasions I have been prompted of the spirit of the Lord to say to people who had prepared large dinners for me when they discovered that I am indeed a seer and a man of great spiritual knowledge and wisdom from the Lord;

"I AM A PROPHET OF GOD, AND THAT'S ALL THAT I AM. IF GOD IS NOT TALKING TO ME, THEN NEITHER AM I GOING TO BE TALKING TO YOU AS A PROPHET!"

They invited their families to dine with me, but the ordeal was for the intent that it might be a set up for me to speak into the lives of their family members who would not and did not even attend the services at the church that I had just ministered. They came with money in their hands and they had gifts, some of them did.

They said to me; "well aren't you a prophet?" My answer to them was as I will say to you right now; "I am a Prophet of God's; only!" I don't tell fortune and I don't communicate with the dead! I don't call out the lottery numbers, and phone numbers' and tell people their home addresses!

When I am impressed to call the name of a significant person of your lives, it will only be so by the leading and the unction of the Holy Ghost. And I am what I am by the grace of God; it IS only by God's grace that I am whatever; I am!

There is no spiritual endowment in the bible which receives attack like as to that of the Office of the Order of the Prophetic; other than speaking with unknown tongues; but to a slighter degree of attack!

As disrespectful as the people of many of the churches are as it

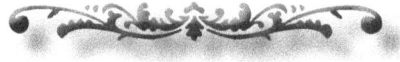

relates to people speaking in tongues; those who are recognized and thus labeled as to being real true prophets of the Lord are targeted much heavier, and disdained as a vocal representative of the Lord.

The people of the churches would much rather have an individual in the churches performing a comic show; telling jokes about the church and people in the churches for a laugh; than to have one who has been called and endowed from on high with the power to not only speak into the life of the people of the churches, but one who has been even more blessed and empowered to speak and break the binding bans of wickedness over the lives of the people calling those things out in the spirit, and out of their lives.

Now we do know that there are certain types of prophets/prophetess that are preferred in the churches, who stand before the people to speak blessings over the people; often lying to the people for the sake of getting them to give money, in very large proportions!

Many that are truly gifted of the Lord from before their birth have chosen never to surrender their gift to the Lord to be used for the glory of the Kingdom of the Lord.

People are called by God; but few are chosen; this is where the faith of God is intertwined with the Prophetic Order in the lives of them who are indeed walking in the Office as a Prophet or Prophetess.

People in the churches are arguing about who can and who ought not to speak as a prophet/prophetess in the churches; often very ignorant of the scripture.

There is quite a bit of teachings in the churches relative to prophets, though very slanted arduous and distorted; sometimes it is viewed and purposed to prevent those who may indeed be called as a prophet; or prophetess(female) keeping them from operating to

the fullest potential of their gift in the spirit. The word of the Lord says that *"the spirits of the prophet are subject unto the prophet";* not to the pastor! *{I Corinthians 14:32}*

Pastor's; in certain churches are sending the prophets to hell over the pulpit because the prophets in their churches will not come under their authority and control.

They are teaching that the prophet ought to shut up and not speak without their permission; under some conditions this is correct as a prophet of God you are never to cause uproar and confusion among the church!

NOTE: ~ just because they say that you are going to hell doesn't make it to be so; "we ought to obey God and not man." Amen! Some just refuse to hear from the prophet of God; period!

It is not as easy to dissuade a called servant of the Lord as it is to embarrass the people of the churches who have been filled with the Holy Ghost; as they begin to speak with unknown tongues.

Too often the ministers from the pulpits will turn the scripture on them to use it against them to prevent them from flowing in the gift of tongues during their services, and in their churches!

In actuality what is exposed most assuredly is the fact that they are not equipped to interpret the utterance of the tongues; and more often they have come under conviction of the spirit exposing the truth that they have not been filled with the Holy Ghost themselves!

Although many of the religious advocates who prevent speaking with tongues in the churches reach for the scripture, which says they should *covet to prophesy;* they often refuse to allow prophecy in their churches either; mostly they never allow it!

Perhaps you have discovered that the people in most of the

churches are really excited about your ministry and that they are eager to have you to come and to speak to their congregations?

Let me suggest to you that you ought to pump your breaks in a hurry, because there is somethings that either you have missed, you have not been taught sufficiently concerning the behavior of the prophetic and the flow of the spirit?

Or, you are just rebellious chasing money and you choose to close your eyes to the ungodliness; wickedness; the sinfulness of the people in the churches; or maybe it's just that you are guilty of these things yourself!

As we embark on this topic of discussion, I am aware that many of you are quite biblically astute and literate of the scripture as it relates to the prophets and to the prophetess in the bible, and of how it was that they operated in the spirit of the Lord; you are familiar to the method of their speaking and to the authority of which they carried about in their own bodies, as a prophet of the Lord.

I do not purport to be able to educate everyone that have been called to the Order of the Prophetic; but I am determinately intent on speaking to all that have an ear to hear what the spirit of the Lord is saying to them through this chapter.

I am of the opinion that those who have been called and ordained to the order of the Prophetic, but have also dedicated themselves and have totally surrendered their whole spirit, soul, and body to the Lord; they are much more purely connected to faith in God!

Not that they have any particular monopoly or authority of faith more than others; but they stand in the presence of faith continually and perpetually, by the will and the admonition of the Lord! Those who are of the Order of the Prophetic are required to live closely to the Lord.

Faith is extremely important to the Prophetic order because that particular spiritual endowment is in divine connection to the natural and to the spiritual atmospheres in the earth often at the will and the leading of the Lord, at a seconds command!

As a prophetic servant in the Kingdom of the Lord, there is not a moment or a second in time that the flow of faith and of the spirit can be hindered, stopped or otherwise blocked in any way!

If you are indeed a scholar of the scripture; you know that in the old testament of the King James Bible; the prophets were called upon at a moment's notice to show forth the intent and the power of God to the people of the earth.

The awesomeness of the Prophetic Order is in the fact that God speaks person to person; even mouth to mouth with the prophets.

God is so awesome and powerful, that He by the aid of the Holy Ghost will teach those in the Prophetic Order by many means through the scripture and by the practical application in the working manifestation of the spirit and the power of God.

The sure faith of God knows those of us that have been called of God to be in the office of the Prophetic.

"Faith; Knows Who Have the Gift of Prophecy."

King Saul went out with his servants looking for his father's asses which had been lost; he went seeking the seer that was of that region; who by the way was Samuel.

When he found Samuel and communed with him for a while; Samuel said to Saul go this way and you will come upon a band of prophets going up to prophesy, join them and the Lord will show you where to find the asses.

The asses were indeed found; Saul went up with the prophets and God gave Saul another heart where he was turned into another man.

Saul began to prophesy with the other prophets so to the point in fact that people began to say; "is Saul now among the prophets?"

Saul had begun to prophesy; but make no mistake about it, he had not begun to work miracles, and bearing signs and wonders from God; as a Prophet.

He was endowed with the prophetic utterances, whereas he could speak the spoken word of admonition; of knowledge and of wisdom prophetically.

Those who are endowed with the gift of prophecy can speak sure words of prophecy as the spirit give the utterance. The Prophet or Prophetess can speak word of knowledge or wisdom; foretell and forth-tell of the things to come as spoken to them of the Lord; but at will as led of the spirit.

God will allow those who have the gift of prophecy to edify the body of Christ; speaking to those who have gathered themselves together in the assembly of worshippers.

The spoken words of those who are gifted to prophesy are often words of encouragement so sharply and keenly intertwined and interwoven with the written word of God and faith.

The hearers of the spoken words of prophecy, who are blessed to hear what the spirit have to say unto the church, leave there determined to continue in the faith; having a mind to go all of the way with the Lord, even to the very end.

Just remember that the working gift of those who walk in the Office of the Order of the Prophetic; is so much more than just an ability or of an endowment to speak a word of prophecy to any

people, and to gain access to their financial means and favor. Absolutely no gift or calling of God is to be diminished or thought to be subpar to any other of the gifts and callings of God.

By faith, walk in your calling and operate in your gift with total confidence and sure authority; knowing that God does not make mistakes!

You are neither called or gifted by accident; God intended to give to you the gift of prophecy or the calling to the Order of the Prophetic.

Before your mother and your father knew you God had already intentionally prepared you to be exactly who you are in the gift and the calling of the anointing of the spirit of the Lord. *{Jeremiah 1:4-6}*

People are struggling and failing trying to be either who they are not in the spirit; or they are trying to compete even desiring to duplicate the ministry of someone else.

The Lord is still saying to us as people of the Lord; *"Be still and know that I am God!"* There is absolutely no room for doubt and unbelief in the realm of the prophetic at any time! If you don't know that God has spoken a thing to you; don't you speak that thing to anyone else!

You have not been called or anointed to tear down other's ministries; and to sow discord among the brethren; neither are you to be uplifted in pride convincing yourselves that you are more anointed than the rest of the people in the Kingdom of God.

You don't need an entourage or a group of followers that follow you everywhere that you go to carry your bible for you, and or a special person to pour your drink for you like the Kings of old; this particular behavior may lead to a desire within you to be reverenced and worshipped?

The more spiritually endowed you become, the more of God is to be seen witnessed and experienced in your presence, and on your life. People ought to always know that you have been with God!

It is not that God has been with you, as if you allow God to follow you everywhere that you go; but it is rather knowing yourselves and making it known to others that you take the Lord with you every-where you go? Better yet, you only go where God leads you through the spirit!

God has been kind to the people of the churches in that He has had mercy on the foolish people who have stood in the congregation of the churches purporting to prophesy; but in this season in this final hour God is going to be more kind to "Faith!"

Since faith knows who is anointed and called of God; the Holy Ghost will begin to visit right in the midst of the people of God, to smite the fake and the false, and even the ungodly prophets who pervert the gift and the calling to the Order of the Prophetic!

Ministers have already begun to fall dead in the pulpit of the churches, and in the midst of the isles of the churches! The spirit of the judgment of God will begin to fall on any people who are dis-order and out of order to the presence of God in the atmosphere of His manifested glory.

People are seeing God move against ministers who have been out of order, and have been leading the people out of order even to the written word of God intentionally; however many people are argu-ing that it is not God's judgment taking place?

Prophets; it's time that we get about announcing the imminent return of the Lord to receive His bride out of the earth. From the housetops it's time to shout it out to the people of the earth; be ready, be ready, be ready!

God is not allowing for you to give sure words of prophecy just

so that people will know that you are a true prophet! But, God; will even allow that sure word to manifest so that even you yourselves as prophetic people of God will know for sure that God will do just what He said that He will do!

God means what he says to us; the word of the Lord is true! So, now we turn a deaf ear to the nay Sayers and to the ungodly, and to all of the non-believers who say that Jesus will not be coming back to receive the church.

If your word of prophecy can come to pass, just know and understand that your word is not greater than the Lord's own word; it's going to happen just like He said it would happen! Jesus is coming back again soon!

God will begin to visit the churches in Judgment that way that He would visit when we worship Him in spirit and in truth; His spirit will be so thick in the atmosphere of the sanctuary that certain people will be running trying to find a hiding place; literally!

When the hand of God begins to move like that in the churches, we will see miracles, signs, and wonders that have never even been imagined before!

Now is the time to prepare and to be ready; make ready them that are assigned to your ministry!

Prophets never get emotionally caught-up and hung-up concerning the people that refuse to hear them. By faith; speak it and get out of the way! Shortly the time will come that when the prophet speaks; they will need but to remove themselves and God will begin to judge according to that word which had been spoken.

Remember the book of Revelation tells us that the Lord says; *"Behold I Come Quickly!"* {Revelation 3:11}

Not enough to announce and to say that you are a prophet of the Lord; it is the hour to be the prophet of God with non-contradicting behavior and

lifestyle attached to you. Go forth prophets of God; tear down and build up where the Lord says to build. Lead the people of God all of the way out to the edge of existence as we know of it today.

Good things must come to an end, so we've been told in the earth! Who says that it's actually good here as much as people are prone to complain and are consistently seeking to get away!

People are desperate to stay here in this place where many people are convinced that they don't even want to be any more. They are planning a one-way exodus from the planet Earth to move away to the planet Mars; they are willing to board a space shuttle to make that journey, not even really sure that they will even be able to make it there safely.

People believe in that possibility, and are willing to invest their money; no return to earth possible; no guarantee that they will ever make it to their final destination; and absolutely no refund!

By faith we are assured through the indwelling power of the Holy Ghost that we will make it indeed to the glorious presence of God. Heaven is prepared and waiting on our arrival; Eternity is laid out and fashioned for our new body, and our glorious reign with God.

Chapter 12

"Faith; Without Works"

Even so faith, if it hath not works, is dead, being alone. Yea, a man may say, Thou hast faith, and I have works: shew me thy faith without thy works, and I will shew thee my faith by my works. {James 2:17-18}

"Faith Works! ~ Have You Worked Faith?"

The picture that faith works; and that it works for all of us, has been developed much clearer for us all now!

There have been so many progressively selfish opinions about the proper working order of faith that has caused most people to be permanently affixed to erroneous ideologies of faith!

Either people have denied the faith of God altogether, or they have taken faith to be nothing short of a religious code key to access financial wealth and gain through the churches?

It sort of burns the insides of the people of the churches when faced with the fact that there are lots of people who really do have

faith in God who will never attend any of their churches?

The people of the churches feel that they should possess the right to examine individuals who are not church attendees, to determine whether or not it is possible for them to have faith in God or not?

So as we open the scripture in the book of James, and see that the writer admonishes us that faith without works is dead:.......

We are more so determined to think and to believe that the meaning ultimately of this particular scripture is relative to what we have personally produced as a faithful member of the church; whether the product produced has any reflection to God; the Kingdom of God; or even to the church that we attend!

Regardless of how we might have embraced faith in God for the truth that it really is; no matter what you might have been able to successfully produce as a member of the church; if your productivity has not been faithful to magnify God, manifesting the awesome love and the presence of God; your works as well as the faith that you should represent is still dead!

So many people; thinking that they might have used faith to get the physical, tangible things that they desired, they have actually misinterpreted the actual framework of faith with the presence of the things that they had gotten.

Most people later determined that it really did not require much effort at all to acquire the stuff that they had received; so if that is all that it takes; perhaps the use of faith just might not be very much work after all?

Lots of people have amassed a great portion of things and of stuff in general; much more than the average individual of the community, but that does not at all suggest that they have greater faith in God!

Many have learned that the secret of having lots of things and

fine stuff is simply the benefiting results of hard work, and wise money management!

Others would not dare at all to confess or to acknowledge that any type of faith had been applied to acquire any of the things that they have.

So you see, to be left to think that faith is better realized and visualized in the things that we have acquired is totally wrong and displeasing to what the scripture has been given for us to know about faith.

Ignorantly people have made declarations as such to the likes of saying; I don't need faith because I have all of the money that I could ever need! In my life time, I could never be broke......?

The manner of which they had gone about to have the things that they have would land many of them in the penitentiary for a long time should it be discovered that they had indeed been illegal and less than honorable in their method of increasing their status.

However; being deceived beyond the reasonable scope of understanding, many who have prospered in their own way believe that they have used a sense of faith to get bye, escaping law enforcement from banning their illegal schemes?

Asking God to allow them to make it this time and they would share the finances of their illegal fortunes with the local churches and with charities of their own choosing?

But don't be so quick to associate your illegal success with the work of faith!

It is not God in Christ Jesus who answers such so called prayers of faith in ungodly schemes and of crimes!

However, knowing that certain people are refusing to come in to total faith and trust in righteousness, holiness, and truth, they are

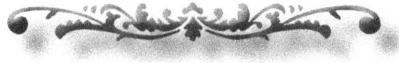

vulnerable to every scheme of sin and of Satan!

Perhaps people need to recognize very strongly and to realistically accept that it is Satan that is spoiling them in their ungodly lifestyles as they happen upon everything that they go after to acquire?

I have had many people both male and female alike to argue with me, telling me that they know that God loves them based on the fact that they should have even been dead, or even locked away in jail for life?

But, they are adamant that it was indeed God who was there with them while they did all of the evil that they were big and grown enough to do, and got away clean! They Think Anyway?

The truth is that many of them have had certain people from the churches to encourage them to believe that even though they were living out-loud in sin, that they were indeed in God's care; no need at all to worry!

The real problem with such people is that they do not discern the spirit of deception; they have been deceived possibly by a demon spirit hanging around the local church.

They believe that they are working for the benefit of the church in their own ways; even though they will never attend nor take part in any of the services of the churches!

They have been deceived to associate their illegal activities and financial contribution to certain of the local churches, as to that of working their faith, so as to avoid dead faith?

They are ignorantly unlearned of the scriptures and totally unbelieving that they have to work their faith within the biblical confines of the scriptures, in Christ Jesus!

Faith; itself; it doesn't die; but what is indeed dead, is that particular idea of faith!

The true definitive clarifying message of *[Hebrews 11:1]*; is taken so far from the spiritual context of meaning and misplaced to the human side of natural thinking that as a result it is left void of the comprehensive revelatory pronouncement of the spirit.

All it is that many people are able to see concerning what they believe to be the rewarding blessings of faith are all of the natural things and the stuff that they are able to brag and to boast about to others who also claim to be people of faith?

In my recent research I have come to know that visibly there are a lot of people who confess to a particular ideology of what they have considered to be faith, even of multiple diversities, idioms of religious expressions; but not all even desire to be people of faith, of God in Christ Jesus!

Many have been willfully deceived and led astray desiring to have what they see that others have acquired; as they will later hear them say that they have faith?

I was taught as were many of the readers of this book; that faith was indeed, you as an individual believer; acting upon what you have believed to be truth!

This statement is often so wrong simply because the truth of God's word has been turned into an outright lie straight from hell; but you might believe to be the truth?

However; my friend, faith is indeed allowing God to act in you, through you, and for you accordingly to the written word of God.

Because you have believed the scripture and have received and accepted it and have found it in your own heart, your mind, and in your own spirit to be the absolute truth!

The detriment in the acquisition of faith is that people are co-dependent and needful of other people, they are alright going in a cer-

tain direction of living as long as it is the direction that many other people alike are going?

They say that God knows my heart and He knows that I can't live without certain things in my life?

I just have to do whatever it takes for me to have those things?

Of course, these same people are disregarding of the scripture;

But seek ye first the kingdom of God, and His righteousness, and all of these things shall be added unto you. But he turned, and said unto Peter, Get thee behind me, Satan: thou art an offence unto me: for thou savourest not the things that be of God, but those that be of men. Then said Jesus, unto his disciples. If any man will come after me, let him deny himself, and take up his cross, and follow me. For whosoever shall save his life shall lose it: and whosoever will lose his life for my sake shall find it.
{St Matthew 6:33; 16:23-25}

Many of the leaders and the people in the churches are materialistic and carnal in their thinking, so they are not willing to apply faith to the written scripture to live according to God's will for their own personal lives.

A very sad indictment against the people of the churches is that many of the people who truly adhere to faith in God and the scripture, they are shunned and labeled as fanatical, suggesting that they have taken the understanding of having faith in God a bit too far?

Even much further than they themselves are willing to go with faith!

It is determined in the thinking processes of so many people, that

faith is working for humanity because of a certain group of people in any given church who are able to walk into a bank only after giving money to the church, and get approval for big loans.

They have large houses and many luxurious cars; they have nice jobs; and let's not forget that they had also been educated to amass the better incomes that they are now receiving.

People may indeed be committed to sow into a certain ministry; but look a little deeper and you will find that many of the same people are not faithful to God according to His word, at all!

Should you begin to converse with some of the said individuals about the greater things of God that are indeed written in the scripture, it doesn't take long to realize that they don't even have a clue about what you are talking about.

They are illiterate of the scripture with the exception to that which is consistently presented to them relative to sowing seed in the church.

People have come to me having very deep issues who have been a member of their own church for a number of years, but having never had their issues addressed nor resolved.

They just keep on giving money and attending the services continually; they believe that they are faithful givers to the ministry, and are even recognized and celebrated as of being such in their churches.

Many of these people are at a loss and in grave disappointment when in need of the Lord due to an illness or a great loss of some kind, they don't even know where to turn in the scripture for their situation.

I find myself often ministering to people who are doing very well financially, they live in their own desired neighborhoods, working

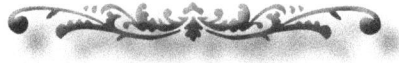

in the field of education on a good salary; but they need God in their lives whereas none of the things that they have can answer or fulfill them.

So then the question comes to the forefront, is it faith that we are seeing or is it that people have adhered to good work ethics and dedication to committed vows for paying the bills on time!

Getting out of the bed going to work even when they didn't feel like it; keeping their record clean from criminal content and a show of genuine integrity?

Too often what has been donned as being faithful is better realized as an individual having been committed to behave themselves according to the learned ethics of their education, and holding fast to the applied commitment for which they have vowed?

Sometimes and more than often, having faith in God; means that we will have to walk and to stand alone in our faithful endeavors, not having others who can even comprehend our stance, as we adhere to our declared show of obedience to God and to His word.

Real faith always reaches forward and stretches into God of all of the ages; no new God; no new faith! The word of God will always give deference to the actuality of faith.

Faith is always allowing us to be built up for the final plan of God for us in the Kingdom of God; therefore we cannot be left wondering and clueless of faith.

We have been taught, only to see the after effects of applied faith, although it was not always the intentions of our instructors to teach us in this manner; they themselves had not delve deeply enough into the present spirit of faith to know what faith actually is.

when the scripture clearly states; "Now Faith;" which is predicated on the present but previously established authority of faith

which is and was with God before the beginning!

Erroneously; many are taught to believe that faith becomes what-ever you might hope for, and eventually it just becomes the evidence of what you have believed?

Wrong; faith is; already what you have hoped for and the mani-fested evidence; even before you ask, hope, and or believe!

In generality we have come to be in existence only after and since faith has been always! So, it is easier to grasp what is presently giv-en to us of other men to understand what faith is supposed to be right before us in the now.

But refusing even to acknowledge that which came before this present now, that has always been established before now, strength-ening the viability to give credence to the obedience of faith in God!

Often, being carnal minded in the thinking processes of hu-man understanding, many people have become lazy and stagnant to reach for the foundational fundamental plants at the depths of God's word that are intentionally placed there for us to retrieve.

As result of our search and find, and they are unbelieving and seriously doubtful that there is more to the scripture than what is visualized at face value on the pages of the bible.

Therefore, we are most adamantly encouraged to adhere to the afterward manifestations of what we would believe is to be faith; rather than to work the revealed understanding of the true actuality of faith in God.

For me; I discovered that the greatest work relative to faith in God is moving myself out of the way!

I have had to learn never to block my own path, believing that I was, or that I had been in authority over whether or not faith worked for me or on my behalf of the ministry to which I have been

endowed. No; God works faith, when we line up and allow for Him to do so!

"The Work; Is it Back Breaking, or Mind Boggling?"

Whether we consider the work of faith as being back breaking or mind boggling to us, that fact is that we have got to get involved with the work of faith.

Faith; being alone, standing all by itself; disallows for the manifested experienced work of faith to be seen and or otherwise realized itself, when those who should be the faithful are disengaged to apply the usage of faith!

Faith will do what it has been designed and created to do with you, but faith is never going to work without you as it was never designed to do so!

Faith sees in the invisible realm of the spirit; faith hears in the midst of sound paralyzing silence, and it speaks the unspoken messages of life; however it must manifest all that has been realized in the supernatural realm through you!

You need to agree with what faith sees, what it says, and for certain with what faith knows.

We know that faith knows the uncertain things, faith uncovers the hidden things of the spirit and of the natural realms; faith clings to truth unrealized, and unlearned that is yet to be revealed to all of mankind and it holds to the expectations that are yet to be engaged in the belly of the believer.

Faith; itself is already infused with the jet-like capabilities to swiftly connect to the natural realm so that the invisible things of the spirit realm can be transformed realities!

In other words, we have working faith that is at its job assign-

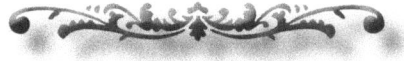

ment consistently while only needing for mankind to set ourselves in total agreement with faith, so as to manifest the produced desires of the heart of man, by faith!

Alike the car lot that has working automobiles that are just waiting to be both sold and purchased; the cars have been manufactured and constructed to work before being driven.

We don't go to the car lot and purchase an automobile with the expectations that we have to install the engine and the transmission in an effort that the auto will run and operate as designed.

Likewise faith has already been constructed; (if you will allow me), to work for us. Faith is in working order even if we never reach for it to allow faith to work in our behalf!

God knows what we need even before we can ask of Him; and God also knows what it will take in effort for those things to be given to us.

Therefore it is not the better wisdom of the Lord to leave faith to us to make things happen for us knowing that alone, we of ourselves, as the people of the earth, that we lack the knowledge and the power to activate the instantaneous combustion of faith to be respondent to our needs and to our request.

As it is faith doesn't even work for so many people because erroneously the wrong assignments have been given for faith that were never ordained or intended for faith to do.

People are adamant to put forth a demand of faith desiring to leave God out of the equation, forsaking to remember that faith is firstly a God thing, then after submitting to the will of God we are included in the practicality of faith to connect to God who can and will fill all things in our lives, through faith.

It is not that we actually put faith to work to make things happen

for us as a result; but the greater reality is that we work an already working faith, which stands waiting for us to get on board for the ride to the destination of our asked for; manifestation!

That of which we have indeed inquired of the Lord for us to have in faith, is already infused and ingrained into faith.

God does not need for any of us to empower faith; faith itself is already empowered by the anointed approval of the word of God and ready; figuratively speaking, the motor of faith is already ignited and idling in position for takeoff in the direction of our request of God through faith.

How could faith in God work for you if it needs for you to make it whatever it needs to be first? God knows much better than you ever will, what it takes for you to be blessed?

Remember; *without faith it is impossible to please the Lord; {Hebrews 11:6}.....*

Most people are not even godly in their thinking or the manner of their choices of living. They have not even allowed themselves to become word oriented to believe the bible, so as to build any faithful adherence.

People avoid hearing the word of God through the teacher, and the preacher; yet they come to church services, but often they are now more determined to be entertained and stroked for the sake of their ego, and of their emotions.

People show up at the churches to be mentally and sometimes intellectually removed from the issues that plague their minds on a daily basis, which may not at all work that which makes for greater faithful adherence as result of the word of God.

So then faith cometh by hearing, and hearing by the word of God.   *{Romans 10:17}*

272

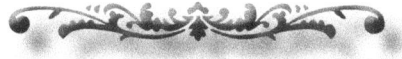

This scripture is not at all intended to suggest to you that faith is created through the hearing of the word of God; faith has already been created and finished! *[Hebrews 12:2]*

But what the scripture does suggest to us is that faith comes into focus more clearly to us through hearing the word of God;

Faith is to be explained and expounded upon to the point that as a faithful being of the Kingdom, we learn to truly walk in the faith that is needed to show forth the glory of God through our daily lives of living among faithless ungodly people, according to the written word of God.

A fancy tickling message may indeed entertain you but it will not work towards the increase of faithful understanding to open you up to a more excellent vision and perception of the faith that is indeed intended to be working on the inside of you.

For unto us was the gospel preached, as well as unto them: but the word preached did not profit them, not being mixed with faith that heard it. *[Hebrews 4:2]*

The preaching that many are hearing these days cannot even be mixed with faith, being that it is so washed out with scientific equations; metaphysics; psychology; psychiatric anomaly good for entertainment and the such like which takes place in most of the pulpits nowadays; and not even according to the word of God.

I have seen some preachers go on for a while talking about the theme from the animated film; "The Lion King!"

I've seen the audience stirred and revved up with excitement over the topic of discussion, and the charismatic speaker; but I have also realized the lack of power and substance to work a greater weight of faith administering grace unto the hearers.

When the preached word that we are hearing cannot be mixed

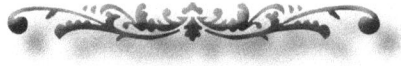

with faith; it is useless and worthless to our hearing. I; personally; cannot even respond to an individual going on and on over the pulpit and PA system for nothing!

The word of God is too important to us and extremely necessary for the benefit of our ability to know God in the fullness of His power, being made conformable to His death;

As we mix faith with the preach word of the gospel of God, faith swings the door open to us so that we are now able to see, to hear, to abide in the truth of God, and to become agreeable to all that God has done for all of humanity through the death, burial, and resurrection of Jesus Christ.

"Allow Faith to Work You!"

Contrary to what we have believed, faith itself must work us; working in us, faith must be allowed to reposition us to stand in the presence of God.

Faith itself, have the ability to not only show us to the Father; but it allows for us to see the Father through the word of God.

Whereas we are positioned in our hearts to accept and to receive the Father according to the written word of God; knowing that there is none like Him in all of the heavens and the earth.

As a result of being taught and trained to put faith to work, faith has become one dimensional to us in that we could never even fathom the truth that faith works a far more exceeding weight of glory in the relationship between God and us.

Faith works on us, in us, and through us from the inside out perspective, whereas what is realized from faith is first realized from the faithful individual that surrenders to the faith on the inside of themselves.

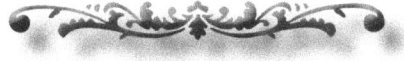

As it relates to faith, I'm going to see it work and realize that it has completed the work before anyone else will ever be able to visualize any manifestations of faith in God through me.

Faith insures that I; myself as the individual of faith show up and show forth myself as a faithful individual, whereas others will be able to see through faith that God is working mightily in me.

It is the assurance of faith that enables me to grow stronger in the manifested presence of God; whereas even the works of the spirit of God show forth in me by greater measure through faith to release God in every atmosphere that I am in.

It is imperative that we begin focusing on the implicit intended working order in the purpose of faith, as it relates to each one of us. Faith is working us even more-so to get the word out to the people of the world that God lives and that He is real!

{Hebrews 11:6,} says; *He that cometh to God must believe that He is;...*

Others are encouraged and convinced to come to God after seeing God work mightily in our lives through faith; thus they now believe that God is real!

"Faith; If It Hath Not Works?"

This is the reason that James opens part B; of this particular scripture, saying; *"yet a man may say;"* in closer scrutiny of this scripture we glean the reality that someone had seen something that would be responsible for igniting this verbal exchange between two individuals.

One man is clearly saying to another individual, you have works; but I have faith!   In other words; I see what you've got, I see what you're working with; but I know what I have also.

The truth is that nothing but a working faith is going to produce

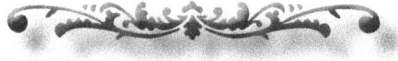

that which flows from the Kingdom of God, on the behalf of the children of faith; who ask of Him in faith.

It is indicative of the people of today, who are dedicated workers in the churches and the communities, who have no actuality of faith in God to show forth.

Faith mirrors the spirit of God wherever it is found, no one is going to be filled with working faith who cannot show that God is alive on the inside of themselves.

Faith is so powerful that it doesn't ask our permission to reveal God in us; it does what it has been created to do on the inside of us.

When the scripture says to us; *"faith without works is dead;"* what we need to understand is that as we refuse to allow faith to work in us according to the activation of the written word of God, faith has to lay dormant, inactive on the inside of us, unable to produce the manifested presence of God in us to fill the atmosphere for every believer and to the unbelievers as well.

The truest purpose of faith working in me is that men may see God in me; to see the works which glorify the Father which is in heaven.

What we are in need of more is the surrendered obedience to faith through the word of God. Faith will work if we just surrender to it, and stop trying to hold on to faith as a prize possession, only!

God has already ordained the works of faith through the written word of God; people are now trying to force works through faith that were never ordained of God in the beginning.

There is no hocus pocus or magic in faith; faith is more powerful and accurate than any magic or a trick show.

We see physical natural works of the flesh going on around the churches now that are ascribed and assigned to faith that have noth-

ing at all really to do with the God given agenda of faith.

We see car washes, Chicken and Bar B Q dinners sold; and we also see dinners and banquets for homemade local church organizations around the local churches that will boost the morale of the people but it will never increase the faithful adherence of the people in the churches.

The people of the churches receive more trophies and certificates than they ever receive of the gifts and the fruit of the spirit; as result of the lack of definitive teaching of faith.

Many of the churches nowadays create programs and services to motivate the membership of the churches, but far too often they are found to have dropped the ball as it related to the teachings of faith.

It is erroneously assumed that people automatically are knowledgeable of faith; what it means to have faith in God; what faith is; what faith does and what faith can really do for you.

We soon realize that people have an accurate record many times of what someone told them about faith!

In many instances they can produce no scripture basis for their understanding of faith, even though everything of the word of God is to be done and experienced through faith.

"Understanding Faith; That Is Thought to Be Dead?"

Faith is alive and living among the living and the dead! As God is; so is faith being eternal, as we have never read nor will we ever read that faith will die and be done away with!

It is my belief that one day as we will have gone to live forever with the Lord that faith will be there to congratulate those of us who had been faithful, even unto death.

Perhaps it may even be a portion of our reward to meet faith that

had already made our acquaintance to lead us to the presence of God on the throne.

Let's consider those who have died already in the faith of God in Christ Jesus; they are forever branded and stamped faithful and will not be forgotten of who they were and are.

When the trumpet sounds and the dead in Christ shall rise first, it is faith that will know who we are, every one of us, both the living and the dead.

God identifies us through faith; faith will not deny any of us who have been faithfully washed in the blood of the Lamb of God! Thus we see a continued activity of faith even after we might have gone in our graves; faith still works.

Anyway my friends, as the scripture admonishes us that faith without works is dead; again we need to understand that faith is therefore rendered to a dormant state of motionless inactivity in the life of everyone that disallows the working activity of faith to be in forward motion having momentum of the manifested activity of God in their lives.

The production of faith is inactive and cannot produce the desired expectations of believing God, as God will give to us nothing that we have refused to ask God for in faith believing that He will indeed give us those things.

Again I state that faith was indeed alive before the living were ever created and formed from the dust of the ground. So if faith can actually die who could kill it, and how would you go about killing something to which there is absolutely nothing at all natural about it? Where would you shoot it or stab the knife into it?

As a matter of the fact, where is the body of faith to be handled and manipulated for the sake of destroying faith? How would you choke the life out of faith seeing that there is no neck to grasp it

around its throat cutting off the oxygen supply?

Mind you that these types of things can only happen in the natural; faith is indeed spiritual!

Faith is agreeable to the life of God on the inside of every individual; doesn't matter who you may be and of where it is that you reside and dwell on the face of the earth, faith stands in agreement.

Even your past ungodly ancestors didn't have the power to block you from having faith in God!

The devil himself, have tried to cause as much unrest as possible to those persons who were connected to generational discourses of faith, through unbelief; but the spirit of the Lord always prevails.

No one on the outside of your body can stop the activity of faith in your life. Faith obeys the God given assignment to produce life in the spirit as life had already been ruled upon and agreed to in the birthing process where we all that are here on the face of the earth came forth to live and to be alive; faith was in that process also, as God never works without faith.

God believed in faith before you and I could ever have an opportunity to believe in God through faith! You may have been blinded at one point in your life lacking understanding of faith, but faith itself have never been blind, and can never be blinded!

There is absolutely no such thing as blind faith; I've wanted to say that for decades now; there it is!

Faith always sees and is also responsible for allowing God to give sight to our ability to see in the natural and for restoring the sight to the blind who themselves cannot see, haven lost their ability to see.

Ignorantly people have assigned some really crazy things to the actuality of faith; perhaps seeking to lessen the powerful authority of faith; but only know and realize that faith is too powerful as

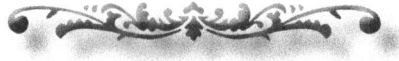

a shield itself, to ever be touched by such disingenuous desires for faith by the unbelieving.

Faith is going nowhere; it must reign until the end of God; of which there is no end to God; He is eternal and eternity is forever! If you can't see your works of faith, neither can anyone else!

Never forget the fact that faith is internal and personal; others have no real bearing on whether or not you actually have faith in God!

Those of us who teach and preach the word of God, can only hope and trust ourselves through faith that the hearers are internalizing the truth of our messages of faith in God.

That that we are given to do around the churches and in the communities cannot establish the work which must be applied to faith in God; so many people are guilty of participating though grudgingly agreeing.

How faithful can it be that you are doing things for the church or for the community, that you absolutely despise and would never do such things without being asked to do them only so that others can see your so-called works of faith?

As a result of the entertainment needs that we as people seem to maintain, having stress over the top on a daily basis; we allow such rediculous animated descriptions and definitions to our faith in God.

For an instance, faith can neither be still born nor comatose? Faith is neither born as a baby, nor buried in a grave as a result of death. We adhere to such playfulness as a result of refusing to be serious about the things that are relative to God.

Too many people are not serious about God!

Faith is not at all a play thing; you can't take faith and put it up

on a shelf until you are ready for it, because there is something that we want that only faith can get it and deliver it to you!

You can neither lose faith nor find faith; faith knows where you are at all times, under all circumstances.

Just know that the assignment of faith is not at all to follow you into every pit, dungeon, and den of the devil. It is our ordained place and our assignment to follow faith to the very end of our natural existence.

If faith can't go then we ought to stay out ourselve!

While faith is a mystery in itself, whenever we search the scripture we soon discover and we learn that there is nothing mythological at all about faith or the acquisition of faith.

You don't have to be a special person to respond to faith in God or to apply faith that has been given to every man on the face of the planet, whether they choose to acknowledge faith in God or not. You don't need a special robe, a hat, nor a special colored light bulb in an effort to work faith; ~ Just Do It!

Through the word of God, we are enlightened of the multiple benefits and blessings that are awarded to us that walk in faith. It is extremely detrimental to even approach the idea about faith without opening the written word of God, in the holy bible.

You don't ever teach faith anything as faith is already all knowing, as is God who gave us Faith; faith teaches us everything when we will just simply listen and pay attention and hear; and open ourselves spiritually in effort to see what it is showing us.

The word of God is to faith as the blood is to our bodies! Faith in God is loaded like a nuclear bomb just waiting to explode for our benefit; only we need to be informed of the fact that faith works for us through love and the word of God.

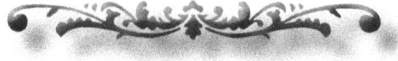

Feelings and emotions; ideas and suggestions; neither stirrs faith for us nor does it pull the plug on faith denying our ability to touch God.

There will be time that we will have to step aside from all of these things to release ourselves to walk in faith; to pray in faith; to live faithfully to the word and to the will of God.

Faith is never at all concerned about its welfare or life; faith is eternal therefore its life is also eternal!

Faith lives through sickness and through the death of all who have died upon the face of the earth, even through the death, burial, and the glorious ressurection of Jesus Christ our Lord and Savior.

So now our greater focus is on the fact that faith with works is alive and thriving to deliver us to our final destination, which is in heaven with the Father.

Chapter 13

"Faith" ~ For Finances" ***

From whence come wars and fighting among you? Come they not hence, even of your lust that war in your members? Ye lust, and have not; ye kill, and desire to have, and cannot obtain; ye fight and war, yet ye have not, because ye ask not. Ye ask, and receive not, because ye ask amiss, that ye may consume it upon your lust.   *{James 4:1-3}*

"We NEED FINANCES, But We DESIRE to Have MONEY!"

We are going to vigorously explore the differences between having money; and finances. While the two can very respectfully be viewed as one and the same, there is a very viable difference between the two.

If you are alike I am, myself; you have prayed for many years asking God for the money needed for the welfare and the well-being of your family, only to find yourselves falling short often of having the money that you think that you really need, or would just simply desire to have continuously available to you at all times.

Even though you have been awarded the ability to pay the bills and to cover the needs of the family; you have productive employment and good health, but still you may find that you are still very low and strapped for cash between the bills; from month to month.

It's been through the need of money that I have come to the revelation of this mystery as to the reason that my prayer for money seemed to have always been denied or at least unheard for all of these years?

Very poignantly; the scripture speaks expressively about money and how it is that we are to handle our money; how we should give to the work of God; paying tithes; feeding the hungry, sharing with them that have need and so on… And the scripture also speaks to the fact so many people are stingy with their money, and uncaring of those who are in need of help.

Now therefore thus saith the Lord of host; Consider your ways. Ye have sown much, and bring in little; ye eat, but ye have not enough; ye drink, but ye are not filled with drink; ye clothe you, but there is none warm; and he that earneth wages earneth wages to put it into a bag with holes Thus saith the Lord of host; Consider your ways.   {Haggai 1:5-7}

Amazingly so many of the leaders who are adamantly trying to convince the people of their churches that they are not doing what God requires, which is evident in the lack of finances they are experiencing in their livelihood; after much scrutinizing, they have been found to be recipients of what the bible calls; "Filthy Lucre!" (Dirty Money)…….

I added this scripture for the sake of some people of the churches who are convinced that money is the earthly reward for living righteous and holy before the Lord. They are adamantly teaching people that if your money is not flowing like everyone else in the

284

ministry, that it is indication that you are not living a life that is indeed pleasing to the Lord; there is something indeed wrong with you? The word of God is right and we need always to pay attention to the written word of God.

In faith, we are given to know whenever a financial crisis is the work of demonic attack; the price of sin that we are in while we yet think that we are living in holiness, but we allow for iniquity to be found in our choices of living as we claim to be worshipers; and finally it may be a real true test and trial of faith!

Most of the same ministers who tried to feed that foolishness down my throat were the same who went out of their way to cheat me out of the money they owed me for services that I had rendered to their ministries. They know what they agreed to pay me for a certain time, but they extended the service for much longer than they agreed; but refused outright to be honorable, concerning me.

So many others have come to me over the years with similar stories from certain leaders in the churches who are making them to feel as if God doesn't love them the same as He love other people in the churches who are a bit more fluid in their own financial flow.

Here in this chapter you may find why it is that certain people who seem to have more money in their churches seem to often have less of the presence and the power of the Lord flowing in their lives as well. While less money doesn't mean less God in the life of an individual; more money certainly does not suggest that one is living a life that is indeed pleasing to the Lord; according to His word.

There are some people that God has to take through the process of financial struggle and ruin, for the sake of implanting a much greater conviction to make them much more effective in their ministry to the people of faith. Their trials will enable them to get the teachings of faith right according to the scripture. Far too many people are suffering as a result of erroneous teachings of faith.

The true understanding of receiving finances from the Lord has been made available to me through praying and fasting according to the word of God. Sincerely praying for certain things, even in faith; is not always the answer to receiving what you may have asked the Lord for when you are in error asking amiss.

The people of the Lord do not always know what it is really that they are asking for of the Lord. God has no real issue with us having the finances that we need; God has a problem with us having the money that we love so greatly; and having great Love of Money!

I was awakened early in the morning hours by the spirit of the Lord; I heard Him say to me; "I NEED FOR YOU TO STOP ASKING ME FOR MONEY; AND ASK ME FOR FINANCES!"

This instruction and admonition of the Lord has got everything to do with the hidden desires of our hearts and even of the undis-covered evil capabilities that lie dormant on the inside of every in-dividual! Most every individual is capable of doing things that are contrary to the will and to the word of God. Just having the right amount of money, and or the right knowledge of money making schemes to get away with doing those types of things!

Your money poses absolutely no threat to the plan of God for the people of faith in God, and doesn't scare God and cause Him to be concerned that they may never need Him; are you serious? But, neither does it impress God to the point in fact that you can estab-lish any special favor with God; money doesn't buy you access to the throne, faith is the only open access to the presence of God!

If and whenever you allow it to be so, that you believe that your money changes the rules of your status with God, your money can and will get you into serious trouble with God! Respect the fact that your money doesn't even have the power or the ability to be a sug-stitute for the shed blood of Jesus Christ. The blood of Jesus estab-lished me; and you for that matter; nothing but the blood of Jesus!

I would not say to any individual that they don't need to have the money that they do have; but I would admonish them to re-examine their motives and their purpose for handling their money and their attitudes behind it. Put the money aside even from sowing seeds and step into faith that will allow for you to sow a faith seed with your money. Your faith gift can begin to produce a harvest for you the very monent that you set your heart to give the seed!

So many people have the money which suggest that they ought to be living in the penthouse, but their lifestyles and even the manner in which they have acquired their money are down underneath the basement, underground living lower than a dog, with the snakes who themselves always come above the ground to slither around on the earth.

And when Simon saw that through laying on of the apostles' hands the Holy Ghost was given, he offered them money, Saying, Give me also this power, that on whomsoever I lay my hands, he may receive the Holy Ghost. But Peter said unto him, Thy money perish with thee, because thou hast thought that the gift of God may be purchased with money. Thou hast neither part nor lot in this matter: for thy heart is not right in the sight of God. Repent therefore of this thy wickedness, and pray God, if perhaps the thought of thine heart may be forgiven thee. For I perceive that thou art in the gall of bitterness, and in the bond of iniquity. {Acts 8:18-23}

Faith in God does not operate in and through iniquity and sin; outright unrighteousness, and wickedness. All the likes of the such will hinder and even paralyze the actual ability of faith to touch God, other than to reach out to God through repentance for the sake of being saved, set free, and delivered, to be changed from that state of sinfullness; to walk in holiness, truth and the Present Love of God.

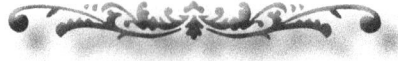

"Money"; alone of itself is left to the imagination to do whatever one's heart may desire for them to do; however "Finances"; is that element of money that is given for an individual to fulfill their purposeful obligations and that which had been avowed of them when they signed and applied their signature to the contractual documented agreement.

Money enables you to indulge in the lust of your mind and of your heart, fulfilling all of the fantasies of your own evil and wicked imagination; nothing stops you from having and from doing whatever you desire when you have the money that it takes to do and or to have whatever it is that you desire.

So many people who have lots of money, their heads are held up so high that it is no wonder that a strong wind have not burst their lungs! We often wonder why it is that people with money act that way?

The truth is that they really can't help but to be responsive to the spirit that money itself will bring with it to any recipient whose worship and respect of the dollar, is greater than that of the worship and reverence for God. When money is all that you want, you have to be subject to all that come with the responsibility of having just money alone without God to influence your spirit, mind, and your attitude concerning the money that you have.

The reason that many people who are saved that end up usually giving away the money that they have received; the spirit of guilt comes along with the truthful fact that others are less fortunate than them.

Others, refusing to pay tithes to God; have allowed their money to be without the borders of protection that the spirit of the Lord would give to them knowing that their money had been given to them for the sake and the purpose of financing their livelihood and ministries. This is the reason that it is so detrimental to play the lot-

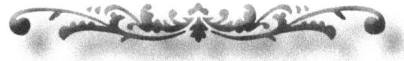

tery instead as a believer in Christ?

Those who play the lottery are playing for a chance to just have money; even as much money or more than the other people that they may be aware of who have lots of money? Regardless of the reasons or the purpose for which the other people may have been so monetarily enlarged; the focus that many people will have is that they have the money that they desire to have for themselves.

It is not often the understanding that the other people may also be monetarily astute to manage money and or to carefully distribute to the needs of others without going broke, as result of scholastic studies and Federal Government approval. Perhaps they have taken the time to sit in the library or on the couch in their own homes for that matter to read and to study, even over the internet, to gain understanding about the INS and the OUTS of having money.

It has always been gravely disappointing to me that a professional athlete had been made rich upon signing a contract to play professional sports; but by the time they retired from their sports career they had squandered their money through partying and splurging, spending at every opportunity, now since their career had ended they've gone broke without a dime!

The worst thing, in my own opinion; was for them to realize that they now have money to have and to do whatever their hearts had ever dreamed of doing. They never really assumed the responsibility assure that they would be secured futuristically. They never made any investments that would show forth the fact that they had indeed been made rich through their own applied athletic skill.

Most of them became so arrogant and haughty in their spirits as a result of their new found financial status; they refused to have financial advisors or money managers to assist them and to help to insure that they have a nest egg to fall back on should the need arise. They should have had a viable plan for the future of their money;

also having a knowledge powerful enough to cause them to control their money. It makes me sick to the stomach to see people who have been so rich to end up in the penitentiary as a result of mishandling even their own money.

See; we are not quite as watchful when our care and concern is all about money alone; as we should be consciously and cautiously aware of what happens to our finances!

Many people who are not rich have the ideas that if ever they are to become rich, they would never ever allow themselves to be poor or broke ever again; they think anyway!

They think that they would carefully and watchfully apply their money to the right types of investments for the sake of growing the invested amounts to even greater proportions; much more than they had initially put in?

Most people who eventually get lots of money, they usually see the money fade away like a vapor of smoke. They've never known the skill or the sensibility of the need to restain themselves, refusing to buy everything available for purchase! You can't spend money and keep money all at the same time!

Only, money alone of itself, even with secular knowledge and skill, it is yet vulnerable to the wicked schemes and the evil plots of educated crooks and robbers who operate from platforms of legally authorized investment organizations.

Those who lurk behind the monitor screens of the computer, they are now more criminally astute to hack into the bank accounts and into the computer systems to steal the money of as many as they can.

Money; alone, is tied to our ego and our lust, to our social status in the community; we allow money to dictate the neighborhood in which we desire to live; the car that we desire to drive, even the

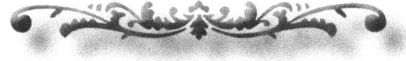

grocery store chain that we desire to shop in. I have met a lot of people who have what I will call "Money~Muscle"; they are strong at moving things and certain people around as a result.

Money can mean a lot to an individual until they are faced with many of the challenges of life that come along to try the integrity of their character and their health; in many cases neither money nor finances are able to assist the individual to the point in fact that they are no longer under the attack.

Truthfully; the careless outright apprehensive chase of money have landed countless people in their graves, having never reached the height of their desired financial class of perfection, or status.

The people of the world seem to understand the art of sowing the types of seed that are indeed going to spring up one day out the blue to come back and cause the sower of the seed to reap very painful harvest; regretfully!

However; the people of the world seem to blow a fuse at the idea of sowing seed of faith in God in the churches, even when upon scrutinizing, it is found to be legitimate and clean, and righteous before the Lord.

"Satan's Influence and Your Money!"

For the love of money is the root of all evil:
which while some coveted after, they have erred
from the faith, and pierced themselves through
with many sorrows.   *{I Timothy 6: 10}*

I had often wondered about the differences between the people of the world and the people of the church as it related to having money? By the grace of God; the wisdom was given to me that the differences are gleaned and comprehended through the under~standing of the integrity of having finances!

Understanding the necessity to properly apply finances will not allow for those of us who are willfully obedient to the financial management of our money, to misappropriate our money irresponsibly spending in spite of the known obligation to tithe first; and to pay our bills.

The churches are filled with religious gamblers; they give offerings and sow what is supposed to be seeds of faith! The only return they are looking for and expecting is for more money to come to them as result of minimum seed to which they had sown before.

Erroneous teaching and preaching in the churches have outright driven the people of many of the churches wild; they think and believe that God now owe them for bringing their money to the church even though they had no faithful intention to give the seed before they even left their homes.

People are mad and angry at God for having been misled to give offerings at the church; they gave their house note payments; their car payments; the money for paying their utility payments, only to come up behind the eight ball; they lost everything!

This is what the possession of money will do for an individual, it always leave them thinking that since the money have been given to them, they are at discretion to do with their money as they have pleased to do so, but often disregarding the need for their own financial obligation!

Now they think that God has done them wrong because it looks as if the plug has been pulled out allowing for all of their stuff sink down the drain right out from beneath them! But, never did they ever stop to think that they had done God wrong in that they did not faithfully appreciate God for blessing them to pay their obligation.

Acting upon the stewardship awarded to them; which would have even put them in better standing with both God and man alike;

they never thanked God!

Married couples that win the lottery often end up with the disaster of the relationship as the actual award for winning all of the money.

Many couples, who loved each other through the lower income levels of living together as husband and wife, split up in divorce court over the now huge bank account and their inability to agree on how, when and where the money is to be spent!

I have even heard of couples splitting over where to place their tithes, or over whether or not to pay tithes to the church, citing that the amount is too much of their money to give to the church. Believe me, the devil knows where the money is and he knows how to influence you to go and get it!

Weak people who chase money will often also be found doing anything and everything to get their hands on it. God knows that we need finances, but Satan knows whether the love of money has been lodged in our hearts; mainly because he put the drive to have money there in our heads.

Love not the world, neither the things that are in the world. If any man love the world, the love of the Father is not in him. For all that is in the world, the lust of the flesh, and the lust of the eyes, and the pride of life, is not of the Father, but is of the world. And the world passeth away, and the lust thereof: but he that doeth the will of God abideth forever. {I John 2:15-17}

The problem is more often than not, that people are guilty of looking at what their neighbors have. Also we as people allow ourselves to think that if they have it than we can to!

As kids we watched the cartoon "Popeye", he would sing a song to "Brutus" which said; "I can do anything you do", "Anything you

can do I can do better!" We were being setup mentally as children to become very covetous and competitive towards our neighbors friends and our family members; even competitive to the people of the churches.

People are so driven in their heads, their hearts, and in their spirits to have lots of money; that they have allowed the local churches to be viewed as a great big joke to them, and have even foolishly charged God as being responsible for the behavior and the attitudes of the people in the churches.

Although they themselves are demonically driven to sinfully chase money; i.e.: to rob, kill, steal, cheat, and to do everything else that they can think of to get money, they are outraged at the idea of seeing people who love money being at the helm of the leadership of the churches.

Amazingly, the only real differences that the people of the world really want to see as it relates to the people of the churches is that they don't want to see them live as lavishly as they do themselves as a leader or as a member of the churches.

Somehow, the more carnal minded thinking people don't quite believe that having faith in God; and having the necessary finances to live responsively should ever marry!

The people of the world are demonically affixed to believe that less to possibly none as it related to having any money, that it looks so much better on the people of faith that are indeed saved, sanctified, and Holy Ghost filled.

Faith in God is what dictates that we have the right to prosper and to increase above our own established ability to have the things that we could have on our own without the word of God and faith to guide us to allow for God to do it for us.

"Faith" knows where the need for finances is among all of the

faithful realm of them that trust in God; and when God will release them to us that continue to trust in God through faith for the financial need that we have.

Money is found in the stream of enticement to entangle us into the bondage of the world, entrapping us to the need of more and more money than even before.

Money has such the innate ability to run out much sooner that we were ready for it to be gone from our grip.

Even of those people who think of themselves to be financially secure, they are more insecure and vulnerable to the threat of losing every dime of their money by any means of which everyday life situations or the enemy deem suitable to take it from them.

Unfortunately, many in the churches have been deceived to believe that whatever they get themselves into, no matter how they might have gotten there, that they can pay their way out of it!

This is another reason that so many people are mad with the churches ability to manipulate an offering from the people who attend the church.

The realization is in the fact that people have come to understand that they need so much more than the money that they already have!

People are leaving the churches by a large percentage; as the pastors in many of the churches offer nothing more to the people than what they already bring with them; which is money!

I would not be too quick to embrace such an idea as to think of my money as being acceptable enough to move the omnipotent God to deliver me from the devastation of my life; especially when I am directly the cause of my own plight.

It doesn't take a rocket science to see and to understand that leadership of the churches are either lacking the power of God or that

they have never been endowed and connected to the power of God to enable the people of the churches to be saved set free and delivered from the power of sin and from the cares of this world.

Far too many seated as the leaders in the churches care more about the money what the people bring with them than they do for the actual person who brings the money.

God; has been reduced to the slot machine or to the likes of being the bigger ATM; even though righteousness and holy living is needed so much more, through the power of the shed blood of Jesus Christ.

Many people who are broke and financially depleted and downright living lowdown in poverty might not be in that predicament they are in had they been living for the Lord; saved and disciplined in the understanding of their finances.

God wants so much more for all of us than to just fill our bank accounts, He desires to fill us with His' spirit! The benefits of being filled with the spirit of God are realized only after we have been filled indeed.

It is not at all enough to talk about the spirit of God and to have corporate conversations about being filled with the spirit of God. Let faith out of the box and be filled with the Holy Ghost!

You will never understand the awesome benefit of having finances until you have received the Holy Ghost! There is not enough biblical teaching on having lots of money alone; as God has ordained so much more for all of us to experience as a result of finances in the Kingdom of God, as a faithful steward.

Every system of the world ought to be coming to the churches for the understanding of the spiritual security of finances, as result of tithing to release the power of God, rather than having all of the entities of the world coming into the churches to do workshop and to conduct seminars about money.

But thou shalt remember the Lord thy God: for it is he that giveth thee power to get wealth, that he may establish his covenant which he swear unto thy fathers, as it is this day.   The blessing of the Lord it maketh rich, and he addeth no sorrow with it.   {Deuteronomy 8:18; Proverbs 10:22}

Wealth ~ a large amount of money or possessions; the state of having plenty of money or possessions; an abundance or great quantity of something; economics the value of assets owned by a person or a community.

The abundance of wealth is not instantaneously amassed by acquiring or inheriting a heaping pile of money alone; else everyone who has suddenly become rich perhaps would never become broke ever again.

However, I am convinced that one will never get wealth or become wealthy without the aid of being financially structured over the process of time. The application of financial responsibility sets the platform standard for the balance of economic wealth.

Wealth rests on the principle foundation of practicing restraint from riotous spending to acquire unnecessary stuff simply because one has the money to afford it!

Spending intelligence requires the discipline of a much less inflated ego of feeling entitled to purchase and to have everything that money can buy, even though you are able to afford it with ease!

One may have the money to afford an Island that is located out in the middle of the ocean deserted away from the land; that island may be purchased at an affordable price for a rich individual; but only to sink and go under the water in a powerful storm, never to been seen again as a piece of land above the water.

Although the purchase of the piece of land might have been the

business of that which is to be determined as a risky financial transaction; it is of the better business mentality to never spend just for the protection against losing everything that has been spent, for a possible loss in totality.

A smart business mind would check the availability of the property's insurability for sake of securing the investment of the property should such a disaster from the surrounding water befall the land; whereas the buyer could recoup the investment preventing them from losing everything that had been spent on the purchase.

We must trust God in faith for finance; much more for the padlock security wall of faith to shut the ingrained fear of knowledge which comes with having a hefty respectful financial base.

Money alone of itself does not really equate to what is believed in America as financial security! We believe that those who have the great sums of money that they are at rest and at peace as a manner of conducting the management of their money as a regulated behavior of controll spending.

A closer examination of the rich people that refuse faith and God; reveals that they are frequently on the edges of committing suicide and losing their minds should something really drastic happen to their money?

Many of them have been completely robbed of their ability to sleep and to eat; their nervous systems have been shot to pieces, worrying over the stability of their money! We all need to have faith in God, but in some instances they need to have faith in God even more-so than some of the rest of us.

Job; was the richest man in the land of Uz; he had it all to lose, as he had gained it all through the uprighteousness of faith and of trust in God; in his whole heart.

When studying the book of Job; it is appearent that Job became

the target of Satan long before he wondered into the presence of God to enquire of Job. God knew already what was indeed tearing at the spirit of the devil concerning Job?

It wasn't Job's money and possessions that had the devil all bunched up and itching to attack the man of faith in God; it was the fact that Job had an allegiance to God that was indeed untouchable!

Naturally, his things and the stuff that he possessed were as vulnerable to the weather conditions of the present atmosphere. Take into consideration that there were also theives and robbers, and murderes in that day as well as they are here today.

Flood dissasters and fires are not brand new to this day and time of which we are living in now. However, even as God has kept us from those things although they happen frequently, God kept Job from them also.

It wore the enemy out that God would never allow for any of the dissasters to happen to Job or to any of his possessions! The devil uses people of tody's churches to say to people like Job; "You Ain't All That!"

But faith causes God to think that you are all of that and then some; You're His; you belong to Him!

The faithfulness of Job; caused God to place an hedge about all of the things and the stuff; even all about the family of Job; and of his servants.

Everything that Job had, the Lord placed and angelic hedge of protection around it and above it and even underneath it! The devil tears away at stuff in an attempt to get inside to tear you apart from believing and having faith in God.

He could not even tear in nor break in to Job's property or surroundings because of the hand of God.

The devil doesn't care about your stuff; he is not really concerned about your great sums of money and how it may be that you had gotten the money; not as many have been led to believe that he is indeed.

What bothers the devil indeed is whether or not you are going to trust God to keep it for you? The greatest determination of the enemy is to keep you in a knot emotionally, blocking your ability to stand faithfully trusting in God to be the keeper and the protector of everything that you have.

Satan; said to God concerning Job; "Take your hand away, remove your protection, and I will touch the faithful allegiance of the man! (paraphrasing) Satan wants always to cause the hand of God to be removed from you; he can never influence the hand of God and neither can he ever show God that He doesn't need to protect you; as he is the accuser of the brethren.

But, the devil is a sneaky adversary against you; he will make you to believe that God wants to take all of your money and give it away to the poor.

Faith allows for us to realize that we are simply trusted with the greater portions in this life; as they are not all given to us for just us! God simply says to us; hold this for me, and I will show you where to place it into the possessions of them that need it?

But, He also promises to us that if and when we give to the poor that we lend it to the Lord! By faith we know that God is ever watching over us to see and to know when we have obeyed Him through faith.

In ministry I posed the question to the people in attendance; I aked them; "what would you give, if you knew for a fact that God is going to give it all back to you and even more?"

In faith, whenever we give anything, we are giving it in God; but

we are giving it to God as well! Faith causes the combustible exchange between us and God: we pull the trigger and cause God to fire right back at us giving back to us!

We grew up in church singing that you can't beat God giving no matter how you try! The more you give the more He gives to you; just keep on giving because it's really true.

You can't beat God giving! Faith for sowing financial seeds silences the devil and the enemy of our realtionship with the Giving Father in Heaven; and it paralyzes all of his tactics and activities concerning our wealth!

The devil keeps people believing that the preachers at the churches are stretegic in taking all of the hard earned money that you have for themselves, and all other sorts of fallible tales?

But here's why: when Satan can convince you that you don't need to faithfully cover your finances and all of the things that you have acquired with your money through tithing and giving money to the churches and to charities, he is causing you to prevent God from placing His hands over you and your stuff to protect you and to keep you from Satan!

Yes; that's right! Satan can't stop the hand of God over your life and all that you possess; But, You can stop God and prevent Him from Keeping you! You have been worrying and too concerned about all of the wrong things for way too long.

Both the doctors and the morticians will get a great big chunck of your money as a result. Who will get all of the rest that is left behind; you may never know?

As an individual it is so important to know why it is that we are determined to spend the money that we have chosen to spend on whatever, whenever, and wherever it is that we will have chosen to spend it.

You have got to know why you are spending the money, and the effect that spending will have on your own financial status.

It is not at all the will of God for us to work all of our natural lives and have absolutely nothing to show for our labor. The scripture tells us that a father leaves and inheritance for his children; but what do you have to leave when you will have spent it all on your ability to purchase stuff, just because?

I have heard some people say that they were going to spend every dime of their money; they were not leaving anything for their children to fight over when they are gone from the presence of this world. That is the attitude of an individual that had never learned the respect of finances to the point of increasing to get wealth.

As I gain the understanding of the powerful driving force of having finances, I also want to leave the strength of financial understanding with my children in that they may never have to fight the financial struggles that I had to battle for the sake of making a better life for them.

It is my dream to leave them in better shape than I have ever been in, thus leaving this corner of my world much better than I found it to be when I realized that I was indeed here in it.

It is very important for a couple to work together on the finances and to make agreeable decisions as it relates to the financial stability of the household and for the family.

In faith they ought to sow seed together in agreement, and never behind one another's back. Too many people are doing the right thing but in the wrong manner.

Faith knows when we as a married couple are united as we ought to be; we don't get an undeserved pass to reap the benefit of faith as a couple when we are divided against one another praying in two separate directions concerning our finances, even the both of them

may have legitimate ideas and financial dreams.

While it is remarkable to have two individual dreamers to come together in marriage and living together in one domain; it can also become the detriment of the marriage for the two of them to aspire to activate their dreams from the balance of the very same financial base of the home.

Of course depending on the spending allotment of the finances, two dreamers of the same household can become successful in simultaneous business ventures.

I was once told by an individual who was indeed standing on the outside looking into my situation; that my problem wasn't getting and or of having money, but that it was indeed perhaps my own ability to manage my money?

My wife has an accounting degree from the University of Texas at Arlington. She and I often had the conversation of applying that kind of skill and of knowledge to account for and to handle somebody else's money, while not being accountable for the care of your own money.

It is just in this season of which that I am writing this book that I have been able to understand the spiritual but financial warfare that has taken place against us for years!

In no manner is faith in God to be determined as weakness or of some type of societal deficiency as it relates to financial growth stimulation and or even of the management of money.

This is a true statement; I have heard several statements made relative to the fact that those of us who faithfully believe, that we have God; but they that refuse to believe in God; they have all of the money?

They believe that God and faith is for the weak people who have

not applied the opportunities to acquire money in this society of living, and that perhaps that most people of faith are not smart enough to have the money that they have being the educated secular influences of the world.

Faith dictates that we communicate with the God of the universe to show us how to manipulate and to master our own money circumstances, through the proper financial respect and structure.

Faith opens us up to the knowledge from the Lord to know how to keep our blessings and to maintain them. It is never the intention of the Father in Heaven to give to us blessing of any kind that we ourselves never intend to keep and to maintain being faithful stewards who are indeed thankful to have received the blessings.

As the churches have taught us for many years now, they have taught us primarily how to give; God is clearly teaching us how to receive, and to have, and to be in control of our own financial conduct both in and on the outside of the church!

But, even more so as faithful members of the churches and of the society of which we live, the Lord wants for us to learn in our daily living to be respectful stewards as we go about our daily affairs.

Remember the scripture tells us that *"the blessing of the Lord it maketh rich"*; but I have found that a greater percentage of the people who have indeed been born again of the spirit of the Lord, that they have not been blessed to receive the true riches of the Lord for the simple reason of the fact they have been seeking the Lord and praying to Him for money instead of praying for finances!

God desires to give to you the money that need in abundance, even to the point of making you rich; but the finishing statement of that particular verse of scripture tells us that *"He addeth no sorrow with it."*

God knows through faith when we are indeed prepared and

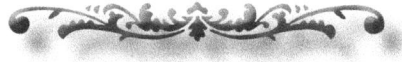

equipped for the money that He desire to give to us, in that we won't let the money divide us from the love of God; or to allow the spirit of the money to change us making us to become very sorrowful; but financially increased!

Perhaps so many people are being left with insufficient finances for the simple fact that their heart and their motives is indeed wrong; they are just waiting for the opportunity of having the right amount of money to carry out the hidden hideous motives of their hearts?

Check the motives of your heart; check the spirit of un-forgiveness down on the inside of you relative to the people who have done you wrong financially; the banks that might have cheated you out of your money; the utility companies that might have overcharged you; the mechanic who might have intentionally misled you to have so-called repairs done to your automobile that were never actually needed or perhaps never done?

Check your heart concerning the contractor who quoted you a certain price for home repairs or for remodeling; then changed the price on you fraudulently?

Perhaps alike I have done in past times; you sowed money into a ministry for a building fund for a new building project which never came to pass?

You're still angry because you've been made to feel that you paid for nothing, when in fact you were never supposed to be paying for anything you were sowing a financial seed!

Many people nowadays stand in a line to give money to a so-called prophet; only to realize that you have been deceived and lied to for the sake of getting your money; the prophecy never came to pass, for many years now, you're still waiting on the manifestations of the words given.

God can never be duped or tricked through faith, whatever is in the heart of an individual, whatever the true motive of the heart is, He knows!

You can't just expect for God to overlook all of the sludge in your heart; the anger, the spirit of revenge; you know that you plan to get those people back for what they had done to you concerning your money as soon as you get the money to do so!

I have been in churches when they started calling on people to come down to bring a certain amount of money to give for a seed;

But immediately I began praying and seeking the Lord; there were times that spirit of the Lord said to me no' that's not me; other times they were indeed led of the spirit of the Lord to have people sow a seed, the Lord did not have to speak to me because I did not have the money to sow the seed, I knew that it was not for me.

It is out of order for the people of the churches to tell the people in attendance to go over to someone else that you might know in the church to borrow the money; you and the Lord know that you are strapped and tapped out at the very end of your financial allowance for the month, and you won't be able to pay the money back as you might have been led to make the promise to do so.

People have lost friendships because they gave the money after borrowing it from another member in the congregation, but have been unable to pay it back; neither would the one who loaned the money forgive the debt!

Borrowing the money from that particular individual was never a faith transaction! Even in such a situation it became obvious that the individuals obedience to the minister was of faith in God. There is a difference in obedience, and obedience of faith in God; have faith in God; not the minister or your pastor!

Far too many games concerning money are being played in the

churches and in all the realm of those who faithfully believe in God.

People will say write three things on a piece of paper and seal it up in an envelope with a certain amount of money and sent to a particular ministry, by faith people are sending the money and the request.

But are now enraged with the idea of giving to the church as a result of not receiving anything that they had asked the Lord through the letter and the financial seed?

God neither blesses disobedience or anyone who is blatantly living disobediently to the scripture in their daily affairs, but on purpose.

Your state of disobedience ought to let you in on the fact that you are being deceived and duped to give your money.

Money itself is always money; however the motives that people have for the usage and for their need of money along with the systemic atmosphere of money; describe the idea cloud of spending, banking, and or even investing.

The allowed atmospheres of money in our society are either corrupt or they are seen as honest and ethical.

Money falls into the definitions relative to how it is either used or misused; while the money never changes in any society; how it is that we choose to use the money changes from day to day.

Chapter 14

"You Can't Fool Faith!"

But let him ask in faith, nothing wavering. For he that wavereth is like a wave of the sea driven with the wind and tossed. For let not that man think that he shall receive anything of the Lord. A double minded man is unstable in all of his ways. [James 1:6-8]

"Faith Stands In the Truth about Us"

Have you ever taken notice of how it is that people rather enjoy being deceptive in all of their living practices, especially to the church; but on the other hand they totally despise being deceived?

The blood of deceptive individuals seems to boil at the very notion that someone else had been dishonest with them.

Some way or another people seem to have been led to believe that it's actually okay to mislead others just as long as they themselves are never misled and deceived?

Many people have confessed to having been washed in the blood of Jesus and filled with the Holy Ghost; they say that their lives have been changed; but it is only a short span before the truth of their deception is revealed.

Too often, the people of the churches no longer have the time to know the truth about the people anymore.

The leadership of the churches has often fallen short at knowing whether people have truly repented to God; the church refused to follow up with them even after the deceivers had been exposed and forgiven for their deception by the people at the church.

Faith knows the real truth about you at all times, and it knows when you haven't given up on the idea of being deceptive. While you can never fake the presence of God; you can be deceiving and quite deceptive in the presence of the faithless and to those who have no discernment working on the inside of them.

As you make~believe; pretending as if you have just met Jesus Christ; or as if you are sensitive to the presence of the Lord?

In the Pentecostal churches where people dance in the spirit and maybe run around the sanctuary in the presence of the Lord; I have witnessed people take to the aisles of the churches to act like everybody else, but of course only to come up short of true praise!

The spiritual plight of many people who have been in the church for the balance of their days on the earth, who profess to be of the body of Christ; without being cognizant of the truth of the spirit which works within themselves; from what should be realized as the new found life in Christ Jesus, they have thought themselves to be hiding and sheilding some things about them-

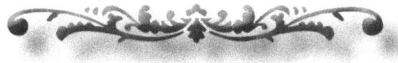

selves away; yet they remain the same as they always were being ignorant that you can't hide from God; or fool faith in God!

They come forward to present themselves as if they are ready to receive Christ in their lives, but they are totally confused and unlearned perhaps of the fact that they cannot have both sin and the savior simultaneously!

So many people want both this and that; they want Jesus Christ; and Satan; they want peace and warfare!

Teaching should clarify and give freedom in the mind and in the spirit~man, relative to the truth about having faith and being active as a result of the faith that is truly on the inside of an individual.

Having Christ in one's life, in an effort to be changed, every individual will have to come to a consensus to make a clear decision of which one it will be!

God has dealt to every man the measure of faith; so as the questions are often why did God give to every man, woman, boy, and to every girl this measure of faith; too often it is overlooked and passed as a thing that everyone just simply ought to know.

The truth is that not everyone has been made aware of the truth about faith.

The truth is; there is no one on the face of the planet earth, who has Jesus in their heart without having received Him; just as the bible says that they are to receive Him.

A few simple things that I will say to everyone that reads this, is that; to receive Jesus means that you have rejected the world and Satan!

Receiving Jesus also means that you are letting go of every~thing in your heart and mind that would keep you from receiv~

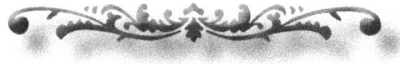

ing Jesus whole heartedly! It means that your determination is to repent; which means to change direction in the way and the manner of which you are living, thinking, and doing things in your life on a daily basis.

Most carnal minded people of the local churches would want to begin arguing right about here; trying to justify themselves about the things that they are not doing that are wrong?

People; begin to try and to justify their choices of living, and their reasons for not reading the bible or praying as they should. They begin talking about all of their charitable deeds of giving food and clothing, and even the times that they have shared their money with the poor and the less fortunate.

To listen to them talk, you soon hear them saying out of their own mouths, that they have got their lives all figured out! Yet there is something missing in their lives that they can't seem to get a hold of on their own recognizance, all by themselves!

The problem often come in when people "cry uncle" at the cares of this world and of this life determining to give in and to give up!

They bow to the fact that there are simply somethings that they can't do for themselves. They are not going to be able to just say well forget about it and hang it up; things need desperately to be done that they can't fine the strength or the ability to do for themselves!

The souls of mankind cry out for God every day in so many ways; but because of rebellion and sin, people are filled with controlling spirits which keeps them bound to the things which have kept them and will keep them separated from the love and relationship with God; through Jesus Christ.

God knows that we all need Him; you know that you des-

312

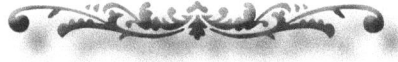

perately need Him; your life is about to spiral, if it is not already spiraling out of control.

And just in case you have never been informed, faith knows that the reason that your spirit-man is not at all fulfilled, is because you have rejected the giver of faith through the only begotten son of God; Jesus Christ!

At every instance that you try and attempt to avoid accepting Jesus Christ as Lord and Savior of your own life; faith is aware of your choice, and actual choosing.

Faith sees you and know when you've reluctantly walked the aisles of the church supposedly to give your heart to God; but vowing within yourself to walk right back out to the life that you had before you ever came to the church.

Even after you will have made confession out of your mouth, my friend; faith is constantly aware of you and your actual condition; faith always know just where you are in your life.

But, with no determination to change or to spiritually connect with the savior to really have anything change in your life; faith is fully aware of whom you are; still!

Faith knows just what chased you to the altar of God in the first place; knowing that it wasn't at all your love and desire for God through His written word and the selfless sacrifice of His son on the cross of Calvary.

Faith knows that it was the fear of almost losing your life out there in the world living in sin and total disobedience to the word and to the will of God!

You ran in as a safety measure to ensure that you might not have to die and go to hell; it was again your determination to control the outcome of your life, disregarding the fact that you

will still be judged before the Lord after you die anyway!

You will never hear the one, unmistakable voice of God; speaking to your heart through the distraction of the confusion that you fail to silence! As I go forth to minister to you, my purpose for speaking is to open your minds and your spirit to faith so that the Father in heaven can speak to your heart.

Moses; said to the people of Israel; *"The Lord our God; is One Lord!"[Deuteronomy 6:4]* How do you propose to distinguish the "One True Voice" of the Lord with so many other voices going on in your head?

As you stand to declare an end to your life as a sinner and to receive Jesus Christ as your savior; faith hears the different voices of the past conversation questioning the authenticity and need for being saved from sins that arise as you purport to tune in to hear Him speak to your heart.

See, faith is always aware of which voice it is that you are listening to, because faith knows the voice of God; since before the igniting of both the entrance of the beginning of time and of the creation and the natural process of forming man from the dust of the ground.

My friend you need to understand and never forget this fact for as long as God lives; faith will silence hearing your voice before it ever ignores and fails to listen to the voice of God!

It is utter deception to think that you have the ability to instruct the faith on the inside of you that doesn't exclusively belong to you!

The faith on the inside of every man belongs to God, and it has already been instructed by and through the written word of God; regardless of your arguments on the fact that man was used to pen the written word!

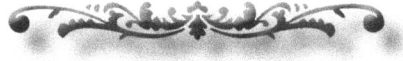

{Psalms 119:89 ~Forever, O Lord, thy word is settled in Heaven}

Faith was even in the garden of Eden; already knowing the voice of God; as people are so mis-taught, or rather under-taught as to the real truth of what it was that got Adam and Even removed from the garden?

It wasn't just the act of actually eating from the tree of knowledge of good and evil which was the very object of the word of God's commandment; that being the very reason that the actual fruit that was eaten is not biblically mention nor described.

It was that they both chose to listen to another voice of reasoning against God's instruction, which was and is still today, the wrong voice!

God; had already said; but then Satan comes along having influenced the serpent's subtle skills to beguile the woman, and said something else!

I have come to realize that in this life we will have many influences both good for us and often many bad influences trying to lead the way for us to adulthood; and to both failure and for success.

People; written articles; and broadcast journals; all of which our parents might both approve of or would definitely have disapprove of had they any knowledge of the fact that those individuals and things were attempting to persuade us in any form?

Once we have been influenced to do certain things we will never have to be persuaded to do them ever again; it is to the likings of the lessons that we had been taught which keep on teaching us.

At best, if at all, we have to be persuaded never to do those things ever again; many times having to face stiff penalties and

dire consequences!

The greatest gift given to mankind upon the face of the earth, in my own opinion, is the gift of teaching!

So many people of the Five-fold ministries of the Kingdom of God; seem to rather dodge the opportunity to teach; they choose rather to preach very entertainingly shouting out loud to the very top of their voices just in the right tune to the organ, and or to give flattering words of preferred prophetic utterances?

I have seen it for myself {They [pro-phe̱l-Lie}; they seem to feel as if teaching belittles them in the eyes of the people of the churches; as if they are not high enough on the ministry scale when they can't tune the people of the churches up for the coming week?

The lack of teaching is the actual reason that people worldwide; are throughout the churches feeling as if even God is fooled by them?

Many times even after the teacher will have dismissed the class, the lessons taught will continue teaching us for many years even after we will have long since finish the course of that particular classroom assignment of studying the word of God.

Many of our teachers have passed on to their graves awaiting their eternal judgment and place of everlasting assignment, but the lessons they taught us still yet lingers fresh in the spirit of our minds, as we will never forget the things they taught us.

The only reason that we are even able to learn other things and even to mentally grasp greater interrogative measures of thought on things more enlightening to our minds is the direct result of the things that we had already been taught and received in our minds.

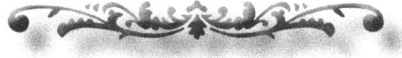

"What's In Your Closets?" "Faith Knows!"

Nowadays, more and more people are determined to mesh the truthful reality of the church of God in Christ Jesus; and the sinfully existing ungodly spirit and system of the world into one sphere of acceptance.

As if God who created the world never knew the difference in the world's influence and Satan, and what He gave to the world in His own begotten son through the power of the written word of the Holy Bible and faith.

Voices have the power of influence and with every conversation the voice or voices speaking to your understanding, can bring forth an influential grasp upon your thinking and of your mind causing you to do or to behave a certain way even against the better judgment of your own will and desires.

Faith understands the reasons that you have behaved the way that you do, in that it is aware of the things that you have hung up in the closets of your mind; you've got too many hang ups that you're okay with!

You have more of a relationship with the hang ups in your closet than you will ever have with the savior unless you get delivered and be filled with the "Holy Ghost."

Faith is also aware as to whether or not those things are locked away and locked down in the closet of your minds awaiting deliverance, or if and when they are allowed to roam freely through the process of thinking within your own reasoning, being the things which determine the choices of your life for you?

Many people approach God through the teaching of, or simply through the purported suggestive worldly ideas of what if, or even if God exists, having many contrary things suppressed and deeply embedded in the back of their minds, holding them

there as an alternative option to choose from, just in case they change their mind on choosing Christ.

I do believe that as the church we are consistently handicapping the people offering them opportunities to try Christ rather than encouraging them to receive Him as the only Lord and Savior! We should be vigorously challenging people to let God try you!

We were the ones broken and in non-working order in our lives; in need of the all working God to touch our lives to change the order of things in our lives to make it right.

We say to people; won't you just give God a chance; as if to suggest that God just may not work for all people? God can do everything; but fail! God; works!

The all-conquering God; never misses nor fails when it comes down to changing the lives of any people; He can do it!

His formula for us being helped and changed is that you come to Him through the eternally manifested word of Jesus Christ; who lived and died on the cross, was buried in the grave, but rose from the dead and the grave on the third day; having conquered death, hell and the grave; and with all power in His hand!

He will never be dead ever again; as a man on the earth, it is appointed only once for a man to die and after the death comes the judgement. Jesus Christ; was and will always be the eternal flame of God's Living Life; burning with Truth, Grace, and Love!

Sometimes the problem is the former teachings of the other forms of religious practices that you were forced to adhere to as a child coming up, that you have locked away in your mental closets that you plan to keep no matter what, as instructed by your past teacher and instructors, that are totally wrong according to the written word of God.

318

Faith; is staring right at those things that have already been erected as the road map to get you wherever it is that you will ever need to go in life and a wall against the truth about the almighty everlasting God; that you had chosen before coming to Christ.

The wrong teachings are detrimental to our future welfare as we tend to follow after the things that we might have been taught.

Many people have been taught to never ever read the Holy Bible, neither to enter into any of the churches which believe and adhere to the biblical instructions written therein.

Regretfully, I have lived to meet people who grew up in homes where it was truly forbidden, having dire consequences as a punishment, to ever speak the name of Jesus under that roof or on the premises of that home or place of living!

It takes the agreement of your own choosing to do a certain thing, then it requires for you to develop the practical habit to continue that particular behavior.

Faith knows that some of the things that you have attached yourself to were even done through blood rituals and the pronouncement of covenant vows and demonic chants selling your souls to Satan!

Faith knows the many attempts that you might have made to free yourself, only failing at every attempt being reminded of the promises that you made to that vice; saying out your own mouth to it, that you would be there for life!

You have no real way of knowing what spirit is working in you except the spirit of the Lord reveal them and truthfully make you aware, through faith. Even in an occult where you may have been given the demonic rite to choose which spirit, or

spirits that you would allow yourself to in-house in your own spirit and mind; people are always deceived and lied to, as Satan is the father of every lie and he cannot change or be changed; therefore you've been lied to! But without the spirit of the living God; you can never know it!

Faith knows about all of those little gods that you have on the inside of you in the closet that are fighting and struggling to be ruler and lord of your living experience; as they could never be lord of your life because life itself belongs to the everlasting Eternal God who gave life to all beings. Life belongs to God for-ever; you might as well let Him be the Lord of your life!

"Faith Knows; Who You Love!"

Through the scriptures we are made aware that faith works by love. But not just because we have a love for a certaing thing or for any certain persons; but faith works by the "Love of God."

It is that way perhaps for the fact that faith is directly in contact with God; who cannot be tricked or deceived, as God knows every-thing that there is to ever know. Since God knows; faith also know and is always made aware of the things which concern you.

Faith knows what love affair you are intertwined into, whereas you are attemping to motivate faith to move God to manifest the de-sires of your heart.

So many people are determined to sway the meaning of the word of God to be agreeable with the desires and the comprehensive rea-soning for wanting the things that are burning on the inside of them.

Of course, many things are not necessarily a need, they are just things that we want and are intrigued to see if we can move God to give those things to us on the strength of what we are calling faith anyway?

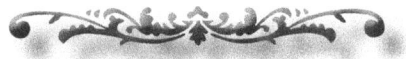

You need to know and to understand that faith knows when your heart is not even turned towards God's written word. In these present generations of so-called faithful people of the churches, we see people who are indeed still in love with the world!

The people of the world; the sociable excitement and entertainment in the world; and with the free inhibited lifestyles of the people in the world, that refuse to be ruled and governed by the writing of the scripture.

Your heart is at issue when you are holding on to the ways of doing things and of obtaining things using methods that are outside of the written word of God. I have learned that we have trust in the things that we love!

It only stands to reason the we have developed a sense of love having been introduced to the ways of the world firstly before coming to the Lord to be saved.

We are most familiar to the former ways of the flesh and of the sinful ways of the world's influence, for which we have been in the practice of employing those methods since long before being made knowledgeable of having faith in God.

Love not the world, neither the things that are in the world. If any man love the world, the love of the Father is not in him. For all that is in the world, the lust of the flesh, and the lust of the eyes, and the pride of life, is not of the Father, but is of the world.
[I John 2:15-16;]
Jesus said unto him, Thou shalt Love the Lord thy God with all thy heart, and with all thy soul, and with all thy mind.   [St. Matthew 22:37]

We have no real problem knowing that the Father in heaven loves us; the scripture tells us over and over again that we are the objects

of God's affection and Love; everything that God has done, He did it for us. However, we struggle to know and to be sure that everything that we are doing, that it is all for the glory of God!

It is a commandment of the Lord that we let our lights shine so that men can see our good works, which glorify our Father in Heaven. We intend to be seen doing the things that we do, but our intellectual designs are geared towards just being seen by other people.

More often than not, people are not even thinking of the Lord when doing things; people never even give a thought about what the Lord is saying concerning their deed? People want to do what they want to do period and regardless of how is going to effect them and how it will have an affect on others as well.

The fact is that people are in love with their own desires and their plans for the way that they have chosen to live and to do things in their lives on a daily basis. You have to Love God in order to even have a desire to develop in your own heart, soul, and spirit that you are going to do things God's way.

Most people are hungup on the fact that they had been doing things in ways that are totally against the written word of God; in their minds those ways worked just fine for them, even though they have suffered immensley, having experienced the most dreadfully painful circumstances and situations that living wrong and foul can bring to them, as result of their choices.

We live in societies now that strongly suggest the we educate our minds to think scientifically and technically; people's minds are so full of the world's knowledge and ways of thinking, that they have deceived themselves to believe that they can out think God?

"Faith Knows What You Are Feeling"

My God the pain and the suffering that so many are carrying on

the inside of themselves. People are become masters of covering up the feelings and the emotions that rest deeply within them.

But, they are usually hiding having learned to camoflague the truth about them from most of the people that they have come into contact with, for the fact that it's been proven that other people can't always be trusted with the most painful details about another individual.

Other people feel that they have to share what you are feeling on the inside of you with other people even though you might have asked for them to keep the matter confidential?

As it relates to feelings and the emotions that are commonly natural to us, we want other people to know what we are feeling on a consistant basis, but we don't want our feelings to be turned and used against us!

Sometimes we may think thet other people in the churches are really stronger and more spiritually mature?

They seem to have forgotten what it's like to be in pain, or to be in agony for any number of reasons?

The idea of spiritual warfare has been totally wiped out of their minds! They can't imagine why you would be experiencing the spiritual, physical; or even the financial attack that has been sent against you?

I am not an advocate of people suffering in silence, as we are built to only suffer for just so long, and then we need a remedy and a solution to the cause of the pains that we are experiencing. So many people are deciding more and more on taking the matter into their own hands.

They are determining to solve the matter which concern them in their own signatured manner, but outside of the manner prescribed

in the written scripture? Too often as of late; their chosen methods for ridding them of the pains and the suffering has been suicide!

People feel many different things on the inside of themselves that calls for the need of explanations and comprehensive illustrations to imagine and to pictorialize the truth in their natural minds.

Their belief is that their own imagination can and will produce suitable explanations to make sense of the written word of God.

Only; people need desperately to understand that imagination at best only produce feelings and stirs the emotions of an individual. The problem is that feelings cancel out faith; faith canceled out can not allow an entrance into the presence of God.

Whenever we find ourselves outed and blocked from entering into the presence of God; we will also find that we have been set to the outer realms of the blessings and the miraculous power of God!

As powerful as faith is indeed, the enemy has still found ways to deceive those who aspire to faith, and believing in the eternal presence and reality of God.

If things were left to feelings alone people would not have a chance with God; as it is often feelings that we have to fight off and work on stilling our feelings and silencing the negative sirens of the emotional alarms that come upon us when we need to get in touch with God the very most.

People feel the spirit of depression and suppression, and even the spirit of oppression may come with the alerting of a feeling of utter hopelessness; because so many people are accustom to feelings and emotions, the blessings of the Lord have also been given the assignment of feelings of euphoria and excitement in the spirit of their mins.

However, not always are excited people thankful to the Lord for

the blessings that they have received; they are just emotionally built up on the inside of themselves.

Feelings are dangerous, in that they can cause an individual to believe and to emotionally embrace things about God that are untrue and out of character; according to the scripture.

The trials which come upon us are not intended to make us to feel anything in particular, they are come however to cause us to better know and to understand the ways that God cares for us, and how God operates according to us.

Through the lack of teaching and erroneous teachings in the churches, many people are allowed to feel as if God in many ways is unfair towards them. The natural normal things which come upon us on the earth are too often the results of our own natural and spiritual negligence!

Clearly we are at fault and the reasons that so many things have happened in our lives, it has not been God at all who is the one responsible for most of the disappointing occurences in our lives. I have discovered and learned that real true faith in God never disappoint us; nor does faith ever let us down.

Faith knows that many people prefer to rely and to totally depend on whatever we are able to feel. It's all about the tangible physical things that most people choose to trust in; but they also rust and corrupt in those same feelings.

People need to be in control of the outcomes of their lives, they need to be able to take the credit and be able to say that they are responsible for their own lives in every way.

Just because an individual my feel that they are responsible for their lives, doesn't make it to be so. If not faith; there is always someone else that just may be responsible for the status our your life, rather you'd like to think of that as the truth or not.

Those who came before us in the earth are in a sense responsible for our lives in one way or another?

As simple as it is, we would not even be on the face of the planet had it not been for our parents; and for their parents; and on and on all of the way back to Adam and Eve in the Garden of Eden.

Life is a setup and it cannot be left to the control of feelings and emotions, as there is too many erroneous spirits of the mind which trigger and set them off, causing our minds and our senses to steer us away from the written word of God in the earth, turning our heart away from God; the Father in Heaven.

Many people have their prayers hindered and often unanswered as result of their own intrusive feelings and emotions that assassinate faith and trust in the Lord Jesus Christ.

The need to touch our Lord Jesus Christ in prayer through faith, will call for the need to silence whatever we are feeling at the time that we engage ourselves in prayer.

Our mouths will be saying one thing in prayer, but our feelings and our emotions will be having another conversation altogether, on the inside of us.

This is utter confusion and the total annihilation to the expected answer to prayer. Check yourselves while you pray and see if you are even talking to the Father in Heaven; don't allow for your feelings and emotions to set your prayers off course unintentionally altering the destination of your prayer.

Faith is right here with us right now, even as we open our mouths having begun to pray; but your own feeling and your emotions will literally hinder you and stop the connection to the faith that is positioned and standing right in the midst of your desire to pray to the Father.

The bottom-line is that you can never and you will never, ever fool faith! As we have discovered in this book; you may not have known or have understood what faith in God indeed is; it doesn't cancel out the fact that faith knows what and who you are, even when you don't know yourselves!

Faith is never clueless or shut up away back in the dark concerning the true purpose and the factual connection between us and our God who created Humanity. We belong to God; thus God gave us the ability to be reconnected with Him since the fall of man back in the Garden of Eden.

Hebrews 11:1 ~ NOW, (attention; hello; come to yourselves; the matter is on this wise; look up from where you are and stop what you are doing; IMMEDIATELY AND ALL AT ONCE; INSTANTLY)

FAITH IS the SUBSTANCE ~ (the Kingdom Systen in Real Time of every second on the second; minute by minute; hour by hour; day by day; week by week; month by the month; year by the year; battle upon battle; experience to experience; revelation to revelation; the provision; the solutions; the healing; the protectin; the guidance; the care for you and of all that is yours; the transforming powerful ability to bring forth all that you can ask for, that you think that you know that God will do for you)

of THINGS HOPED FOR, ~ (the things that you ultimately expect from God; and only from God! The things that sink deeply into the realm of the spirit, even deeper than you could ever imagine in your heart, and in the swiftness of the thinking processes of your minds)

the EVIDENCE ~ (the gathered, collected particles of the hidden things of the spirit realm that come into the reality of the NATURAL REALM OF HUMANITY; for

the benefit to show forth the factual truth that God AN-SWERS and RESPONDS TO FAITH)

of THINGS NOT SEEN. ~ (even though you might have thought of the things that you desired deeply in your heart and called it forth in your minds according to the scripture; that which has been believed for and trusted that God would do them, was yet invisible and stayed in the realm of the Light of the Lord)... WTJR. 2018

Faith calls the things of the hidden spirit realm into view and into focus; whereas we could not see them even though they were indeed in existence, but in the invisible spirit realm in God; initially. When we need faith, and however it is that we may need for faith to work for us; and wherever it may be that we are; faith is already available.

Knowing how to activate faith, and activily responding to the need to activate the power of faith is what we need in an effort to see things change right before our very eyes.

God is real; as we approach the throne of God to enquire of Him; we must never approach the throne only believing, questioning and guessing; but we must come before the Lord Knowing that He Is in-deed God!

NOW, FAITH IS................................. NOT FOOLED!

Chapter 15

"Faith; When God is Silent?

But the Lord is in his holy temple: let all the earth keep silence before him. [Habakkuk 2:20]
Be silent, O all flesh, before the Lord: for he is raised up out of his holy habitation. [Zechariah 2:13]

"Calling; but, no answer; searching; but, can't find Him?"

Faith is that one thing that the enemy is consistently trying to shake loose from us, if not that he is able to shake us loose from faith.

Let's always remember that faith is the inner-connectivity that fastens us to the almighty God in Christ Jesus, through the power of the Holy Ghost we are sealed in and covered to the likeness of a welded connection.

That makes us a most formidable opponent to the powers of

darkness in the earth's realm.

So whenever we are challenged to believe that our greatest connection has abandoned us or otherwise gone silent on us, those are the times that we should immediately tap into faith to hear the silent message of faith in God through worshiping because we know that it is not possible. As immature children of the Lord; there may indeed be times that we feel that God has gone silent on us.

Time lapses are not allowed, pouting and sulking over a possible disconnect, refusing to talk to the Father in prayer because we are caught away in our feelings!

To defeat you possibly in one of the most crucial times of a need, it only takes a the employment of your feelings and your emotions to make the next decisions of your life, to signal the enemy that you have totally lost your focus on the Lord.

God; is quite frequently quoted, as saying to us; "I will never leave you or forsake you!"

Instead of using those words against God for an opportunity to complete a sinful ungodly behavioral act of the flesh, step out of your feelings and stand right back smack dab in the middle of faith understanding that it is never about a feeling but always about faith; never abandon faith!

Even when you might not hear Him speaking to you in a trial, or in a time of needing direction, or clarity; use those words to know that in spite of all that is enveloping you at the moment; God is still there! Use the assurance of those words to be the covenanted promise of God!

Dig a bit deeper to receive the message of His silence, because He is saying something to you indeed! We will get into that a little later on in the chapter.

Many of the silly little attacks on the almighty ability of our God's love for us and His will to see that we make it to the assigned destination of our own purpose in this life, is nothing more than an attempt to shrink God to an inferior image too small to testify of His omnipotence, and to His extreme incomparable greatness.

Remember; we were taught that God holds the power of this world in the very palm of His hand which gives us the indication that His vastness is greater than anyone can even imagine.

Of all of the things that I have read in the scripture concerning the attributes of God; shrinkage is not at all one of them!

Among the denominational spectrums and of the religious communities at large; one of the greater arguments is that God doesn't speak to mankind anymore; for which the churches heads are willing to debate this argument among each other!

It is an argumental debate that can indeed be solved on our knees, if we simply will ourselves to prayerfully test the theory; thus giving God the right to indeed still speak to humanity; but they must all tune in to the spirit frequency of the Holy Ghost speaking to us!

It's not even fair to say that God is silent; when in fact so many of the people are being taught inadvertently not to even consider listening for Him; since He doesn't talk or speak audibly.

Many of the churches are determined to convince people that there just can't be a possible reality of hearing an audible voice of God speaking anyway; so skip the idea of God speaking to them. God has been speaking to the world outwardly through the written word of the Holy Bible.

It is my determination to be fair to our God in this dialogue; as so many people have charged God so unfairly in accusing Him of not speaking to them.

God does yet speak to us here in the earth; He has indeed finished creating the earth and all that is in the earth; but He has not finished the purpose for which everything had been created!

God is so much wiser and intelligent than any of us will ever be; He is not going to struggle to speak with humanity with all of the noise pullution and confusion of which voices of authority to listen to?

Many refuse reluctnatly to teach the people that God speaks internally to each of us; on the inside where the spirit of God resides.

As it is, many of the people are confused, not at all knowing what to expect from God just in case He does speak to them?

It is not our position to try and to tell God how to speak to us when He does speak. If God is indeed silent, it is for sure that the bible is chocked full of the reasons that he may not be speaking on certain conditions? Check the word of God to know the truth!

They say that He will only speak to your heart, although ones heart may be corrupt and wicked filled with un-forgiveness and hatred; people's hearts are filled with racial indifferences; they feel that they have a right to judge other people based on their assumption of another person's guilt of sinfulness; or the color of their skin?

God knows the condition of our hearts, and while it just may be that our hearts have muted our hearing, disabling us from being able to hear the voice of God speaking to us; God is yet speaking.

It is our own responsibility to keep our hearts right before the Lord.

The heart is deceitful above all things, and desperately wicked: who can know it? I the Lord search the heart, I try the reigns, even to give every man according to his ways, and

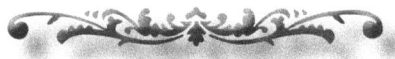

according to the fruit of his doings.   [Jeremiah 17:9-10;]
Create in me a clean heart, O God; and renew a right spirit
within me.   [Psalms 51:10;]
Keep the heart with all diligence; for out of it are the issues
of life.   [Proverbs 4:23;]

The spiritually mature in the faith; who understand that God will speak to your spirit; they have been spiritually enlightened through the indwelling power of the Holy Ghost and the truth in the written word of God.

It is never the intention of those who may indeed be more spiritually aware than others to cause them to feel inferior, their intentions are to inform them of fact that you have got to get into the spirit by firstly allowing the spirit of the Lord to be at rest on the inside of you.

God is a spirit, and they that worship Him must worship
Him in spirit and in truth.   {St. John 4:24}

You should never approach the idea of speaking with God from the standpoint of a conversation as you would speak to a member of your family; or for some people, in the same manner as they would speak with their animals and their pets. You must understand that God is a spirit!

Being ignorant of the spirit or of the working order of the spirit will most definitely hinder your ability to communicate with the Father in the spirit.

No liar can ever come before the Lord demanding that God speak with them relative to their dilemma. Neither should sinners approach God seeking to have His to regulate the condition of their wicked alliances?

For an instance: an adulterous man or woman should never seek God to manipulate their adulterous love to leave their spouse to

come and to be with them!

In such situations you have silenced the voice of God; but the word of God is yet speaking loudly; insistently!

Most people believe that the only truth necessary in coming before the Lord is in acknowledging that He is Lord; however we must be truthful about our individual status.

Knowing the truth about me is one thing, as we all know the truth about ourselves; but our willingness to acknowledge the truth about ourselves is another thing altogether.

The prophet Isaiah; when he came into the presence of the Lord, he began to acknowledge his present status to the Lord. He said unto the Lord;

………..*"woe is me! For I am undone; because I am a man of unclean lips, and I dwell in the midst of people of unclean lips: for mine eyes have seen the King, the Lord of host."*
{Isaiah 6:5}

The prophet Isaiah never wasted any time, immediately he began to acknowledge the real truth about himself. Of course God already knows the truth about you; but He must be assured that you know that truth about you also.

Stop trying to force God to communicate with the unfaithful fragmented confused shell of the person that you supposed to be.

God know who you're supposed to be; but He sees who you really are! God desires to talk with you, and not just a raggedy image of which it is that you think you are!

The make believe you can never talk to the all true and real God! While you're struggling to know the real from the true; God knows truth firstly; fake and that which is indeed false stands out in light of the truth as that of being sore rotting and exposed having no real

right to even exist in the presence of God!

What is it then? I will pray with the spirit, and I will pray with the understanding also: I will sing with the spirit, and I will sing with the understanding also.
{I Corinthians 14:15}

There is a spiritual language dialogue that can only be acquired through the indwelling power of the spirit itself. No one will ever be able to teach you the language of the spirit, because you have to exit your mental grasp to the understanding of the natural realm to enter into the free uninhibited flow of the spirit realm.

As we are taught in the word of God we are made aware of the truth and the love that God have for us. Seeking to know spirit alone of itself can cause you to be spiritually deceived and entangled with the spirit of darkness not knowing the word and the spirit of God's Love.

God is Love; the spirit of God is Love; the love of God is spirit; so as you enter into the love of God; you will find yourself likewise entering into the spirt of God.

The apostle Paul spent a lot time conveying to us that, that which is flesh is flesh; that which is spirit is spirit. Even as of this late generation of so-called smart and intelligent believers, people are still struggling trying to scrunch the two realities in to one existence.

It's like trying to combine the visible and the invisible into the same reality. You will never be able to see what was never there, and neither can you make that which is there in the natural disappear. And if you could make a thing disappear, you could never deny the fact that it was there at first.

You will never be able to combine hearing and silence into the very same instance or the very same reality; but neither will you be able to combine verbally speaking and silence!

In order to speak you must open your mouth and begin to maneuver your jaw, using your teeth and your tongue, and your vocal chords.

Silence is going to require you to close your mouth, and to still the movement of your jaws, also stopping the vibration of the sound which flows from your vocal chords.

Many people are in trouble as they attempt to enter into the realm of the spirit; they are determined to deny the fact that God said it from the beginning; whatever it might have been! God; said; "let there be" and it is; to this very day!

God said; it was good, and it is so! On the other hand; lots of people are consistently speaking in error, saying to other people that God said; when He has not said anything at all!

Sometimes my friend, it is not that God is silent, as much as it is that He was never even speaking at all during the times of which you might have decided to listen for His voice!

My love for you as a child of the most high God goes very deeply into my own heart and my spirit; so much so that I endeavor to encourage you to let go of that place of doubt and deception; thinking and believing that God is ignoring you.

Release the anger and the disappointment of what might have appeared to have been the failed connectivity in the fellowship of the spirit; God Loves You!

Any reader of this book can say that they agree with the messages over the pulpit, but are you yet aware of exactly where it is that your hearing is located?

How do you hear the Lord speaking to you? When you hear a voice speaking to you, are you spiritually discerning of the Lord's voice; are you sure that it is even the voice of the Lord?

The enemy is consistently vying for your attention on a daily basis; are you watchful to know when it is the voice of Satan trying to deceive you and to make you feel as if it is God?

Sinful; wicked; unbelieving and doubtful people are not going to be awarded the benefit of having God speak to them in an open dialogue.

Only through the written word of God are we truly made aware as to what to expect from God as He speaks to us.

As a matter of the fact, when we read the bible we see where God indeed have spoken and will speak because He does speak; however, His method of speaking is often hinged on the purpose for which He is speaking to a person.

Repentance changes our status before the Lord, which also changes our eligibility for being awarded the open access through faith in God; to hear the Lord speak to us, in any and every way that He choose to speak to us!

I have heard a strong message admonishing the people in attendance to hear the voice of God speaking to them, but almost immediately they switch and begin telling the people not to expect an audible voice from the Lord.

I listened as they made an attempt to suggest what the people should be listening for when God speaks. To this day I still can't tell you what it was that they were trying to convey to the people in the churches. They appeared to have been confused themselves, which was coming through very clear in their message.

Many of the churches argue the idea of Apostles; Prophets; who are the direct mouth-pieces of God to speak to the existing body of believers.

Although the bible speaks of both true prophets and of false

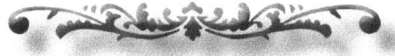

prophets; they embrace the idea of false prophets and totally disregard true called apostles and prophets of God.

So, to many of the so-called believers, God is always silent in all manner and expression of His eternal being; simultaneously they agree that God doesn't change.

This kind of rhetoric is spewed out to the people of the churches while they are admonished to adhere to faith in God.

It is no wonder that so many of the people in the churches are totally confused and scrambled like a mixed bag of nuts concerning faith and being able to hear the voice of God.

People are sitting in the midst of the move of God in the worship service, but they are doubtful as to whether, what they are seeing; the miracles of healing and deliverance, casting out demons; if it is even real or some sort of an optical illusive trick show.

Thank God; that; "AIN'T NOBODY GOD, BUT GOD!"

If I were God for even a moment or two, I would not speak to so many of the people who doubt that I am even who I Am! He that comes to God must believe firstly, that He is God! *[Hebrews 11:6]*

That's right, people doubt Him, but they want to hear from Him; they prefer to test God much rather than to be tested by God. In all actuality, people prefer to be heard by God, they don't really have a true desire to hear God; or to hear from God by the way of His prophets and apostles.

Whenever people come before God they want God to believe that they are real, while they doubt that He is even real and true. They doubt His existence, but pray mightily He will believe in the need to fix the things that are wrong in their natural existence! People come before the Lord discombobulated, bewildered, and totally confused!

The teachers and the teaching in many of the churches desire to

silence God in these modern times? Some churches don't embrace the Old Testament, while others totally disdain the King James Bible all together; more Americanized versions of the bible are preferred.

Many churches behave as if the four books in the New Testament writings of the Gospel of Jesus Christ is all that really matter of the scripture. The moment that they reach the book of The Acts of The Apostles; it would appear that the rest of the bible has been muted; thus it is now silent to them!

As we go deeper in the dialogue of whether or not God is ever silent, and where it is that faith stands as a result in those times, we are going to also deal with the problem of deafness among the people! Most of them look to God and say to Him; I can't hear you!

In an effort to truthfully say that God has been silent concerning you; it is imperative that you acknowledge that you have surrendered your hearing to faith and the word of God, to utter the silence of everything else of the systems of the earth that speaks; intentionally by default you can't hear any of them any longer. You have set yourselves to hear nothing elso but the voice of God?

What have you done to increase understanding; knowing the difference in faith, the things that you believe and of the other systems of the world that might have an ability to produce in the natural realms of humanity?

One of the greater hindrances of faith in God is that people are led to believe that it is our portion to tell faith what to do, how to do, and or even when and where to do whatever it is that we as human beings desire for faith to operate.

People of theological studies argue the validity and the authenticity of the written word and of the reality and the total deity of God; leaving me to understand that they really do not believe the bible or God!

The Same people are dead set on their definitions of faith and of the abilities and functional manners of which faith can be used or put into action.

Through the very same erroneous definitions of faith in God; they don't mind going out of their way to support any people who in so many ways may be suggesting that faith in God doesn't work for them?

Figuratively speaking; people are shaking their finger in the face of God saying to Him; talk to me! Even of the people who are saved and serving the Lord; so they say, anyway; they spend no time in the word of God at all which would enable for them to clearly have God to speak to them through the word of God; but they are adamant that He is silent!

People by the scores are standing in the line at the churches to re-ceive a word; quote~unquote; from the prophet of God; they come bearing big money in effort for the prophet to give a word that will give them direction and a sense of peace for the situation that they are presently experiencing.

I'm amazed at how it is that people believe that they are prepared to hear from the Lord? They think that their ears are opened, but it is for sure that they're bibles are closed on a daily basis; they are imprisoned in their own spirits, and in their own minds!

Multiples of times the scripture admonishes; "he that hath an ear to hear, let him hear what the spirit has to say unto the churches."

While it is that you are determined that God is truly silent con-cerning you; my question to you is; how would you even know that God is indeed silent when you don't even have an ear to hear what God is saying?

The average people of the Christian churches worldwide don't even have an ear to hear what the spirit of the Lord is saying to

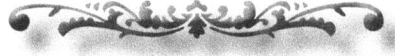

them! This is evident in the lack of interest that is shown to attend a prayer service!

We all have witnessed that people will show up at the church for any other type of a service at the church, until, unless it is for the purpose of praying corporately to touch the heart of God collectively.

Whenever the announcements are given during the Sunday services, when the announcement for prayer to be held at the church on Tuesday evening is made; you could hear people all over the sanctuary say; "well that's only prayer, I'm not coming all of the way out here for that!"

The truth is that they had it all wrong, and they lacked the understanding that prayer is the most important part of the Christian life; it is that part which enables an open dialogue between us and God in the relationship.

There is an undercurrent of disgruntled believers all across the board, complaining that they can't seem to connect with God during the most trying times of their lives?

They don't have a regiment for prayer on a daily basis, or personal time for studying their bible; yet they complain that God is silent! Faithlessly, they are desiring to maintain a communication with the Father in Heaven, overlooking that fact that such communicable reverential esteem is only realized through faith in God; initially.

"Silence Is On You!"

After all that has been written and said relative to God ever being silent; let me encourage your understanding in knowing that God is never silent!

But we should be silent enough to listen to what God has said already, which has all bearing on whatever it is that God is saying in

this time of our existence.

Perhaps I may be a bit instrumental in helping us to place silence where it really belongs.

This chapter opens with the scripture; *Habakkuk 2:20... But the Lord is in His holy temple; let all the earth keep silence before Him; .....*

I can remember a senior citizen who would quote that scripture to me all of the time, but the true revelation of the scripture evaded my inner comprehension for many years.

As of late, the spirit of the Lord begin to reveal the meaning of the scripture, as so many people began coming to me for the understanding as to why it seemed that God was silent and not speaking to them?

Rather than truly being able to meditate on their questions concerning God's silence; I would hear the scripture speaking to me; let the earth keep silence before Him....

Once I settled down enough to hear what the spirit of the Lord was indeed saying to me, it donned on me that God had already spoken!

The answers to our dilemmas and our situations had already been given in the scripture. In other words, it is not always necessary that God speak to us concerning our individual plight of circumstances, being that if we would follow the mandate of the scripture, chances are that we would never have even been in the position to have such occurrences and happenstances to be brought about in our lives.

So the scripture urges us to hush and to listen to what God is already saying to us in the scripture; disregarding our opinions and our thoughts on the subject of our lives! "Whatever God says is always right; He's right the first time!"

No matter how you pray and fast, you are never going to influ-

ence God to say something other than what He has already spoken for us to follow and to obey.

Even though we might have been in the church for all of our natural lives, that doesn't create some sort of special platform for us to move God against the settled establishment, of the written word of God!

So many people can't seem to get it; they have been going through the very same thing for decades, when the answer is in the fact that may need to hurry up and be quiet, and study to listen and to hear the word of God which had been written and established even before you ever came to the earth.

Your arrival to the earth was no surprise to the Lord, and neither did you have to be squeezed into the existence of mankind, forging a need for the word of God to be altered for your sake!

The greatest plight in human existence is that the people of these latter generations have way too much to say! They are adamantly resistant, and rebellious to what God has said through the written word of God! They are determined that their spin on the word is much more meaningful and enlightening than the revelations given through the spirit of the Lord, through prayer, and studying the word of God; which has been settled in Heaven forever.

Most people who are indeed struggling to hear the spirit of the Lord speaking are often most assuredly dealing with a perverted ideology of what it really means to have faith in God!

The accepted spirit of perversion which has gotten people to agree with same-sex relationships; the legal usage of illegal drugs; and to bringing unholy things in to the houses of worship; has all been designed to attack your understanding of having faith in God!

This is the reason that there is such aggressive fighting against the established landmarks of holiness and righteousness.

All that it takes to pervert what God has said to us already is to replace the voice of God; with my voice or the voice of any other individuals, or spiritual entities!

Many of the same people who have deemed God as haven been silent, they never meditate in the word of God; neither day or night; but they go out of their way to join Yoga class to blanket their minds, in an effort to relax their minds, to relieve themselves of stress, and or to clear their minds of the things of which really need to be attended unto; they think anyway?

Willingly they give the attention of their minds to all sorts of things which clutter their thinking, only to try and to take their cluttered minds in a prayer dialogue with the Lord, expecting to hear Him talking to them?

The other means of captivating their minds ability to reason have been chosen and applied firstly above and far beyond the written word of God and Faith.

Amazingly; people want to hear God's response to what some other person on the face of the earth has spoken to them, rather than to hear God's spiritual response to what He has already spoken in the word; so rather than to hear what the spirit has to say, He is deemed to have been non~responsive.

Sort of to the likes of saying to God; Lord; my neighbor John said to me the other day; rather than saying "Father; Jesus said in the scripture; having settled upon what Jesus has spoken in the scripture as the only truth to really need!

People spend time in the court of law, and even in the collegiate classrooms, so much that they are not really aware that they're being intellectually and mentally shaped and emotionally structured to refuse the truth of the scripture, and the reality of God in Christ Jesus.

They may indeed believe that God exist in Jesus Christ; but they have not been postured to know Him in the fullness of His spirit and power!

Alike our historical brothers and sisters of the Old Testament; people are positioned to receive the idea Christ, but not His Image! *{Hebrews 9; 10;}*

While the image of God reaches the minds of the people in the earth, but only allowing for the greater platforms of questioning the true existence of God; His Presence settles into the heart of mankind, establishing the truth of knowing that God Is indeed who He Is!

Knowing that God is; establishes the foundation for a righteous relationship; opening us up to the presence and to the power of God.

People talk so much because they may have been influence to think that maybe they can alter and or change the idea of who God is or of who God just may not be.

Such people often expose the fact that such idealisms have been imputed into their thinking about God when writing a simple post relative to God; when writing and using such spellings; *i.e. god; G_d; or even Gid!*

They know that they are being watched by those who have influenced their doubt and unbelief; so they conduct their responsiveness in a chat to insure they never offend their instructors.

Remember Jesus taught us in the word of God;
if any man come after me let him deny himself... [Matthew 16:24]

Today's followers of the church, they much rather deny Christ than to deny themselves of the opportunity to sit under such destroyers of the faith in God through their teachings.

Figuratively speaking; these people sort of desire to be able to be

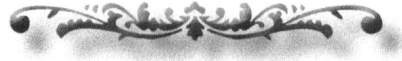

on both sides of the fence, they want to be with us and them at the very same time.

It is almost an all-out war to tell people that they need to be quiet and listen to what the Lord is saying to them, about them! Because of the fact that people are warring within themselves as result of the wrong, and wicked decisions that they have made in their lives, they can't stand to be silent!

Silence turns up the volume of the evil reminders speaking down on the inside of their spirit, replaying the wickedness of their past, most assuredly silence makes one to see the truth of their character and spirit, whether they choose to acknowledge the truth or not.

Most people would like to think that they had gotten away with having done some wicked and evil things to other people, especially since they had not fallen to the ground dead in their tracks as a result. In fear, they're talking louder and louder consistently blocking out the voice of the spirit of the Lord just in case He really is going to speak to them about their behavior, and the need to repent.

How deceived they are, in that God has already required us to repent and to forgive one another, loving one another as we love ourselves.

There are multiple reasons as relating to why people cannot and will not hear the voice of the Lord speaking to them, but none of those reasons will land on any reason such as to the fact that He is silent!

Not so; God is simply waiting on you to be silent and to listen to what has been spoken to you and for you already.

I did a study about 6-7 years ago on God's silence; what I learned was that in many instances, God is silent because He had already spoken, and He is not in a debate with mankind as to whether or not we are going to hear what He has to say in His word!

Regardless of your opinion or your refusal to accept God's word; the only other option outside of listening and hearing to obey God's word is death and destruction.

People are so scrunched and fitted into the ideas of getting whatever they want from the Lord; they totally ignore what the scripture says about what God wants from us.

Erroneously, as people of the churches we are taught how to misuse faith, thinking that faith is as the power of our credit; depending on our credit score, we may or may not be able to acquire the things that we may desire?

You need to be silent because God does not want you to be just like them; He created you to be just like Him; which should be the reason that you are seeking to hear Him speaking to you!

Your own lustful desires have got you thinking that God doesn't want you to have things, whatever those things may be?

If you would only search the scripture for the sake of knowing the truth, you would know that you need to prioritize your search to know God first, through faith, and everything else that you desire would then begin to desire you! *{Matthew 6:33}*

You will never master the ability to tell God what to do; when to do it and how to do it for you! This is a love relationship with the Father in Heaven, but He is not at all insensitive or unknowledgeable of your need; or of your desires.

As we are required to pray to the Father in heaven in the name of Jesus; it is not all about telling Him what you want; it's about positioning yourself in the realm of the spirit to hear Him tell you what He wants from you.

Are you interested in hearing His voice for the sake of having that experience, or are you hearing with the intent to obey His in-

structions whenever He does speak to you?

God knows that when He speaks to you that you are going to take what He had spoken to you back to a leader of a ministry, who has never been acquainted with Him; personally for themselves, only to have them to say to you that perhaps you missed it, because that could not have been the voice of the Lord speaking to you!

God; is right now presently aware of the things that you have been taught and are being taught in a bible study; or in a bible destruction course of study?

Someone may be teaching you that God doesn't even have a voice anymore; what are you listening for?

Be very leery of any person in a pulpit who is more adamant about telling the people what God either won't do or can't do for them!

My advice to you is that they are setting you up to believe that they themselves can do the things that you need for the Lord to do.

No man on the face of the planet will ever be able to replace God to take care of your need; doesn't matter how much money they might have.

You may be falsely led to believe that money can fix all of your problems, only to get money and then realize that you have a need that money can't suffice.

Be honest, it is all because of money that you are driven to your knees to talk with God; if He is not talking to you about the money that you need, you really don't want to hear what He has to say to you anyway! Believe me, faith in God produces so much more than just money!

Hearing God through faith will have you living godly, manifesting the powerful acts of God in your own personal space and at-

mosphere, and it will cause you to be empowered to show to other people the truthful presence of God's Love.

People are adamant about hearing God speak to them, when they have no plan on ever showing Love to people around them, sometimes not even to their families, and friends.

God is Love; you have got to be filled with God's Love; then God's voice will leap forward towards you, whereas you will not have to ask to hear his voice, and neither will God have to ask you to listen to Him speaking to you.

God's Love attracts our attention and it draws us to Him when we have been filled with His spirit which is Love!

You know how attracted you are to people that genuinely love you and show you their love; you have no problem being in their presence. As a matter of the fact, we rather enjoy conversing with the people that Love us, and don't mind showing it!

Real Love has that vacuum effect where it draws everything to it that is in the close proximity to it; so as God is love; you are drawn to His Love for you.

But it is your determination to move away from Him that has your own spirit silenced to the Voice of God?

God; said to us; with loving kindness have I drawn thee…
                    {Jeremiah 31:3}
Be silent, O all flesh, before the Lord: for he is raised up out
of his holy habitation.   *{Zechariah 2:13}*

What is so amazing to me is how that people think that what they have to say now that they have an issue, outweigh the power of what has already been discussed and released into the atmospheric surroundings for all people to take hold of for the sake of governing their livelihood.

What we need most is to remember by faith; the things that come along in our lives only rise up to wedge a divide between us and faith in our risen Lord.

We have faith and the assurance of the Holy Ghost to prevent this from happening, though these types of thing will come regardless of how we may feel or strive to resist such occurrences from happening in our lives.

Perhaps the greater hindrance of hearing the Lord speaking to us may be found in the fact that we are trying to listen for His voice in the midst of the explosive destructive noises of our trials and tribulations; which are the times that we are not necessarily supposed to be listening for the sound of His voice speaking to us!

But we should have been made aware and ready for the coming of such things through a prayer dialogue long before such things could ever happen to us. We should be relying upon what the Lord has already said to us while in communion with Him in prayer.

Faith; reminds us of what the Father has already said to us; as the Lord loves us too much to allow a life filled with evil occurrences and devastating circumstances to slip upon us without warning!

These times of which people have accused God of being silent are to the likeness of taking a class where we never listen to the instructor or to the teacher; perhaps we slept in class; fooled around passing letters and notes to other classmates; daydreaming about the things that we wanted to do after the class had ended?

When the time came to be tested to see whether or not we had learned anything that we had been taught in the class, we soon learned that we had missed out on the necessary lessons, and we failed the test!

Often the spirit of the Lord is calling us to prayer, but we are too sleepy; too busy; much more interested in what's showing on televi-

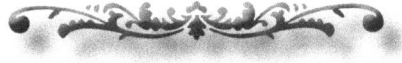

sion; or just simply deciding on procrastination?

We prefer to put off talking with the Lord until we have what we think is an urgency; not realizing that He the Lord is pulling on us to pray because He know that and urgent matter is coming upon shortly!

God already know all things that are going to come upon us, even before they are able to intrude upon our living realities.

So many people raise their children, allowing them to remain distracted while they are trying to speak to them to instruct them about the rules and the possible discipline of the household.

The children respond to them by saying; what did you say; I didn't hear you. They want you to say it again; they need for you repeat yourself.

The parents are at fault for never teaching their children to pay close attention to what they have to say. They allowed their children to take for granted the seriousness of their instructions.

Many developed problems with following instructions and respecting authority. They have been consistently disciplined during school and on their jobs; for which in honesty, they really have not understood why it is that they have been in need of being reprimanded!

Many of the same people have conflicts with the police and the judicial system, always finding them in trouble of some sort?

Unintentionally, they were not being raised to build the mental fortitude of their own recognizance; they have no thinking of truth and of responsibilities to rely upon.

See; it is easier to place the blame on our God; suggesting that He might have indeed been silent whenever they came to Him to discuss their problem with Him.

However, the very same people avoid the teaching sessions of the churches and they go out of their way to avoid at all cost to be absent from all prayer meetings.

They never meet with their pastors and leaders to be taught how to behave themselves in faith whereas they are presented before the Lord; having a faithful demeanor, that is indeed pleasing to the Lord, whereas He will talk to them?

You have got to begin listening to the people of the Lord as they teach to you the word of the Lord, and even as they pray to the Lord corporately, so as to get the purported faithful idea of praying to the Lord, to enter into His presence, then praying to get an answer from the Lord.

Real true sanctified, anointed leaders will teach you to accept whatever the answer might be that you receive from the Lord.

God always see faith; however the reward of hearing Him speak to you only come through the benefit of faithfulness!

Faith turns on the sound of His voice, and it makes His direct message to you audible in the language that you can and will understand!

You will always hear Him talking to you, through faith! Don't make the attempt to hear Him as if He is just blowing with the wind, howling and making a sound that is inaudible to your natural hearing.

Tap in to the word of God through the hearing of faith; in which you will then develop the ability to hear Him as He speaks to you.

Read the word of God until you wear the pages out in the bible; get the word down in your spirit, and you will then discover that God is word; and the word is God!

Get out of your flesh and learn to leave it behind when entering

into the presence of the Lord.

No flesh will glory in His presence; people may indeed be over-whelmed with your flesh; i.e. you look good; you're so fine; they call you King or Queen?

God is never overwhelmed with your flesh, as your flesh is your benefit to exist in the earth realm as a natural created being.

Jesus Christ; is the only flesh of the word; but He is the word given for all flesh! Give up your flesh for the word; the word gave up His flesh for your salvation!

And the word was made flesh, and dwelt among us, (and we beheld His glory, the glory as of the only begotten of the Father,) full of grace and truth.   *{St. John 1:14}*

"*Hope; Faith; and Trust*"

Now, Faith is the Substance of Things Hoped for, the Evidence of Things Not Seen. {Hebrews 11:1}

"*Total Complete Aspect of Living by Faith!*"

Talking about fighting to the finish and hearing the conclusion of the whole matter; that's the time that you can say that you have actually been on the winding roads which brought you to the journey's end right where you are now. A journey doesn't deserve its rank until it has been completed, and then it is successfully declared as an expedition indeed.

Whenever we journey sincerely, there just may be those times that we enquire of the Lord within ourselves, wondering if we are going to make it; will we reach our intended destination?

Affixed just in between the start of our journey and the intended destination are bridges that we will have to cross, otherwise avoiding the need for a boat to cross us over the water beneath the bridge; being a necessary event of our travel. The bridge overpass/underpass is yet a blessing and a benefit of our journey, though often overlooked and disregarded.

Looking at the landscape of the map, we are able to see in direct detail, from the point of starting all of the way to the point of arriving at the projected destination of the journey.

However; having a road map in the grip of your hands means absolutely nothing to being able to reach your destination, if you have no plan on using the map to direct you to none of the places that are listed on that map.

Naturally it would be quite a devastating ride to ignore the directions on the map, as we would have no idea of how long it had been since we had gotten lost on our journey.

We are rather destination and purpose driven, whereas it is the greater determination to overlook if not to omit the traveling process of the journey to award us the blessing of reaching the destination, we would much rather just to be where we are going.

In the words of such likeminded people who would prefer to overlook and to avoid all of the time travel on the roads, they are rather quick to say to you that; "it don't take all of that."

And of course to those of us that have accepted the fact that the journey must be traveled, we often seek the fastest and the quickest method of travel so that the journey is not very long at all.

As we begin applying the things that we hope for in the Lord to faith, ignorantly, we allow ourselves also to believe that all of a sudden we've just began to hope.

In sincere actuality, we most likely might have been void of the true understanding of what it actually means to hope. Many years ago it was made clear to me that many people were not quite comprehensive as to what real hope is.

Hope is not the cartoon suppositions, and make-believe desires of the fictional dramas and the television series of make believe love stories and of the wishful diaries and a schematic plot where luck is the heroic supplier and the giver of those things that could never otherwise be possible for people to ever have.

In our youth we might have been playing outside on what was at first a partly sunny day, there may have been clouds in the sky, but it was not raining initially.

But all of a sudden, rain drops would begin to fall sporadically from the sky, in our immaturity because we wanted to finish playing the games that we were playing; or we want to continue hanging outside with our friends, so we would look to the sky and say; "I hope that it doesn't rain" even though it had already began to shower slightly.

At school during class, the teacher would begin passing out a surprise quiz that we did not know that we were about to be tested on; you could hear several of the students say; "I hope this is not another test."

We learned to practice this kind of thinking methodology relative to hope as we grow older without being properly educated and informed.

While driving we might approach an intersection and see another driver with their signal indicator light turned on, and because they have to slow down their speed to make the turn, we say; "I hope they hurry up and turn; or I hope they are not about to turn right here."

Too often we are allowed to believe that we are in question when applying hope in situations of our lives. Hope doesn't question God; hope, rather, expects God to the very point of trusting that God is going to do whatever we believe for in faith.

Questioning cancels out the actuality of hope and trust in the Lord; as the fact is that everything that we maintain in question, we simply have not as of yet believed.

Doubt and disbelief are the assassins of faith in God; these two negative elements are sure to unplug the powerful connectivity of faith and of God.

These make-believe hypothetical application of negative desires is not at all the hope that is mentioned in the scripture.

I urge you to stay as far away from anything that even sound remotely close to the afore mentioned examples of what might have been thought of as hope, as that type of hope will net you absolutely nothing from the Lord.

As a matter of the fact, it is that type of hope that is responsible for producing what is referred to as a double minded man.

Hope doesn't make God do it, but it does expect for God to do it without wrath or doubting that He can or that He will!

You are looking at the actual reality of a thing; but rather than to accept it for what you see, and then speak to it accordingly as a result, the thing is spoken to as if the person speaking to it has the magical powers to change what they are seeing at that instance.

That is not at all the hope of the scripture! Hope doesn't magically alter the things of our present atmosphere; but it does allow for us to speak to God in reference of faith concerning the things of our atmosphere.

The hope of the scripture actually means for us to ultimately ex-

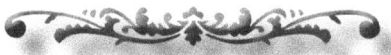

pect for God to bring it to pass for us; all along for a while we had been hoping to turn the attention of God to our situations but void of the true knowledge of the scripture concerning faith in God.

How we learned to hope in what has become most recognized and accepted often as hopeless situations and circumstances; is too often far beyond our comprehension, simply because we like to think and believe that we are dismissive of the process of developing the hope which landed us right on top of the platform foundation to activate the power of faith!

Several years ago I preached a message titled; "HOPELESS FAITH"; it seemed to have stunned several of the people in attendance at that time. The scripture clearly states to us that faith is the substance of the things that we first of all must have hoped for.

We are a generation of people most hopeless and not often at all are we really as a whole, hopeful people in the churches.

The issues are that in our hopelessness, we have been unsuspectingly suspended over the open pit of nothingness, expecting nothing, believing for nothing, not believing that there is even anything to satisfy our curiosity, which could never have led to faith in God in the first place.

As a since of methodology to cure what might have been diagnosed as the faithlessness of most people, measures have been employed to strike up, or to ignite the faith that we believe to be on the inside of people.

Only too often, there has been no consideration of the fact that people are empty and void of hope; they have no expectation of God!

The many generated reasons for such hopelessness among the people of today are just too many to name and too vastly spread across the land to try and to put my pen to it!

I might be writing until this time next year, just on this one topic of discussion to make my point.

I have listened to messages across the pulpits all of my life; the ministers are attempting to lead the people of the churches to have faith in God.

While sitting beneath the voices of spiritual reason, I have on occasion scanned the audience only to discern on the faces of many of the people in attendance, that they have no hope.

Lacking hope would be the only real reason for rejecting and lacking interest in the message of faith.

As we begin to speak on the message of faith in God; many of the people are board to the maximum; outwardly they appear to be totally turned off.

The messages; "Name it and claim it" over the years to the people of the faith in the past, caused the people to think and to believe that they could avoid the process of hoping in God initially!

Hope; precedes the allowed award of approaching faith; hope is as the revealed secret passage to entering into faith in God.

The scripture informs us that without faith it is impossible to please God; but without hope there is no way to even enter the atmosphere of faith.

It is sad to realize that there are people in the churches that are as hopeless and spiritually dead as those who are adamantly sinful and wicked in the living behavior in the world.

Listening to the wrong people and their ideas of faith has allowed for the hope that many have had to be deflated like a helium balloon; everything that would give a spiritual rise to faith has been depleted!

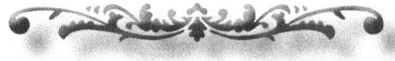

Shame on the teaching instructors of the bible; who adamantly teach faith in God; however passively teaching they are causing the message of faith to become intensively complex even for the more reasonable simplex of thinkers and failing to instruct the people of the churches of the extreme importance of hope in the Lord.

People are seeking to understand and to comprehend what to do to make faith work for them?

On any given day, we can hear people saying that I have tried everything, but still it is not working for me. Even as people read the scripture from cover to cover; how to truly activate faith is lost in the lack of hope.

I was taught and I even learned from a child upwards, that there will never be a time in the history of my life that I would ever be able to say that everybody liked me; and for certain not everyone will love me.

So many of the leaders in the churches are determined to be loved by everyone, they are often caught up in passivity and extreme tolerance.

While they are watchful to allow the people of the churches to live and to behave as they wish to do so, they are also allowing for the people to miss this main ingredient to be overlooked and disregarded.

Many people, who live as they choose to do so, find themselves in hopelessness, relative to being changed and often to being forgiven; they wouldn't dare approach faith to ask the Lord for anything.

The world often gives consenting approval for the people of this world to live as they choose to try everything their hearts desire without any regrets; after all we are only human.

Many have later found themselves to be remorseful for having

stretched themselves behaviorally beyond the respectful boundaries and it doesn't at all make them feel very good about what they have done.

They tell themselves that they have no regrets for having the fun of a life time, and breaking all of the barriers and going beyond every limit; only they can't seem to get the monkey off of their backs, or the stench of sin and the stain of sins filth off of the surface of their skin; they need help.

If sin were really our only problem well we would all be totally eradicated and tucked away in the religious package for heaven.

Often even greater than sin is the destruction of self which stands in the way to prevent us from repenting, or of even feeling the guilt that might be upon us as a result of sin and of self.

Self is even powerful enough to silence the need for God in our lives; we really don't need an adversary to deter us from doing what are indeed the right things, as people are often totally self-absorbed and selfish to the greatest degree.

Self tells us that we want to do the detestable and to experience the wicked things in this life; but it also blocks us from seeing and from focusing on the penalties of those actions.

Most often, before we go ahead and persist to do the wrong things, we are triggered and alerted on the inside of us to think again about the actions that we are about to take.

We later learn to regret not listening to the voice on the inside of us telling us not to do the things that we had done.

This is indeed the conditions for which the Lord has suggested for all men to come to Him just as they are, while most people are attempting to use the word of the Lord against Him; showing up at the houses of worship looking like runaway slaves and criminals;

God's appeal is to the soulish and the spiritual conditions that we may be in. Whenever we had allowed for our spirit and our emotions to be tied up in a knot, is the time that we need to have been running to the Lord to have the attached chords of guilt and shame severed and slashed in the power of the blood to be loosed from our beings.

While being pumped up of ourselves to do what we want to do, in those times of consenting ourselves to be stupid and sinful, we are not realizing that it is going to be those same consenting measures of self that will be confronting us when it comes to the point of needing to repent and or even to ask the Lord to deliver us from the unexpected binding holds of guilt and of the prideful shame that attacked our desire to hope in the Lord.

It is self that is standing in the way of us believing that God is good enough to help us, to save us and to set us free! Rather, all it is that we are able to hear speaking on the inside of us is that we are not good enough for God!

When you can't believe you can't hope either; self will talk us out of believing that we could ever hope for God to work it out for us!

So much time is spent going over the failures and the mistakes of the past which when given the proper glance of the behavior of most people perhaps they ought to be ashamed, but the scripture has supplied a remedy for that.

Jesus has the power to wipe the slate clean as if there had never been any infractions committed that would have cause such deep embarrassment.

How simple is it for us to understand according to the scripture that without hope there can be no faith; while faith is there eternally affixed to all of humanity, we will never be able to successfully connect to faith in God without assuredly hoping for God in our lives.

Just as a rocket cannot and it will not even be launched from its launching pad to lift into the sky without rocket fuel, nothing that we will ever desire of the Lord can ever be lifted to His presence without the fuel of hope, to ignite the fire of faith in God.

Faith is the extinguishing furnace that consumes away all of our desires and our needs in the fire of God once our hope has elevated our expectations; once in the hands of faith they are no longer desires or a need, they then become the manifested answers and the realities of the things that we have hoped for.

As well as it is a fact that people really do want to know of the reality of God in Christ Jesus; they need to know the realistic Love of God which cares for us all delivering the things that we ask for of Him through faith.

Hope; doesn't create faith, which is already created and made to be adhered unto of all mankind of the entire scope of humanity in all of the earth, hope helps us and strengthens our determination to reach God; satisfying the prerequisites of faith.

Hope is the playing field of faith whereas we are enabled to stretch out and to reach up into the extensive complete atmospheric realm of all that is of God indeed through faith.

Wherever God is faith is there also, thus in the times of our need, being that we are already in faith, we are likewise in God; right then and there.

Faith reaches into the heavens and brings God to us; right to us in the realm of the earth.

In truth, we have only almost scratched the surface of whatever faith in God can do for us.

The limited ability of mankind to mentally and to emotionally grasp just so much of what faith in God can do for us has also limit-

ed our ability to understand and to comprehend the unlimited powerfully ingrained ability of faith to reach up into the invisible realm
and to draw out the things that without faith could only be wishful
thinking for us, to be made visible manifestations of reality to us.

"So Here Is the Reasons That We Trust In God"

In faith I choose to let God do it for me; in trust I refuse to question that He did it for me. In faith I believed God unto righteousness
which pleased God; in trust I unapologetically refused to doubt His
Love for me.

In faith I listened to hear what the spirit of the Lord would say
to me; in trust I settled on what God has spoken in the word of God
knowing that it will never change, as the word can never be removed.

I trust in God; that being the final and the finishing stance of my
positioning around the truth in the word of God.

It's final, it's set and established forever in every fiber of my own
being; God is not only my choice as my life and living progresses, He
is ultimately now the determinate essence in the reasons that I let go
to allow God in Christ Jesus; through the power of the Holy Ghost
to live in me and through me; through faith!

We were not put here in the earth so that God could live this life
for us, but rather His divine design is that He can and will be allowed to live through us in the earth before all humanity!

So many people flirt with doubt and unbelief after that they have
received the reward of faith, through believing God. They allow
for themselves to believe that they are being smart and intelligent to
examine what, how, and when the Lord did it for them.

They want to check His methodology, and scrutinize His love and
care for us, not able to accept the truth of the word of God concern-

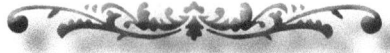

ing God's genuine Love for humanity. They will often say; well yes God did it for me, but I want to know why He did it!

Such behavioral attitude of looking to God side eyed in question, fearful of glorifying God for what He has done, is actually a trust assassination!

Lacking understanding and true integrity of our heart, we allow for trust to bleed to death. In truth, many people who confess to have faith in God; they refuse to totally trust in Him. Many are taught and otherwise encouraged to say to God; "I will let you do this for me; if?"

The conditions that you think that you put on God is never what is to come after faith, only trust is to follow what God has done for you! We believed God to do it for us through faith, now we trust God to keep it done!

People are determined to believe that we can put God to the test behind faith; actually believing that they are doing God a favor by allowing for Him to do it for them.

In total ignorance they are refusing to trust that He is the God of all grace and truth, able to do what He says that He will do! So when God has done the things that many people have asked for Him to do, they struggle to tell other people that it was indeed God that did it.

In fear of trusting in God many people choose to praise God in secret for the things that He has done.

They might share their testimonies with a select few people but they will not be heard sharing the good news of God with anyone that will listen to them, too often they are ashamed and insecure, lacking the proper teaching and instruction from the written word of God that enables them to trust in God!

It is one thing to have God to fix things for us, however we need to trust that whatever God does can never ever be undone.

Trust is the stitching which sewed the thing together, and it is the binding element which seals the finished product permanently. In trust we are woven together with God, in that the things that God will do for us is more-so done to us!

So many people, who confess to being saved, failed drastically, but totally unnecessarily for the total lack of trust; they had the faith to believe it but they lacked the trust to keep it!

They have been taught to trust in the arms of their own flesh to keep themselves saved and living in the will of God; but totally overlooking the fact that they are completely incapable of keeping themselves.

I am thankful to God for all of the many people who have come to Him to be saved; set free; and delivered from sin and from self. Many of the ministers in the churches have settled on the four gospels of Christ; Matthew; Mark; Luke, and John; in the New Testament of the bible.

In their teaching and instruction to the people of the churches they too often have stopped just short of the finished product of God; which is the Holy Ghost!

These particular books of the bible were penned to tell of the goodness and of the awesome works and the miracles of faith that Jesus did while He walked the earth.

The writings detail the journey to the cross, and of all of the interchanging with mankind as He walked among humanity in the flesh. We get an opportunity to know of the genealogy of His human Linage, and a brief history of His family upbringing.

We are made aware of the manner of which Jesus went about

selecting and making disciples of the Twelve endowed Apostles, and the reasons why they were chosen.

Jesus planted many hidden mysteries to be revealed later, right in the midst of the written gospels. Jesus', revealed Himself as God; though mere men were unable to receive Him as the equal person of God in the flesh;

He is Emmanuel (God with us) the manifested word of God who became flesh and dwelt among us in the earth.

Jesus is the expressed image of God in the flesh; He came to let men see God; He came to let mere men touch God in the flesh. He came to redeem man in the flesh from the penalty of sin and of death, through the works of sin in the flesh.

Jesus came to reconnect us back to the Godhead of Heaven; Elohim' (Triune God; in Three Persons......

God the Father; God the Son; Jesus The Christ; The Savior; and God the Holy Ghost...

The Paraclete ~ one who goes along side to help...

This is all revealed and penned truth in the writing of the Four Gospels of God; the revelation of who Jesus Christ is; why He came to the earth; why He left the earth; and why He's coming back again.

Those who lack trust in the finished works of Christ Jesus while He walk the earth in the presence of all Humanity, can never receive Him and be transformed to live with Him in eternity.

However, many of the ministers are intentionally leaving off the part of the Holy Ghost as the final part and the completion of the Godhead.

The Holy Ghost is sent to seal it all up unto the day of redemption. John 15 teaches us that He is the spirit of truth; but I must also

inform you that He is also the spirit of Trust!

He is that part of God that eradicates any and all doubt and question of the authenticity in the truthful existence of God!

With exception to those who choose to blaspheme the truth of the Holy Ghost; there is not an individual on the face of the planet earth that has come into contact and the presence of the Holy Ghost; that have any doubt as to whether or not it is God!

Anyone that has ever been shocked or electrocuted have no question as to the authentic power of electricity! They have been shocked into the reality of the power of the current flowing through the wiring and out of the outlets.

Once you've been touched by the power of the Holy Ghost, there is no more question in the authentic power of God! You will know forever that God is God!

As powerful as electricity is; one could be electrocuted to death and be resurrected by the all-powerful touch of God; God's power is proven to be even more powerful than electricity and all of the damage that it can in fact do.

God has the power to reverse the damage of the electrocution, without having to reverse and to dismiss the fact that an individual had been electrocuted!

John said to the Jews that were questioning Him of his own true character and existence; he said to them; there is one coming after me, that is' mightier than I am; "He will baptize you with the Holy Ghost and with Fire."

Jesus; in His teaching said to the apostles; 'I must leave you; but I will send you another comforter." Jesus says specifically that; "I Will Send You" another comforter.

Those who refuse to be filled with the Holy Ghost, in an effort to

be dismissive of the truth of the word of God; which is that Jesus has sent Him directly to us to live in us; they are more agreeable to teach that the comforter has indeed come into the world; He may not be on the inside of many of us but He is indeed in the world.

While they do believe that He the comforter has been sent into the world; they feel that they have the ability to allow for the Holy Ghost to rest in the atmosphere of Humanity without teaching that He must abide within the spirit-man to keep the souls of them that have been saved.

He has come to activate the eternal power of God in the life of everyman who receives Him! He is the ability to show other men of the world and of otherwise sinful influence that God is yet alive; but now moving and alive in our natural flesh!

Jesus the Christ; Son of the Living God; He knows all things which concerns humanity. He made us having installed the ability to trust in God; God knows that you and I will never have any reason to question or to doubt Him.

Only so many people are attempting to trust in God in Christ without the aid of the Holy Ghost, which is the ignition and the furnace to forever maintain the fire of our faith and trust in God; to keep it burning hot!

If you don't have a burning trust on the inside of you ignited of the Holy Ghost; you need to get rid of the natural idea of trust that has been watered down, doused, and unable to keep you knowing that which the Lord has done and said in your life through the written word of God.

Although you might have acquired an idealistic understanding of knowledge relative to what it means to trust other people, it doesn't bear any resemblance to that of being able to trust in God.

Human beings are able to change their minds thus being able

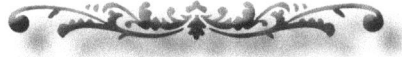

and apt to change their position on a decision which have the power to destroy the integrity of the ability to be trusted.

Many will teach of salvation who also fails to teach of the fire of the Holy Ghost; simply because as a teaching instructor you have to possess the Holy Ghost to effectively teach people about the Holy Ghost.

We have failed to realize just how serious of a matter it really is to have so many people of the churches running around with a natural idea of the meaning of trust.

They have been to the library and have looked through the dictionary and have read the definitions of the meaning of the word trust.

Only that word form of trust in the dictionary is derived from the natural ability to confide in another natural being.

It is paramount that we learn to trust through the spirit of the Lord by the aid of the Holy Ghost; as trusting in God will only be made manifested through the working of the spirit.

When we are tested tried and tempted to sin against God, these are of the most assuring times of the fact that we serve a God who is; and can be trusted with us in all manner of our need and will not deny us or let us down.

He will neither fail us nor betray the trust that we have in Him. If it is our will not to sin against God nor to live an outright sinful lifestyle; we very desperately need to trust in the Lord to keep us from all of the evil of sin and of self.

Whatever has been brought to pass through faith, trust will keep it in tact, even if it is our thinking about what God has done that trust will help us to maintain the acknowledgement of the fact.

My heart bleeds for those who have made the attempt to trust in

God, who had never hoped in the Lord to the point of faith in God to see the things hoped for come to pass.

So many things that have been out of order are now being brought back into the proper order for the sake of allowing the relationship with the Father in Heaven to be made manifest as the Father originally intended.

In an effort to really trust in God you have got to know God by faith through repentance, which will ensure that you have made the true connection for the benefit of having a right relationship with Him.

Too many people are attempting to initiate trust in God of whom they are not even sure of Him being who He says that He is through the writing of the Holy Bible.

Trust can never be initiated through doubt and unbelief; these two negative elements of the spiritual realm must be solved and absolved before trust can be laid out on the table as an option.

So many people attempt to make the final things to be the first things. They have no proper respect of the divine order of God, which only makes for a dismal failure to properly connect to God through the written word of God and it allows for grave disappointment relative to receiving God so that we can be who God intended for us to be from the beginning!

The people of the worldly influence are looking at the people of the churches, disdaining the confusion and the lack of faith to trust in the God of the Universe.

They hear what we confess out of our mouths, but they see what we do in a crisis, and in the most troubling times of our lives. They see us even when we weren't aware of the fact that they were even looking at us!

We must trust God enough to care about what it is that people actually see whenever they enter into our spaces of living.

Trusting in God means so much more than being a regular attendant to the services at the local churches; it means that we are required to keep on moving through the storms and the rain; through sickness and through pain; no matter what has come upon us we must keep a praise on our lips and maintain worship in our hearts towards God.

Remember, John, says that we that worship God; that is in fact if we are going to worship Him; that we must do so in the spirit, and in Truth.

Trusting in God means that we are not hesitant to spill the details of our lives to Him; while we are determined to worship and to reverence God as the almighty Creator that He is.

Trust sets us on a leveled platform to worship God; whom our eyes have never seen! Trust allows for us to disregard the pains and the disappointments of life and to set our focus on God knowing that trough worship; He sets His focus on us!

No need at all to worry about what we are going through knowing that we have the all-powerful God who cares about us.

We must be willing to bring all things into the divine order in an effort to see to it that God will change things for us and to transform our lives.

So many people are seeking the Lord through the obstructions and the screens of the flesh and all of the many questions and uncertainties of the flesh.

Those types of things have caused for hope, faith, and trust to be displaced, incomplete and totally out of the proper order.

There has to be the alignment of Hope, Faith, and Trust; the align-

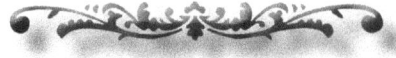

ment brings into clear focus of the reality of our relationship with the Father in Heaven through our trials and our tribulations.

The tougher things get for us in this world, the stronger our grip has to become as to never even entertain the idea of forsaking our trust in God.

Holding on to God is the only way that the people of the world who have not come to God in Christ Jesus as of yet will know for sure that what we have is indeed real and true.

I TRUST IN GOD................... 2018

God Sees Faith ~ But He Rewards

"FAITHFULNESS"

"BE FAITHFUL"

WILLIAM THOMPSON JR

www.ingramcontent.com/pod-product-compliance
Lightning Source LLC
Chambersburg PA
CBHW062000090426
42811CB00006B/997